3rd Workshop on Computational Approaches to Subjectivity and Sentiment Analysis 2012

(WASSA 2012)

Jeju Island, Korea
12 July 2012

ISBN: 978-1-62276-598-0

Printed from e-media with permission by:

Curran Associates, Inc.
57 Morehouse Lane
Red Hook, NY 12571

Some format issues inherent in the e-media version may also appear in this print version.

Printed by Curran Associates, Inc. (2012)

For permission requests, please contact the Association for Computational Linguistics
at the address below.

Association for Computational Linguistics
209 N. Eighth Street
Stroudsburg, Pennsylvania 18360

Phone: 1-570-476-8006
Fax: 1-570-476-0860

acl@aclweb.org

Additional copies of this publication are available from:

Curran Associates, Inc.
57 Morehouse Lane
Red Hook, NY 12571 USA
Phone: 845-758-0400
Fax: 845-758-2634
Email: curran@proceedings.com
Web: www.proceedings.com

Introduction

In the past years, the quantity of contents generated by users on the Web, in social networking sites, fora and microblogs has reached an unprecedented level. All this data adds on to the contents generated in traditional media, such as newspapers, bringing additional factual, as well as a high quantity of opinionated and subjective information. In the context of the society in which we live, where sifting through the immense quantities of information to gather knowledge has become a must, the challenge of processing opinionated and subjective information is becoming more and more a focus to the Natural Language Processing (NLP) research communities worldwide.

In the past decade, the interest in proposing computational methods to deal with subjectivity and sentiment in text has grown constantly from the NLP community. However, although the subjectivity and sentiment analysis research fields have been highly dynamic in this period, much remains still to be done, so that systems dealing with subjectivity, sentiment and, more generally, affect in text, can be reliably used in critical decision-making environments. Moreover, the new means of communication and user connection, in microblogs and social networks, become more and more relevant to these two tasks, as the contexts (internal and external) of the information communication process bring about new challenges and applications to be explored.

Inspired by the above-mentioned issues and the objectives we aimed at in the first two editions of the Workshop on Computational Approaches to Subjectivity Analysis (WASSA 2010 and WASSA 2.011), the purpose of the third edition of the Workshop on Computational Approaches to Subjectivity and Sentiment Analysis (WASSA 2012) was to create a framework for presenting and discussing the challenges related to subjectivity and sentiment analysis in NLP and its applications, in traditional and Social Media contexts, from an interdisciplinary theoretical and practical perspective. WASSA 2012 was organized in conjunction to the 50th Annual Meeting of the Association for Computational Linguistics, on July 12, 2012, in Jeju, Korea.

At this third edition of the workshop, we received a total of 31 submissions, from a wide range of countries, of which 11 were accepted as full papers and another 4 as short papers. Each paper has been thoroughly reviewed by 3 members of the Program Committee. The accepted papers were all highly assessed by the reviewers, the best paper receiving an average punctuation (computed as an average of all criteria used to assess the papers) of 4.6 out of 5.

The main topics of the accepted papers are the creation and evaluation of resources for subjectivity and sentiment analysis in a cross-lingual and multilingual setting, subjectivity and sentiment analysis using semi-supervised and supervised methods in different types of texts (although the accent this year has been undoubtedly on Social Media texts) and affect detection in context. Additionally, the WASSA 2012 authors have enhanced the analysis of these phenomena beyond the traditional intra-textual aspects, towards the reader and writer intentions and interpretations, and have also analyzed the application of subjectivity and sentiment reseach in NLP to real-life, relevant scenarios (such as the detection of socially unacceptable behavior in online contexts).

The invited talks reflected the multimodal and interdisciplinary nature of the research in affect-related phenomena as well. Prof. Rada Mihalcea, from the University of North Texas, presented a talk on "Multimodal Sentiment Analysis", linking the textual aspects of affect detection to affect detection in para-textual contexts. Prof. Janyce Wiebe's talk concentrated on the language ambiguity in the subjectivity analysis area. In her keynote on "Subjectivity Word Sense Disambiguation", she showed the importance of distinguishing among objective and subjective usages of word senses.

This year's edition has shown again that there is a demonstrated and increasingly growing interest in the topics addressed by WASSA and that the knowledge disseminated through this forum and the associated publications is bringing an important contribution to the research in subjectivity and sentiment analysis.

We would like to thank the ACL 2012 Organizers for the help and support at the different stages of the workshop organization process. We are also especially grateful to the Program Committee members and the external reviewers for the time and effort spent assessing the papers. We would like to extend our thanks to our invited speakers – Prof. Rada Mihalcea and Prof. Janyce Wiebe, for accepting to deliver the keynote talks.

Secondly, we would like to express our gratitude for the official endorsement we received from SIGSEM (the ACL Special Interest Group on Computational Semantics), SIGNLL (the ACL Special Interest Group on Natural Language Learning) and SIGLEX (the Special Interest Group on the Lexicon of the Association for Computational Linguistics).

Further on, we would like to thank the Editors of the "Computer Speech and Language Journal", published by Elsevier, for accepting to organize a Special Issue of this journal containing the extended versions of the best full papers accepted at WASSA 2012.

We would like to express our gratitude to Yaniv Steiner from the European Commission Joint Research Centre (Italy), who created the WASSA logo and to Miguel Ángel Varo and Miguel Ángel Baeza, from the University of Alicante, for the technical support they provided.

Last, but not least, we are grateful for the financial support given by the Academic Institute for Research in Computer Science of the University of Alicante (Instituto Universitario para la Investigación en Informática, Universidad de Alicante).

Alexandra Balahur, Andrés Montoyo, Patricio Martínez-Barco, Ester Boldrini
WASSA 2012 Chairs

Organizers:

Alexandra Balahur
European Commission Joint Research Centre
Institute for the Protection and Security of the Citizen

Andrés Montoyo
University of Alicante
Department of Software and Computing Systems

Patricio Martínez-Barco
University of Alicante
Department of Software and Computing Systems

Ester Boldrini
University of Alicante
Department of Software and Computing Systems

Program Committee:

Khurshid Ahmad, Trinity College Dublin (Ireland)
Sivaji Bandyopadhyay, Jadavpur University (India)
Nicoletta Calzolari, CNR Pisa (Italy)
Erik Cambria, University of Stirling (U.K.)
José Carlos Cortizo, European University Madrid (Spain)
Michael Gamon, Microsoft (U.S.A.)
Jesús M. Hermida, University of Alicante (Spain)
Veronique Hoste, University of Ghent (Belgium)
Mijail Kabadjov (Mexico)
Zornitsa Kozareva, Information Sciences Institute California (U.S.A.)
Rada Mihalcea, University of North Texas (U.S.A.)
Saif Mohammad, National Research Council (Canada)
Karo Moilanen, University of Oxford (U.K.)
Rafael Muñoz, University of Alicante (Spain)
Günter Neumann, DFKI (Germany)
Alena Neviarouskaia, University of Tokyo (Japan)
Manabu Okumura, Tokyo Institute of Technology (Japan)

Constantin Orasan, University of Wolverhampton (U.K.)
Manuel Palomar, University of Alicante (Spain)
Viktor Pekar, University of Wolverhampton (U.K.)
Paolo Rosso, Technical University of Valencia (Spain)
Josef Steinberger, European Commission Joint Research Centre (Italy)
Ralf Steinberger, European Commission Joint Research Centre (Italy)
Veselin Stoyanov, John Hopkins University (U.S.A.)
Hristo Tanev, European Commission Joint Research Centre (Italy)
Maite Taboada, Simon Fraser University (Canada)
Mike Thelwall, University of Wolverhampton (U.K.)
José Antonio Troyano, University of Seville (Spain)
Dan Tufis, RACAI (Romania)
Alfonso Ureña, University of Jaén (Spain)
Erik van der Goot, European Commission Joint Research Center (Italy)
Piek Vossen, Vrije Universiteit Amsterdam (The Netherlands)
Marilyn Walker, University of California Santa Cruz (U.S.A.)
Janyce Wiebe, University of Pittsburgh (U.S.A.)
Michael Wiegand, Saarland University (Germany)
Theresa Wilson, John Hopkins University (U.S.A.)
Taras Zagibalov, Brantwatch (U.K.)

Additional Reviewers:

Elena Lloret, University of Alicante (Spain)

Invited Speakers:

Prof. Dr. Rada Mihalcea, University of North Texas (U.S.A.)
Prof. Dr. Janyce Wiebe, University of Pittsburgh (U.S.A.)

Table of Contents

Conference Program

Thursday July 12, 2012

(8:30) Opening Remarks

(8:40) Invited talk (I): Prof. Dr. Rada Mihalcea

Multimodal Sentiment Analysis
Rada Mihalcea

(9:35) Invited talk (II): Prof. Dr. Janyce Wiebe

Subjectivity Word Sense Disambiguation
Janyce Wiebe

(10:30) Break

(11:00) Session 1: Subjectivity and Sentiment Analysis in Social Media

Random Walk Weighting over SentiWordNet for Sentiment Polarity Detection on Twitter
Arturo Montejo-Ráez, Eugenio Martínez-Cámara, M. Teresa Martín-Valdivia and L. Alfonso Ureña-López

Mining Sentiments from Tweets
Akshat Bakliwal, Piyush Arora, Senthil Madhappan, Nikhil Kapre, Mukesh Singh and Vasudeva Varma

SAMAR: A System for Subjectivity and Sentiment Analysis of Arabic Social Media
Muhammad Abdul-Mageed, Sandra Kuebler and Mona Diab

Thursday July 12, 2012 (continued)

(12:30) Lunch Break

(13:30) Session 2: Affect Detection and Classification (I)

Opinum: statistical sentiment analysis for opinion classification
Boyan Bonev, Gema Ramírez Sánchez and Sergio Ortiz Rojas

Sentimantics: Conceptual Spaces for Lexical Sentiment Polarity Representation with Contextuality
Amitava Das and Gambäck Björn

Analysis of Travel Review Data from Reader's Point of View
Maya Ando and Shun Ishizaki

Multilingual Sentiment Analysis using Machine Translation?
Alexandra Balahur and Marco Turchi

(15:30) Break

(16:00) Session 3: Affect Detection and Classification (II)

Unifying Local and Global Agreement and Disagreement Classification in Online Debates
Jie Yin, Nalin Narang, Paul Thomas and Cecile Paris

Prior versus Contextual Emotion of a Word in a Sentence
Diman Ghazi, Diana Inkpen and Stan Szpakowicz

Cross-discourse Development of Supervised Sentiment Analysis in the Clinical Domain
Phillip Smith and Mark Lee

POLITICAL-ADS: An annotated corpus for modeling event-level evaluativity
Kevin Reschke and Pranav Anand

Thursday July 12, 2012 (continued)

(17:30) Session 4: Applications of Subjectivity and Sentiment Analysis

Multimodal Sentiment Analysis
(Abstract of Invited Talk)

Rada Mihalcea
Department of Computer Science and Engineering
University of North Texas
P. O. Box 311366
Denton, TX 76203-6886, U.S.A.
rada@cs.unt.edu

Abstract

With more than 10,000 new videos posted online every day on social websites such as YouTube and Facebook, the internet is becoming an almost infinite source of information. One important challenge for the coming decade is to be able to harvest relevant information from this constant flow of multimodal data. In this talk, I will introduce the task of multimodal sentiment analysis, and present a method that integrates linguistic, audio, and visual features for the purpose of identifying sentiment in online videos. I will first describe a novel dataset consisting of videos collected from the social media website YouTube, which were annotated for sentiment polarity. I will then show, through comparative experiments, that the joint use of visual, audio, and textual features greatly improves over the use of only one modality at a time. Finally, by running evaluations on datasets in English and Spanish, I will show that the method is portable and works equally well when applied to different languages.

This is joint work with Veronica Perez-Rosas and Louis-Philippe Morency.

Subjectivity Word Sense Disambiguation
(Abstract of Invited Talk)

Janyce Wiebe
Department of Computer Science
University of Pittsburgh
Sennott Square Building, Room 5409
210 S. Bouquet St., Pittsburgh, PA 15260, U.S.A.
wiebe@cs.pitt.edu

Abstract

Many approaches to opinion and sentiment analysis rely on lexicons of words that may be used to express subjectivity. These are compiled as lists of keywords, rather than word meanings (senses). However, many keywords have both subjective and objective senses. False hits – subjectivity clues used with objective senses – are a significant source of error in subjectivity and sentiment analysis. This talk will focus on sense-level opinion and sentiment analysis. First, I will give the results of a study showing that even words judged in previous work to be reliable opinion clues have significant degrees of subjectivity sense ambiguity. Then, we will consider the task of distinguishing between the subjective and objective senses of words in a dictionary, and the related task of creating "usage inventories" of opinion clues. Given such distinctions, the next step is to automatically determine which word instances in a corpus are being used with subjective senses, and which are being used with objective senses (we call this task "SWSD"). We will see evidence that SWSD is more feasible than full word sense disambiguation, because it is more coarse grained – often, the exact sense need not be pinpointed, and that SWSD can be exploited to improve the performance of opinion and sentiment analysis systems via sense-aware classification. Finally, I will discuss experiments in acquiring SWSD data, via token-based context discrimination where the context vector representation is adapted to distinguish between subjective and objective contexts, and the clustering process is enriched by pair-wise constraints, making it semi-supervised.

Random Walk Weighting over SentiWordNet for Sentiment Polarity Detection on Twitter

A. Montejo-Ráez, E. Martínez-Cámara, M. T. Martín-Valdivia, L. A. Ureña-López
University of Jaén
E-23071, Jaén (Spain)
{amontejo, emcamara, maite, laurena}@ujaen.es

Abstract

This paper presents a novel approach in Sentiment Polarity Detection on Twitter posts, by extracting a vector of weighted nodes from the graph of WordNet. These weights are used on SentiWordNet to compute a final estimation of the polarity. Therefore, the method proposes a non-supervised solution that is domain-independent. The evaluation over a generated corpus of tweets shows that this technique is promising.

1 Introduction

The birth of Web 2.0 supposed a breaking down of the barrier between the consumers and producers of information, i.e. the Web has changed from a static container of information into a live environment in which any user, in a very simple manner, can publish any type of information. This simplified means of publication has led to the rise of several different websites specialized in the publication of users opinions. Some of the most well-known sites include Epinions[1], RottenTomatoes[2] and Muchocine[3], where users express their opinions or criticisms on a wide range of topics. Opinions published on the Internet are not limited to certain sites, but rather can be found in a blog, forum, commercial website or any other site allowing posts from visitors.

On of the most representative tools of the Web 2.0 are social networks, which allow millions of users to publish any information in a simple way and to share it with their network of contacts or "friends". These social networks have also evolved and become a continuous flow of information. A clear example is the microblogging platform Twitter[4]. Twitter publishes all kinds of information, disseminating views on many different topics: politics, business, economics and so on. Twitter users regularly publish their comments on a particular news item, a recently purchased product or service, and ultimately on everything that happens around them. This has aroused the interest of the Natural Language Processing (NLP) community, which has begun to study the texts posted on Twitter, and more specifically related to Sentiment Analysis (SA) challenges.

In this manuscript we present a new approach to resolve the scoring of posts according to the expressed positive or negative degree in the text. This polarity detection problem is resolved by combining SentiWordNet scores with a random walk analysis of the concepts found in the text over the WordNet graph. In order to validate our non-supervised approach, several experiments have been performed to analyze major issues in our method and to compare it with other approaches like plain SentiWordNet scoring or machine learning solutions such as Support Vector Machines in a supervised approach. The paper is structured as follows: first, an introduction to the polarity detection problem is provided, followed by the description of our approach. Then, the experimental setup is given with a description of the generated corpus and the results obtained. Finally, conclusions and further work are discussed.

[1]http://epinions.com
[2]http://rottentomatoes.com
[3]http://muchocine.net
[4]http://twitter.com

2 The polarity detection problem

In the literature related to the SA in long text a distinction is made between studies of texts where we assume that the text is a opinion and therefore solely need to calculate its polarity, and those in which before measuring polarity it is necessary to determine whether the text is subjective or objective. A wide study on SA can be found in (Pang and Lee, 2008), (Liu, 2010) and (Tsytsarau and Palpanas, 2011). Concerning the study of the polarity in Twitter, most experiments assume that tweets[5] are subjective. One of the first studies on the classification of the polarity in tweets was published in 2009 by (Go et al., 2009), in which the authors conducted a supervised classification study of tweets in English.

Zhang et al. (Zhang et al., 2011) proposed a hybrid method for the classification of the polarity in Twitter, and they demonstrated the validity of their method over an English corpus on Twitter. The classification is divided into two phases. The first one consists on applying a lexicon-based method. In the second one the authors used the SVM algorithm to determine the polarity. For the machine learning phase, it is needed a labelled corpus, so the purpose of the lexicon-method is to tag the corpus. Thus, the authors selected a set of subjective words from all those available in English and added hash-tags with a subjective meaning. After labelling the corpus, it is used SVM for classifying new tweets.

In (Agarwal et al., 2011) a study was conducted on a reduced corpus of tweets labelled manually. The experiment tests different methods of polarity classification and starts with a base case consisting on the simple use of unigrams. Then a tree-based model is generated. In a third step, several linguistic features are extracted and finally a final model learned as combination of the different models proposed is computed. A common feature used both in the tree-based model and in the feature-based one is the polarity of the words appearing in each tweet. In order to calculate this polarity the authors used DAL dictionary (Whissell, 1989).

Most of the proposed systems for polarity detection compute a value of negativeness or positiveness. Some of them even produce a neutrality value. We will consider the following measurement of polarity (which is very common, indeed): a real value in the interval [-1, 1] would be sufficient. Values over zero would reflect a positive emotion expressed in the tweet, while values below zero would rather correspond to negative opinions. The closer to the zero value a post is, the more its neutrality would be. Therefore, a polarity detection system could be represented as a function p on a text t such as:

$$p : \mathbb{R}^N \to \mathbb{R}$$

so that $p(t) \in [-1, 1]$. We will define how to compute this function, but before an explanation of the techniques implied in such a computation is provided.

3 The approach: Random Walk and SentiWordNet

3.1 The Random Walk algorithm

Personalized Page Rank vectors (PPVs) consists on a ranked sequence of WordNet (Fellbaum, 1998) synsets weighted according to a random walk algorithm. Taking the graph of WordNet, where nodes are synsets and axes are the different semantic relations among them, and the terms contained in a tweet, we can select those synsets that correspond to the closest sense for each term and. Then, it starts an iterative process so more nodes are selected if they are not far from these "seeds". After a number of iterations or a convergence of the weights, a final list of valued nodes can be retrieved. A similar approach has been used recently by (Ramage et al., 2009) to compute text semantic similarity in recognizing textual entailment, and also as a solution for word sense disambiguation (Agirre and Soroa, 2009). We have used the UKB software from this last citation to generate the PPVs used in our system. Random walk algorithms are inspired originally by the Google PageRank algorithm (Page et al., 1999). The idea behind it is to represent each tweet as a vector weighted synsets that are semantically close to the terms included in the post. In some way, we are *expanding* these sort texts by a set of disambiguated concepts related to the terms included in the text.

As an example of a PPV,the text *"Overall, we're still having a hard time with it, mainly because we're not finding it in an early phase."* becomes the vector of weighted synsets:

[5]The name of posts in Twitter.

```
[02190088-a:0.0016, 12613907-n:0.0004,
01680996-a:0.0002, 00745831-a:0.0002, ...]
```

Here, the synset `02190088-a` has a weight of 0.0016, for example.

3.2 SentiWordNet

SentiWordNet (Baccianella et al., 2008) is a lexical resource based on the well know WordNet (Fellbaum, 1998). It provides additional information on synsets related to sentiment orientation. A synset is the basic item of information in WordNet and it represents a "concept" that is unambiguous. Most of the relations over the lexical graph use synsets as nodes (hyperonymy, synonymy, homonymy and more). SentiWordNet returns from every synset a set of three scores representing the notions of "positivity", "negativity" and "neutrality". Therefore, every concept in the graph is weighting according to its subjectivity and polarity. The last version of SentiWordNet (3.0) has been constructed starting from manual annotations of previous versions, populating the whole graph by applying a random walk algorithm. This resource has been used by the opinion mining community, as it provides a domain-independent resource to get certain information about the degree of emotional charge of its concepts (Denecke, 2008; Ogawa et al., 2011).

3.3 Computing the final estimation

As a combination of SentiWordNet scores with random walk weights is wanted, it is important that the final equation leads to comparable values. To this end, the weights associated to synsets after the random walk process are L_1 normalized so vectors of "concepts" sum up the unit as maximum value. The final polarity score is obtained by the product of this vector with associated SentiWordNet vector of scores, as expressed in equation 1.

$$p = \frac{\mathbf{r} \cdot \mathbf{s}}{|\mathbf{t}|} \tag{1}$$

where p is the final score, $\mathbf{r}$ is the vector of weighted synsets computed by the random walk algorithm of the tweet text over WordNet, $\mathbf{s}$ is the vector of polarity scores from SentiWordNet, t is the set of concepts derived from the tweet. The idea behind it is to "expand" the set of concepts with additional ones that are close in the WordNet graph, corresponding to those synset nodes which have been activated during the random walk process. Therefore, terms like *dog* and *bite* (both mainly neutral in SentiWordNet) appearing in the same tweet could eventually be expanded with a more emotional term like *hurt*, which holds, in SentiWordNet, a negative score of 0.75.

4 Experiments and results

Our experiments are focused in testing the validity of applying this unsupervised approach compared to a classical supervised one based on Support Vector Machines (Joachims, 1998). To this end, the corpus has been processed obtaining lemmas, as this is the preferred input for the UKB software. The algorithm takes the whole WordNet graph and performs a disambiguation process of the terms as a natural consequence of applying random walk over the graph. In this way, the synsets that are associated to these terms are all of them initialized. Then, the iterative process of the algorithm (similar to Page Rank but optimized according to an stochastic solution) will change these initial values and propagate weights to closer synsets. An interesting effect of this process is that we can actually obtain more concepts that those contained in the tweet, as all the related ones will also finalize with a certain value due to the propagation of weights across the graph. We believe that our approach benefits from this effect, as texts in tweets use to suffer from a very sort length, allowing us to expand short posts.

Another concern is, therefore, the final size of the PPV vector. If too many concepts are taken into account we may introduce noise in the understanding of the latent semantic of the text. In order to study this fact, different sizes of the vector have been explored and evaluated.

4.1 Our Twitter corpus

The analysis of the polarity on microblogging is a very recent task, so there are few free resources (Saša et al., 2010). Thus, we have collected our own English corpus in order to accomplish the experiments. The work of downloading tweets is not nearly difficult due to the fact that Twitter offers two kinds of API to those purposes. We have used the

Search API of Twitter[6] for automatically accessing tweets through a query. For a supervised polarity study and to evaluate our approach, we need to generate a labelled corpus. We have built a corpus of tweets written in English following the procedure described in (Read, 2005) and (Go et al., 2009).

According to (Read, 2005), when authors of an electronic communication use an emotion, they are effectively marking up their own text with an emotional state. The main feature of Twitter is that the length of the messages must be 140 characters, so the users have to express their opinions, thoughts, and emotional states with few words. Therefore, frequently users write "smileys" in their tweets. Thus, we have used positive emoticons to label positive tweets and negative emoticons to tag negative tweets. The full list of emoticons that we have considered to label the retrieved tweets can be found in Table 1. So, following (Go et al., 2009), the presumption in the construction of the corpus is that the query ":)" returns tweets with positive smileys, and the query ":(" retrieves negative emotions. We have collected a set of 376,296 tweets (181,492 labelled as positive tweets and 194,804 labelled as negative tweets), which were published on Twitter's public message board from September 14th 2010 to March 19th 2011. Table 2 lists other characteristics of the corpus.

Emoticons mapped to :) (positive tweets)	:)	:)	:-)
	;)	;-)	=)
	^_^	:-D	:D
	:d	=D	C:
	Xd	XD	xD
	Xd	(x	(=
	^^	^o^	'u'
	n_n	*-*	*O*
	o	*_*	
Emoticons mapped to :((negative tweets)	:-(	:(	:((
	: (	D:	Dx
	'n'	:\	/:
	):-/	:'	='[
	:_(	/T_T	TOT
	;_;		

Table 1: Emoticons considered as positives and negatives

On the other hand, the language used in Twitter has some unique attributes, which have been removed because they do not provide relevant information for the polarity detection process. These specific features are:

1. **Retweets**: A retweet is the way to repeat a message that users consider interesting. Retweets can be done through the web interface using the Retweet option, or as the old way writing RT, the user name and the post to retweet. The first way is not a problem because is the same tweet, so the API only return it once, but old way retweets are different tweets but with the same content, so we removed them to avoid pitting extra weight on any particular tweet.

2. **Mentions**: Other feature of Twitter is the so called Mentions. When a user wants to refer to another one, he or she introduces a Mention. A Mention is easily recognizable because all of them start with the symbol "@" followed by the user name. We consider that this feature does not provide any relevance information, so we have removed the mentions in all the tweets.

3. **Links**: It is very common that tweets include web directions. In our approach we do not analyze the documents that links those urls, so we have eliminated them from all tweets.

4. **Hash-tags**: A hash-tag is the name of a topic in Twitter. Anybody can begin a new topic by typing the name of the topic preceded by the symbol "#". For this work we do not classify topics so we have neglected all the hash-tags.

Due to the fact that users usually write tweets with a very casual language, it is necessary to preprocess the raw tweets before feeding the sentiment analyzer. For that purpose we have applied the following filters:

1. **Remove new lines**: Some users write tweets in two or three different lines, so all newlines symbols were removed.

2. **Opposite emoticons**: Twitter sometimes considers positive or negative a tweet with smileys

[6] https://dev.twitter.com/docs/api/1/get/search

			Total
Positive tweets	181,492		
Negative tweets	194,804		376,296
Unique users in positive tweets	157,579		
Unique users in negative tweets	167,479		325,058
Words in positive tweets	418,234		
Words in negative tweets	334,687		752,921
Average number of words per positive tweet	9		
Average number of words per negative tweet	10		

Table 2: Statistical description of the corpus.

that have opposite senses. For example:

```
@Harry_Styles I have all day to try
get a tweet off you :)  when are
you coming back to dublin i missed
you last time,I was in spain :(
```

The tweet has two parts one positive and the other one negative, so the post cannot be considered as positive, but the search API returns as a positive tweet because it has the positive smiley ":)". We have removed this kind of tweets in order to avoid ambiguity.

3. **Emoticons with no clear sentiment**: The Twitter Search API considers some emoticons like ":P" or ":PP" as negative. However, some users do not type them to express a negative sentiment. Thus, we have got rid of all tweets with this kind of smileys (see Table 3).

Fuzzy emoticons	:-P	:P	:PP	\(

Table 3: Emoticons considered as fuzzy sentiments

4. **Repeated letters**: Users frequently repeat several times letters of some words to emphasize their messages. For example:

```
Blood drive todayyyy!!!!!  :)
Everyone donateeeee!!
```

This can be a problem for the classification process, because the same word with different repetitions of the same letter would be considered as a different word. Thus, we have normalized all the repeated letters, and any letter occurring more than two times in a word is replaced with two occurrences. The example above would be converted into:

```
blood drive todayy :)  everyone
donatee!!
```

5. **Laugh**: There is not a unique manner to express laugh. Therefore, we have normalized the way to write laugh. Table 4 lists the conversions.

Laugh	Conversion
hahahaha...	haha
hehehehe...	hehe
hihihihi...	hihi
hohohoho...	hoho
huhuhuhu...	huhu
Lol	haha
Huashuashuas	huas
muahahaha	Buaha
buahahaha	Buaha

Table 4: Normalization for expressions considered as "Laugh"

Finally, although the emoticons have been used to tag the positive and negative samples, the final corpora does not include these emoticons. In addition, all the punctuation characters have been neglected in order to reduce the noise in the data. Figure 1 shows the process to generate our Twitter corpus.

4.2 Results obtained

Our first experiment consisted on evaluating a supervised approach, like Support Vector Machines, using the well know vector space model to build the vector of features. Each feature corresponds to the TF.IDF weight of a lemma. Stop words have not been removed and the minimal document frequency required was two, that is, if the lemma is not present in two o more tweets, then it is discarded as a dimension in the vectors. The SVM-Light[7] software was used to compute support vectors and to evaluate them using a random leave-one-out strategy. From

[7] http://svmlight.joachims.org/

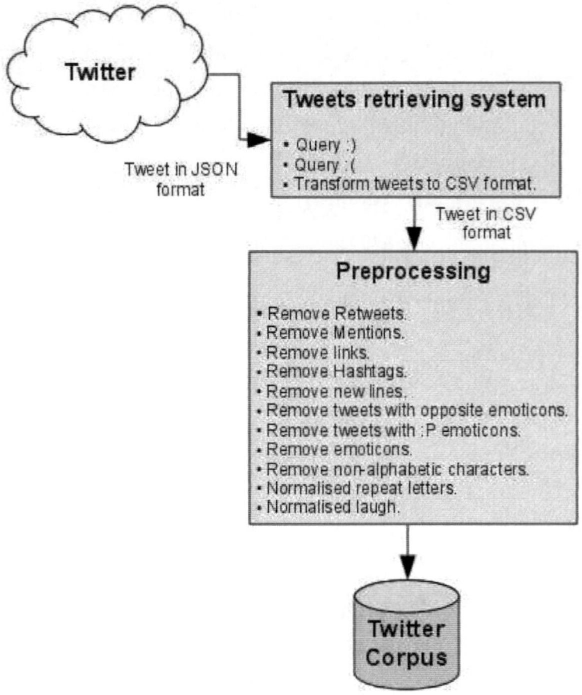

Figure 1: Corpus generation work-flow

a total of 376,284 valid samples 85,423 leave-one-out evaluations were computed. This reported the following measurements:

Precision	Recall	F1
0.6429	0.6147	0.6285

In our first implementation of our method, the final polarity score is computed as described in equation 1. More precisely, it is the average of the product between the difference of positive and negative SentiWordNet scores, and the weight obtained with the random walk algorithm, as unveiled in equation 2.

$$p = \frac{\sum_{\forall s \in t} rw_s \cdot (swn_s^+ - swn_s^-)}{|t|} \quad (2)$$

Where s is a synset in the tweet t, rw_s is the weight of the synset s after the random walk process over WordNet, swn_s^+ and swn_s^-) are positive and negative scores for the synset s retrieved from SentiWordNet.

The results obtained are graphically shown in figures 2, 3 and 4 for precision, recall and F1 values respectively. As can be noticed from the shapes of the graphs, the size of the PPV vectors affects the performance. Sizes above 10 presents an stable behavior, that is, considering a large number of synsets does not improves the performance of the system, but it gets worse neither. The WordNet graph considered for the random walk algorithm includes antonyms relations, so we wanted to check whether discarding these connections would affect the system. From these graphs we can extract the conclusion that antonyms relations are worth keeping.

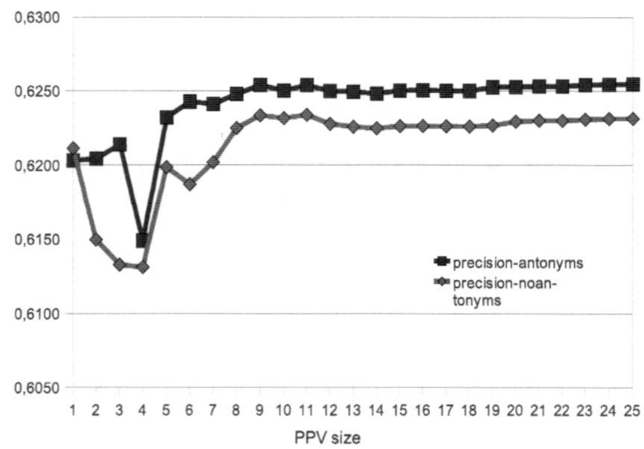

Figure 2: Precision values against PPV sizes

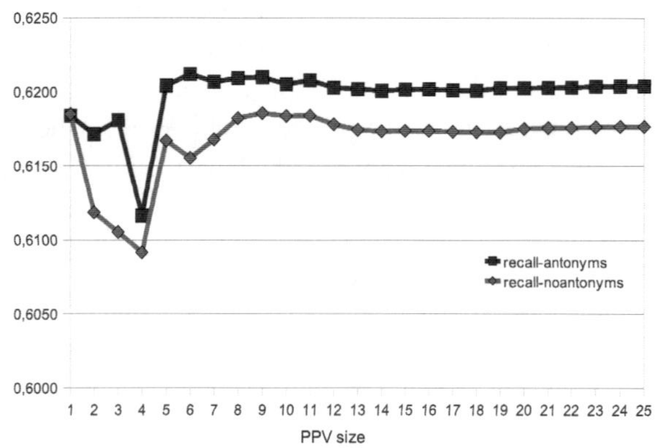

Figure 3: Recall values against PPV sizes

Comparing our best configuration to the SVM approach, the results are not better, but quite close (table 5). Therefore, this unsupervised solution is an interesting alternative to the supervised one.

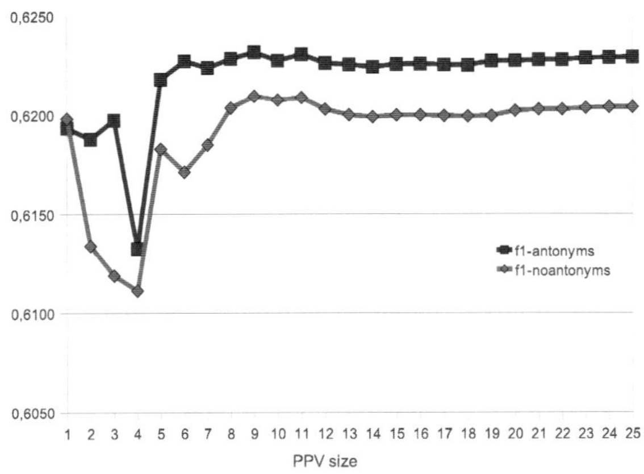

Figure 4: F1 values against PPV sizes

	Precision	Recall	F1
SVM	0.6429	0.6147	0.6285
RW·SWN	0.6259	0.6207	0.6233

Table 5: Approaches comparative table

5 Conclusions and further work

A new unsupervised approach to the polarity detection problem in Twitter posts has been proposed. By combining a random walk algorithm that weights synsets from the text with polarity scores provided by SentiWordNet, it is possible to build a system comparable to a SVM based supervised approach in terms of performance. Our solution is a general approach that do not suffer from the disadvantages associated to supervised ones: need of a training corpus and dependence on the domain where the model was obtained.

Many issues remain open and they will drive our future work. How to deal with negation is a major concern, as the score from SentiWordNet should be considered in a different way in the final computation if the original term comes from a negated phrase. Our "golden rules" must be taken carefully, because emoticons are a rough way to classify the polarity of tweets. Actually, we are working in the generation of a new corpus in the politics domain that is now under a manual labeling process. Another step is to face certain flaws in the computation of the final score. In this sense, we plan to study the context of a tweet among the time line of tweets from that user to identify publisher's mood and adjust final scores. As an additional task, the processing of original texts is important. The numerous grammatical and spelling errors found in this fast way of publication demand for a better sanitization of the incoming data. An automatic spell checker is under development.

As final conclusion, we believe that this first attempt is very promising and that it has arose many relevant questions on the subject of sentiment analysis. More extensive research and experimentation is being undertaken from the starting point introduced in this paper.

Acknowledgments

This work has been partially supported by a grant from the Fondo Europeo de Desarrollo Regional (FEDER), TEXT-COOL 2.0 project (TIN2009-13391-C04-02) from the Spanish Government. This paper is partially funded by the European Commission under the Seventh (FP7 - 2007-2013) Framework Programme for Research and Technological Development through the FIRST project (FP7-287607). This publication reflects the views only of the author, and the Commission cannot be held responsible for any use which may be made of the information contained therein.

References

Apoorv Agarwal, Boyi Xie, Ilia Vovsha, Owen Rambow, and Rebecca Passonneau. 2011. Sentiment analysis of twitter data. In *Proceedings of the Workshop on Language in Social Media (LSM 2011)*, pages 30–38, Portland, Oregon, jun. Association for Computational Linguistics.

Eneko Agirre and Aitor Soroa. 2009. Personalizing pagerank for word sense disambiguation. In *EACL '09: Proceedings of the 12th Conference of the European Chapter of the Association for Computational Linguistics*, pages 33–41, Morristown, NJ, USA. Association for Computational Linguistics.

Stefano Baccianella, Andrea Esuli, and Fabrizio Sebastiani. 2008. Sentiwordnet 3.0 : An enhanced lexical resource for sentiment analysis and opinion mining. *Proceedings of the Seventh conference on International Language Resources and Evaluation LREC10*, 0:2200–2204.

K. Denecke. 2008. Using sentiwordnet for multilingual sentiment analysis. In *Data Engineering Workshop,*

2008. ICDEW 2008. IEEE 24th International Conference on, pages 507 –512, april.

Christiane Fellbaum, editor. 1998. *WordNet: An Electronic Lexical Database*. MIT Press, Cambridge, MA.

Alec Go, Richa Bhayani, and Lei Huang. 2009. Twitter sentiment classification using distant supervision. *Processing*, pages 1–6.

T. Joachims. 1998. Text categorization with support vector machines: learning with many relevant features. In *European Conference on Machine Learning (ECML)*.

Bing Liu. 2010. Sentiment analysis and subjectivity. *Handbook of Natural Language Processing*, 2nd ed.

Tatsuya Ogawa, Qiang Ma, and Masatoshi Yoshikawa. 2011. News Bias Analysis Based on Stakeholder Mining. *IEICE TRANSACTIONS ON INFORMATION AND SYSTEMS*, E94D(3):578–586, MAR.

Lawrence Page, Sergey Brin, Rajeev Motwani, and Terry Winograd. 1999. The pagerank citation ranking: Bringing order to the web. Technical report, Stanford University.

Bo Pang and Lillian Lee. 2008. Opinion mining and sentiment analysis. *Found. Trends Inf. Retr.*, 2(1-2):1–135.

Daniel Ramage, Anna N. Rafferty, and Christopher D. Manning. 2009. Random walks for text semantic similarity. In *TextGraphs-4: Proceedings of the 2009 Workshop on Graph-based Methods for Natural Language Processing*, pages 23–31, Morristown, NJ, USA. Association for Computational Linguistics.

Jonathon Read. 2005. Using emoticons to reduce dependency in machine learning techniques for sentiment classification. In *Proceedings of the ACL Student Research Workshop*, ACLstudent '05, pages 43–48, Stroudsburg, PA, USA. Association for Computational Linguistics.

Petrović Saša, Miles Osborne, and Victor Lavrenko. 2010. The edinburgh twitter corpus. In *Proceedings of the NAACL HLT 2010 Workshop on Computational Linguistics in a World of Social Media*, WSA '10, pages 25–26, Stroudsburg, PA, USA. Association for Computational Linguistics.

Mikalai Tsytsarau and Themis Palpanas. 2011. Survey on mining subjective data on the web. *Data Mining and Knowledge Discovery*, pages 1–37, October.

C M Whissell, 1989. *The dictionary of affect in language*, volume 4, pages 113–131. Academic Press.

Ley Zhang, Riddhiman Ghosh, Mohamed Dekhil, Meichun Hsu, and Bing Liu. 2011. Combining lexicon-based and learning-based methods for twitter sentiment analysis. Technical Report HPL-2011-89, HP, 21/06/2011.

Mining Sentiments from Tweets

Akshat Bakliwal, Piyush Arora, Senthil Madhappan
Nikhil Kapre, Mukesh Singh and Vasudeva Varma
Search and Information Extraction Lab,
International Institute of Information Technology, Hyderabad.
{akshat.bakliwal, piyush.arora}@research.iiit.ac.in,
{senthil.m, nikhil.kapre, mukeshkumar.singh}@students.iiit.ac.in,
vv@iiit.ac.in

Abstract

Twitter is a micro blogging website, where users can post messages in very short text called Tweets. Tweets contain user opinion and sentiment towards an object or person. This sentiment information is very useful in various aspects for business and governments. In this paper, we present a method which performs the task of tweet sentiment identification using a corpus of pre-annotated tweets. We present a sentiment scoring function which uses prior information to classify (binary classification) and weight various sentiment bearing words/phrases in tweets. Using this scoring function we achieve classification accuracy of 87% on Stanford Dataset and 88% on Mejaj dataset. Using supervised machine learning approach, we achieve classification accuracy of 88% on Stanford dataset.

1 Introduction

With enormous increase in web technologies, number of people expressing their views and opinions via web are increasing. This information is very useful for businesses, governments and individuals. With over 340+ million Tweets (short text messages) per day, Twitter is becoming a major source of information.

Twitter is a micro-blogging site, which is popular because of its short text messages popularly known as "Tweets". Tweets have a limit of 140 characters. Twitter has a user base of 140+ million active users[1] and thus is a useful source of information. Users often discuss on current affairs and share their personals views on various subjects via tweets.

Out of all the popular social media's like Facebook, Google+, Myspace and Twitter, we choose Twitter because 1) tweets are small in length, thus less ambigious; 2) unbiased; 3) are easily accessible via API; 4) from various socio-cultural domains.

In this paper, we introduce an approach which can be used to find the opinion in an aggregated collection of tweets. In this approach, we used two different datasets which are build using emoticons and list of suggestive words respectively as noisy labels. We give a new method of scoring "Popularity Score", which allows determination of the popularity score at the level of individual words of a tweet text. We also emphasis on various types and levels of pre-processing required for better performance.

Roadmap for rest of the paper: Related work is discussed in Section 2. In Section 3, we describe our approach to address the problem of Twitter sentiment classification along with pre-processing steps.Datasets used in this research are discussed in Section 4. Experiments and Results are presented in Section 5. In Section 6, we present the feature vector approach to twitter sentiment classification. Section 7 presents as discussion on the methods and we conclude the paper with future work in Section 8.

2 Related Work

Research in Sentiment Analysis of user generated content can be categorized into Reviews (Turney, 2002; Pang et al., 2002; Hu and Liu, 2004), Blogs (Draya et al., 2009; Chesley, 2006; He et al., 2008),

[1] As on March 21, 2012. Source: http://en.wikipedia.org/wiki/Twitter

News (Godbole et al., 2007), etc. All these categories deal with large text. On the other hand, Tweets are shorter length text and are difficult to analyse because of its unique language and structure.

(Turney, 2002) worked on product reviews. Turney used adjectives and adverbs for performing opinion classification on reviews. He used PMI-IR algorithm to estimate the semantic orientation of the sentiment phrase. He achieved an average accuracy of 74% on 410 reviews of different domains collected from Epinion. (Hu and Liu, 2004) performed feature based sentiment analysis. Using Noun-Noun phrases they identified the features of the products and determined the sentiment orientation towards each feature. (Pang et al., 2002) tested various machine learning algorithms on Movie Reviews. He achieved 81% accuracy in unigram presence feature set on Naive Bayes classifier.

(Draya et al., 2009) tried to identify domain specific adjectives to perform blog sentiment analysis. They considered the fact that opinions are mainly expressed by adjectives and pre-defined lexicons fail to identify domain information. (Chesley, 2006) performed topic and genre independent blog classification, making novel use of linguistic features. Each post from the blog is classified as positive, negative and objective.

To the best of our knowledge, there is very less amount of work done in twitter sentiment analysis. (Go et al., 2009) performed sentiment analysis on twitter. They identified the tweet polarity using emoticons as noisy labels and collected a training dataset of 1.6 million tweets. They reported an accuracy of 81.34% for their Naive Bayes classifier. (Davidov et al., 2010) used 50 hashtags and 15 emoticons as noisy labels to create a dataset for twitter sentiment classification. They evaluate the effect of different types of features for sentiment extraction. (Diakopoulos and Shamma, 2010) worked on political tweets to identify the general sentiments of the people on first U.S. presidential debate in 2008.

(Bora, 2012) also created their dataset based on noisy labels. They created a list of 40 words (positive and negative) which were used to identify the polarity of tweet. They used a combination of a minimum word frequency threshold and Categorical Proportional Difference as a feature selection method and achieved the highest accuracy of 83.33% on a hand labeled test dataset.

(Agarwal et al., 2011) performed three class (positive, negative and neutral) classification of tweets. They collected their dataset using Twitter stream API and asked human judges to annotate the data into three classes. They had 1709 tweets of each class making a total of 5127 in all. In their research, they introduced POS-specific prior polarity features along with twitter specific features. They achieved max accuracy of 75.39% for unigram + senti features.

Our work uses (Go et al., 2009) and (Bora, 2012) datasets for this research. We use Naive Bayes method to decide the polarity of tokens in the tweets. Along with that we provide an useful insight on how preprocessing should be done on tweet. Our method of Senti Feature Identification and Popularity Score perform well on both the datasets. In feature vector approach, we show the contribution of individual NLP and Twitter specific features.

3 Approach

Our approach can be divided into various steps. Each of these steps are independent of the other but important at the same time.

3.1 Baseline

In the baseline approach, we first clean the tweets. We remove all the special characters, targets (@), hashtags (#), URLs, emoticons, etc and learn the positive & negative frequencies of unigrams in training. Every unigram token is given two probability scores: Positive Probability (P_p) and Negative Probability (N_p) (*Refer Equation 1*). We follow the same cleaning process for the test tweets. After cleaning the test tweets, we form all the possible unigrams and check for their frequencies in the training model. We sum up the positive and negative probability scores of all the constituent unigrams, and use their difference (positive - negative) to find the overall score of the tweet. If tweet score is > 0 then it is positive otherwise negative.

$$
\begin{aligned}
P_f &= Frequency\ in\ Positive\ Training\ Set \\
N_f &= Frequency\ in\ Negative\ Training\ Set \\
P_p &= Positive\ Probability\ of\ the\ token. \\
&= P_f/(P_f + N_f) \\
N_p &= Negative\ Probability\ of\ the\ token. \\
&= N_f/(P_f + N_f)
\end{aligned} \tag{1}
$$

3.2 Emoticons and Punctuations Handling

We make slight changes in the pre-processing module for handling emoticons and punctuations. We use the emoticons list provided by (Agarwal et al., 2011) in their research. This list[2] is built from wikipedia list of emoticons[3] and is hand tagged into five classes (extremely positive, positive, neutral, negative and extremely negative). In this experiment, we replace all the emoticons which are tagged positive or extremely positive with 'zzhappyzz' and rest all other emoticons with 'zzsadzz'. We append and prepend 'zz' to happy and sad in order to prevent them from mixing into tweet text. At the end, 'zzhappyzz' is scored +1 and 'zzsadzz' is scored -1.

Exclamation marks (!) and question marks (?) also carry some sentiment. In general, '!' is used when we have to emphasis on a positive word and '?' is used to highlight the state of confusion or disagreement. We replace all the occurrences of '!' with 'zzexclaimzz' and of '?' with 'zzquestzz'. We add 0.1 to the total tweet score for each '!' and subtract 0.1 from the total tweet score for each '?'. 0.1 is chosen by trial and error method.

3.3 Stemming

We use Porter Stemmer[4] to stem the tweet words. We modify porter stemmer and restrict it to step 1 only. Step 1 gets rid of plurals and -ed or -ing.

3.4 Stop Word Removal

Stop words play a negative role in the task of sentiment classification. Stop words occur in both positive and negative training set, thus adding more ambiguity in the model formation. And also, stop words don't carry any sentiment information and thus are of no use to us. We create a list of stop words like he, she, at, on, a, the, etc. and ignore them while scoring. We also discard words which are of length ≤ 2 for scoring the tweet.

[2] http://goo.gl/oCSnQ

[3] http://en.wikipedia.org/wiki/List_of_emoticons

[4] http://tartarus.org/m̃artin/PorterStemmer/

3.5 Spell Correction

Tweets are written in random form, without any focus given to correct structure and spelling. Spell correction is an important part in sentiment analysis of user- generated content. Users type certain characters arbitrary number of times to put more emphasis on that. We use the spell correction algorithm from (Bora, 2012). In their algorithm, they replace a word with any character repeating more than twice with two words, one in which the repeated character is placed once and second in which the repeated character is placed twice. For example the word 'swwweeeetttt' is replaced with 8 words 'swet', 'swwet', 'sweet', 'swett', 'swweet', and so on.

Another common type of spelling mistakes occur because of skipping some of characters from the spelling. like "there" is generally written as "thr". Such types of spelling mistakes are not currently handled by our system. We propose to use phonetic level spell correction method in future.

3.6 Senti Features

At this step, we try to reduce the effect of non-sentiment bearing tokens on our classification system. In the baseline method, we considered all the unigram tokens equally and scored them using the Naive Bayes formula (*Refer Equation 1*). Here, we try to boost the scores of sentiment bearing words. In this step, we look for each token in a pre-defined list of positive and negative words. We use the list of of most commonly used positive and negative words provided by Twitrratr[5]. When we come across a token in this list, instead of scoring it using the Naive Bayes formula (*Refer Equation 1*), we score the token +/- 1 depending on the list in which it exist. All the tokens which are missing from this list went under step 3.3, 3.4, 3.5 and were checked for their occurrence after each step.

[5] http://twitrratr.com/

3.7 Noun Identification

After doing all the corrections (3.3 - 3.6) on a word, we look at the reduced word if it is being converted to a Noun or not. We identify the word as a Noun word by looking at its part of speech tag in English WordNet(Miller, 1995). If the majority sense (most commonly used sense) of that word is Noun, we discard the word while scoring. Noun words don't carry sentiment and thus are of no use in our experiments.

3.8 Popularity Score

This scoring method boosts the scores of the most commonly used words, which are domain specific. For example, happy is used predominantly for expressing the positive sentiment. In this method, we multiple its popularity factor (pF) to the score of each unigram token which has been scored in the previous steps. We use the occurrence frequency of a token in positive and negative dataset to decide on the weight of popularity score. *Equation 2* shows how the popularity factor is calculated for each token. We selected a threshold 0.01 min support as the cut-off criteria and reduced it by half at every level. Support of a word is defined as the proportion of tweets in the dataset which contain this token. The value 0.01 is chosen such that we cover a large number of tokens without missing important tokens, at the same time pruning less frequent tokens.

$$
\begin{aligned}
P_f &= Frequency\ in\ Positive\ Training\ Set \\
N_f &= Frequency\ in\ Negative\ Training\ Set \\
& if(P_f - N_f) > 1000) \\
& \qquad pF = 0.9; \\
& elseif((P_f - N_f) > 500) \\
& \qquad pF = 0.8; \\
& elseif((P_f - N_f) > 250) \\
& \qquad pF = 0.7; \\
& elseif((P_f - N_f) > 100) \\
& \qquad pF = 0.5; \\
& elseif((P_f - N_f < 50)) \\
& \qquad pF = 0.1;
\end{aligned} \tag{2}
$$

Figure 1 shows the flow of our approach.

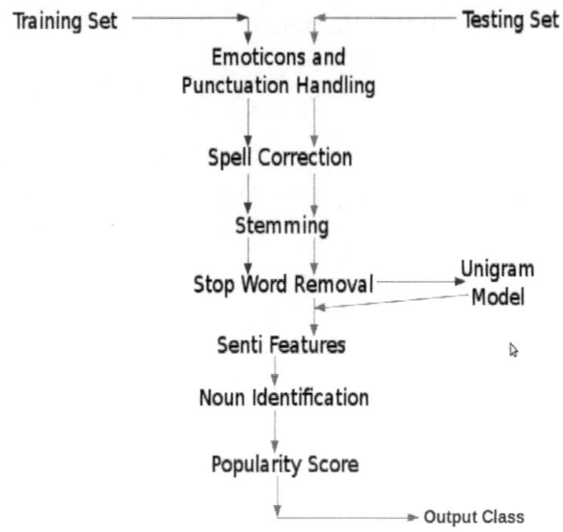

Figure 1: Flow Chart of our Algorithm

4 Datasets

In this section, we explain the two datasets used in this research. Both of these datasets are built using noisy labels.

4.1 Stanford Dataset

This dataset(Go et al., 2009) was built automatically using emoticons as noisy labels. All the tweets which contain ':)' were marked positive and tweets containing ':(' were marked negative. Tweets that did not have any of these labels or had both were discarded. The training dataset has ~1.6 million tweets, equal number of positive and negative tweets. The training dataset was annotated into two classes (positive and negative) while the testing data was hand annotated into three classes (positive, negative and neutral). For our experimentation, we use only positive and negative class tweets from the testing dataset for our experimentation. *Table 1* gives the details of dataset.

Training Tweets	
Positive	800,000
Negative	800,000
Total	1,600,000
Testing Tweets	
Positive	180
Negative	180
Objective	138
Total	498

Table 1: Stanford Twitter Dataset

4.2 Mejaj

Mejaj dataset(Bora, 2012) was built using noisy labels. They collected a set of 40 words and manually categorized them into positive and negative. They label a tweet as positive if it contains any of the positive sentiment words and as negative if it contains any of the negative sentiment words. Tweets which do not contain any of these noisy labels and tweets which have both positive and negative words were discarded. *Table 2* gives the list of words which were used as noisy labels. This dataset contains only two class data. *Table 3* gives the details of the dataset.

Positive Labels	Negative Labels
amazed, amused, attracted, cheerful, delighted, elated, excited, festive, funny, hilarious, joyful, lively, loving, overjoyed, passion, pleasant, pleased, pleasure, thrilled, wonderful	annoyed, ashamed, awful, defeated, depressed, disappointed, discouraged, displeased, embarrassed, furious, gloomy, greedy, guilty, hurt, lonely, mad, miserable, shocked, unhappy, upset

Table 2: Noisy Labels for annotating Mejaj Dataset

Training Tweets	
Positive	668,975
Negative	795,661
Total	1,464,638
Testing Tweets	
Positive	198
Negative	204
Total	402

Table 3: Mejaj Dataset

5 Experiment

In this section, we explain the experiments carried out using the above proposed approach.

5.1 Stanford Dataset

On this dataset(Go et al., 2009), we perform a series of experiments. In the first series of experiments, we train on the given training data and test on the testing data. In the second series of experiments, we perform 5 fold cross validation using the training data. *Table 4* shows the results of each of these experiments on steps which are explained in Approach (Section 3).

In table 4, we give results for each step emoticons and punctuations handling, spell correction, stemming and stop word removal mentioned in Approach Section (Section 3). The Baseline + All Combined results refers to combination of these steps (emoticons, punctuations, spell correction, Stemming and stop word removal) performed together. Series 2 results are average of accuracy of each fold.

5.2 Mejaj Dataset

Similar series of experiments were performed on this dataset(Bora, 2012) too. In the first series of experiments, training and testing was done on the respective given datasets. In the second series of experiments, we perform 5 fold cross validation on the training data. *Table 5* shows the results of each of these experiments.

In table 5, we give results for each step emoticons and punctuations handling, spell correction, stemming and stop word removal mentioned in Approach Section (Section 3). The Baseline + All Combined results refers to combination of these steps (emoticons, punctuations, spell correction, Stemming and stop word removal) performed together. Series 2 results are average of accuracy of each fold.

5.3 Cross Dataset

To validate the robustness of our approach, we experimented with cross dataset training and testing. We trained our system on one dataset and tested on the other dataset. *Table 6* reports the results of cross dataset evaluations.

6 Feature Vector Approach

In this feature vector approach, we form features using Unigrams, Bigrams, Hashtags (#), Targets (@), Emoticons, Special Symbol ('!') and used a semi-supervised SVM classifier. Our feature vector comprised of 11 features. We divide the features into two groups, NLP features and Twitter specific features. NLP features include frequency of positive

Method	Series 1 (%)	Series 2 (%)
Baseline	78.8	80.1
Baseline + Emoticons + Punctuations	81.3	82.1
Baseline + Spell Correction	81.3	81.6
Baseline + Stemming	81.9	81.7
Baseline + Stop Word Removal	81.7	82.3
Baseline + All Combined (AC)	83.5	85.4
AC + Senti Features (wSF)	85.5	86.2
wSF + Noun Identification (wNI)	85.8	87.1
wNI + Popularity Score	**87.2**	**88.4**

Table 4: Results on Stanford Dataset

Method	Series 1 (%)	Series 2 (%)
Baseline	77.1	78.6
Baseline + Emoticons + Punctuations	80.3	80.4
Baseline + Spell Correction	80.1	80.0
Baseline + Stemming	79.1	79.7
Baseline + Stop Word Removal	80.2	81.7
Baseline + All Combined (AC)	82.9	84.1
AC + Senti Features (wSF)	86.8	87.3
wSF + Noun Identification (wNI)	87.6	**88.2**
wNI + Popularity Score	**88.1**	88.1

Table 5: Results on Mejaj Dataset

Method	Training Dataset	Testing Dataset	Accuracy
wNI + Popularity Score	Stanford	Mejaj	**86.4%**
wNI + Popularity Score	Mejaj	Stanford	84.7%

Table 6: Results on Cross Dataset evaluation

NLP	Unigram (f1)	# of positive and negative unigram
	Bigram (f2)	# of positive and negative Bigram
Twitter Specific	Hashtags (f3)	# of positive and negative hashtags
	Emoticons (f4)	# of positive and negative emoticons
	URLs (f5)	Binary Feature - presence of URLs
	Targets (f6)	Binary Feature - presence of Targets
	Special Symbols (f7)	Binary Feature - presence of '!'

Table 7: Features and Description

Feature Set	Accuracy (Stanford)
f1 + f2	85.34%
f3 + f4 + f7	53.77%
f3 + f4 + f5 + f6 + f7	60.12%
f1 + f2 + f3 + f4 + f7	85.89%
f1 + f2 + f3 + f4 + f5 + f6 + f7	**87.64%**

Table 8: Results of Feature Vector Classifier on Stanford Dataset

unigrams matched, negative unigrams matched, positive bigrams matched, negative bigrams matched, etc and Twitter specific features included Emoticons, Targets, HashTags, URLs, etc. *Table 7* shows the features we have considered.

HashTags polarity is decided based on the constituent words of the hashtags. Using the list of positive and negative words from Twitrratr[6], we try to find if hashtags contains any of these words. If so, we assign the polarity of that to the hashtag. For example, "#imsohappy" contains a positive word "happy", thus this hashtag is considered as positive hashtag. We use the emoticons list provided by (Agarwal et al., 2011) in their research. This list[7] is built from wikipedia list of emoticons[8] and is hand tagged into five classes (extremely positive, positive, neutral, negative and extremely negative). We reduce this five class list to two class by merging extremely positive and positive class to single positive class and rest other classes (extremely negative, negative and neutral) to single negative class. *Table 8* reports the accuracy of our machine learning classifier on Stanford dataset.

7 Discussion

In this section, we present a few examples evaluated using our system. The following example denotes the effect of incorporating the contribution of emoticons on tweet classification. Example *"Ahhh I can't move it but hey w/e its on hell I'm elated right now :-D"*. This tweet contains two opinion words, "hell" and "elated". Using the unigram scoring method, this tweet is classified neutral but it is actually positive. If we incorporate the effect of emoticon ":-D", then this tweet is tagged positive. ":-D" is a strong positive emoticon.

Consider this example, *"Bill Clinton Fail - Obama Win?"*. In this example, there are two sentiment bearing words, "Fail" and "Win". Ideally this tweet should be neutral but this is tagged as a positive tweet in the dataset as well as using our system. In this tweet, if we calculate the popularity factor (pF) for "Win" and "Fail", they come out to be 0.9 and 0.8 respectively. Because of the popularity factor weight, the positive score domniates the negative score and thus the tweet is tagged as positive. It is important to identify the context flow in the text and also how each of these words modify or depend on the other words of the tweet.

For calculating the system performance, we assume that the dataset which is used here is correct. Most of the times this assumption is true but there are a few cases where it fails. For example, this tweet *"My wrist still hurts. I have to get it looked at. I HATE the dr/dentist/scary places. :(Time to watch Eagle eye. If you want to join, txt!"* is tagged as positive, but actually this should have been tagged negative. Such erroneous tweets also effect the system performance.

There are few limitations with the current proposed approach which are also open research problems.

1. Spell Correction: In the above proposed approach, we gave a solution to spell correction which works only when extra characters are entered by the user. It fails when users skip some characters like "there" is spelled as "thr". We propose the use of phonetic level spell correction to handle this problem.

2. Hashtag Segmentation: For handling hashtags, we looked for the existence of the positive or negative words[9] in the hashtag. But there can be some cases where it may not work correctly. For example, "#thisisnotgood", in this hashtag if we consider the presence of positive and negative words, then this hashtag is tagged positive ("good"). We fail to capture the presence and effect of "not" which is making this hash-

[6] http://twitrratr.com/

[7] http://goo.gl/oCSnQ

[8] http://en.wikipedia.org/wiki/List_of_emoticons

[9] word list taken from http://twitrratr.com/

tag as negative. We propose to devise and use some logic to segment the hashtags to get correct constituent words.

3. Context Dependency: As discussed in one of the examples above, even tweet text which is limited to 140 characters can have context dependency. One possible method to address this problem is to identify the objects in the tweet and then find the opinion towards those objects.

8 Conclusion and Future Work

Twitter sentiment analysis is a very important and challenging task. Twitter being a microblog suffers from various linguistic and grammatical errors. In this research, we proposed a method which incorporates the popularity effect of words on tweet sentiment classification and also emphasis on how to preprocess the Twitter data for maximum information extraction out of the small content. On the Stanford dataset, we achieved 87% accuracy using the scoring method and 88% using SVM classifier. On Mejaj dataset, we showed an improvement of 4.77% as compared to their (Bora, 2012) accuracy of 83.33%.

In future, This work can be extended through incorporation of better spell correction mechanisms (may be at phonetic level) and word sense disambiguation. Also we can identify the target and entities in the tweet and the orientation of the user towards them.

Acknowledgement

We would like to thank Vibhor Goel, Sourav Dutta and Sonil Yadav for helping us with running SVM classifier on such a large data.

References

Agarwal, A., Xie, B., Vovsha, I., Rambow, O. and Passonneau, R. (2011). Sentiment analysis of Twitter data. In Proceedings of the Workshop on Languages in Social Media LSM '11.

Bora, N. N. (2012). Summarizing Public Opinions in Tweets. In Journal Proceedings of CICLing 2012, New Delhi, India.

Chesley, P. (2006). Using verbs and adjectives to automatically classify blog sentiment. In In Proceedings of AAAI-CAAW-06, the Spring Symposia on Computational Approaches.

Davidov, D., Tsur, O. and Rappoport, A. (2010). Enhanced sentiment learning using Twitter hashtags and smileys. In Proceedings of the 23rd International Conference on Computational Linguistics: Posters COLING '10.

Diakopoulos, N. and Shamma, D. (2010). Characterizing debate performance via aggregated twitter sentiment. In Proceedings of the 28th international conference on Human factors in computing systems ACM.

Draya, G., Planti, M., Harb, A., Poncelet, P., Roche, M. and Trousset, F. (2009). Opinion Mining from Blogs. In International Journal of Computer Information Systems and Industrial Management Applications (IJCISIM).

Go, A., Bhayani, R. and Huang, L. (2009). Twitter Sentiment Classification using Distant Supervision. In CS224N Project Report, Stanford University.

Godbole, N., Srinivasaiah, M. and Skiena, S. (2007). Large-Scale Sentiment Analysis for News and Blogs. In Proceedings of the International Conference on Weblogs and Social Media (ICWSM).

He, B., Macdonald, C., He, J. and Ounis, I. (2008). An effective statistical approach to blog post opinion retrieval. In Proceedings of the 17th ACM conference on Information and knowledge management CIKM '08.

Hu, M. and Liu, B. (2004). Mining Opinion Features in Customer Reviews. In AAAI.

Miller, G. A. (1995). WordNet: A Lexical Database for English. Communications of the ACM *38*, 39–41.

Pang, B., Lee, L. and Vaithyanathan, S. (2002). Thumbs up? Sentiment Classification using Machine Learning Techniques.

Turney, P. D. (2002). Thumbs Up or Thumbs Down? Semantic Orientation Applied to Unsupervised Classification of Reviews. In ACL.

SAMAR: A System for Subjectivity and Sentiment Analysis of Arabic Social Media

Muhammad Abdul-Mageed, Sandra Kübler
Indiana University
Bloomington, IN, USA
{mabdulma, skuebler}@indiana.edu

Mona Diab
Columbia University
New York, NY, USA
mdiab@ccls.columbia.edu

Abstract

In this work, we present SAMAR, a system for Subjectivity and Sentiment Analysis (SSA) for Arabic social media genres. We investigate: how to best represent lexical information; whether standard features are useful; how to treat Arabic dialects; and, whether genre specific features have a measurable impact on performance. Our results suggest that we need individualized solutions for each domain and task, but that lemmatization is a feature in all the best approaches.

1 Introduction

In natural language, *subjectivity* refers to aspects of language used to express opinions, feelings, evaluations, and speculations (Banfield, 1982) and, as such, it incorporates sentiment. The process of subjectivity classification refers to the task of classifying texts as either *objective* (e.g., *The new iPhone was released.*) or *subjective*. Subjective text can further be classified with *sentiment* or *polarity*. For sentiment classification, the task consists of identifying whether a subjective text is *positive* (e.g., *The Syrians continue to inspire the world with their courage!*), *negative* (e.g., *The bloodbaths in Syria are horrifying!*), *neutral* (e.g., *Obama may sign the bill.*), or, sometimes, *mixed* (e.g., *The iPad is cool, but way too expensive*).

In this work, we address two main issues in Subjectivity and Sentiment Analysis (SSA): First, SSA has mainly been conducted on a small number of genres such as newspaper text, customer reports, and blogs. This excludes, for example, social media genres (such as Wikipedia Talk Pages). Second, despite increased interest in the area of SSA, only few attempts have been made to build SSA systems for *morphologically-rich languages* (Abbasi et al., 2008; Abdul-Mageed et al., 2011b), i.e. languages in which a significant amount of information concerning syntactic units and relations is expressed at the word-level, such as Finnish or Arabic. We thus aim at partially bridging these two gaps in research by developing an SSA system for Arabic, a morphologically highly complex languages (Diab et al., 2007; Habash et al., 2009). We present SAMAR, a sentence-level SSA system for Arabic social media texts. We explore the SSA task on four different genres: chat, Twitter, Web forums, and Wikipedia Talk Pages. These genres vary considerably in terms of their functions and the language variety employed. While the chat genre is overridingly in dialectal Arabic (DA), the other genres are mixed between Modern Standard Arabic (MSA) and DA in varying degrees. In addition to working on multiple genres, SAMAR handles Arabic that goes beyond MSA.

1.1 Research Questions

In the current work, we focus on investigating four main research questions:

- **RQ1:** How can morphological richness be treated in the context of Arabic SSA?
- **RQ2:** Can standard features be used for SSA for social media despite the inherently short texts typically used in these genres?
- **RQ3:** How do we treat dialects?

- **RQ4:** Which features specific to social media can we leverage?

RQ1 is concerned with the fact that SSA has mainly been conducted for English, which has little morphological variation. Since the features used in machine learning experiments for SSA are highly lexicalized, a direct application of these methods is not possible for a language such as Arabic, in which one lemma can be associated with thousands of surface forms. For this reason, we need to investigate how to avoid data sparseness resulting from using lexical features without losing information that is important for SSA. More specifically, we concentrate on two questions: Since we need to reduce word forms to base forms to combat data sparseness, is it more useful to use tokenization or lemmatization? And given that the part-of-speech (POS) tagset for Arabic contains a fair amount of morphological information, how much of this information is useful for SSA? More specifically, we investigate two different reduced tagsets, the RTS and the ERTS. For more detailed information see section 4.

RQ2 addresses the impact of using two standard features, frequently employed in SSA studies (Wiebe et al., 2004; Turney, 2002), on social media data, which exhibit DA usage and text length variations, e.g. in twitter data. First, we investigate the utility of applying a UNIQUE feature (Wiebe et al., 2004) where low frequency words below a threshold are replaced with the token "UNIQUE". Given that our data includes very short posts (e.g., twitter data has a limit of only 140 characters per tweet), it is questionable whether the UNIQUE feature will be useful or whether it replaces too many content words. Second, we test whether a polarity lexicon extracted in a standard domain using Modern Standard Arabic (MSA) transfers to social media data. Third, given the inherent lack of a standardized orthography for DA, the problem of replacing content words is expected to be increased since many DA content words would be spelled in different ways.

RQ3 is concerned with the fact that for Arabic, there are significant differences between dialects. However, existing NLP tools such as tokenizers and POS taggers are exclusively trained on and for MSA. We thus investigate whether using an explicit feature that identifies the dialect of the text improves SSA performance.

RQ4 is concerned with attempting to improve SSA performance, which suffers from the problems described above, by leveraging information that is typical for social media genres, such as author or gender information.

The rest of the paper is organized as follows: In Section 2, we review related work. Section 3 describes the social media corpora and the polarity lexicon used in the experiments, Section 4 describes SAMAR, the SSA system and the features used in the experiments. Section 5 describes the experiments and discusses the results. In Section 6, we give an overview of the best settings for the different corpora, followed by a conclusion in Section 7.

2 Related Work

The bulk of SSA work has focused on movie and product reviews (Dave et al., 2003; Hu and Liu, 2004; Turney, 2002). A number of sentence- and phrase-level classifiers have been built: For example, whereas Yi et al. (2003) present a system that detects sentiment toward a given subject, Kim and Hovy's (2004) system detects sentiment towards a specific, predefined topic. Our work is similar to Yu and Hatzivassiloglou (2003) and Wiebe et al. (1999) in that we use lexical and POS features.

Only few studies have been performed on Arabic. Abbasi et al. (2008) use a genetic algorithm for both English and Arabic Web forums sentiment detection on the document level. They exploit both syntactic and stylistic features, but do not use morphological features. Their system is not directly comparable to ours due to the difference in data sets.More related to our work is our previous effort (2011b) in which we built an SSA system that exploits newswire data. We report a slight system improvement using the gold-labeled morphological features and a significant improvement when we use features based on a polarity lexicon from the news domain. In that work, our system performs at 71.54% *F* for subjectivity classification and 95.52% *F* for sentiment detection. This current work is an extension on our previous work however it differs in that we use automatically predicted morphological features and work on data belonging to more genres and DA varieties, hence addressing a more challenging task.

3 Data Sets and Annotation

To our knowledge, no gold-labeled social media SSA data exist. Thereby, we create annotated data comprising a variety of data sets:

DARDASHA (DAR): (Arabic for "chat") comprises the first 2798 chat turns collected from a randomly selected chat session from "Egypt's room" in Maktoob chat `chat.mymaktoob.com`. Maktoob is a popular Arabic portal. DAR is an Egyptian Arabic subset of a larger chat corpus that was harvested between December 2008 and February 2010.

TAGREED (TGRD): ("tweeting") is a corpus of 3015 Arabic tweets collected during May 2010. TRGD has a mixture of MSA and DA. The MSA part (TRGD-MSA) has 1466 tweets, and the dialectal part (TRGD-DA) has 1549 tweets.

TAHRIR (THR): ("editing") is a corpus of 3008 sentences sampled from a larger pool of 30 MSA Wikipedia Talk Pages that we harvested.

MONTADA (MONT): ("forum") comprises of 3097 Web forum sentences collected from a larger pool of threaded conversations pertaining to different varieties of Arabic, including both MSA and DA, from the COLABA data set (Diab et al., 2010). The discussions covered in the forums pertain to social issues, religion or politics. The sentences were automatically filtered to exclude non-MSA threads.

Each of the data sets was labeled at the sentence level by two college-educated native speakers of Arabic. For each sentence, the annotators assigned one of 3 possible labels: (1) objective (OBJ), (2) subjective-positive (S-POS), (3) subjective-negative (S-NEG), and (3) subjective-mixed (S-MIXED). Following (Wiebe et al., 1999), if the primary goal of a sentence is judged as the objective reporting of information, it was labeled as OBJ. Otherwise, a sentence was a candidate for one of the three SUBJ classes. We also labeled the data with a number of other *metadata*[1] tags. Metadata labels included the user gender (GEN), the user identity (UID) (e.g. the user could be a *person* or an *organization*), and the source document ID (DID). We also mark the language variety (LV) (i.e., MSA or DA) used, tagged at the level of each unit of analysis (i.e., sentence, tweet, etc.). Annotators were instructed to label a

Data set	SUBJ	GEN	LV	UID	DID
DAR	✓	✓			
MONT	✓	✓			✓
TRGD	✓	✓	✓	✓	
THR	✓				✓

Table 1: Types of annotation labels (features) manually assigned to the data.

tweet as MSA if it mainly employs MSA words and adheres syntactically to MSA rules, otherwise it is treated as dialectal. Table 1 shows the annotations for each data set. Data statistics, distribution of classes, and inter-annotator agreement in terms of Kappa (K) are provided in Table 2.

Polarity Lexicon: We manually created a lexicon of 3982 adjectives labeled with one of the following tags {*positive, negative, neutral*}, as is reported in our previous work (2011b). We focus on adjectives since they are primary sentiment bearers. The adjectives pertain to the newswire domain, and were extracted from the first four parts of the Penn Arabic Treebank (Maamouri et al., 2004).

4 SAMAR

4.1 Automatic Classification

SAMAR is a machine learning system for Arabic SSA. For classification, we use $\text{SVM}^{\text{light}}$ (Joachims, 2008). In our experiments, we found that linear kernels yield the best performance. We perform all experiments with *presence* vectors: In each sentence vector, the value of each dimension is binary, regardless of how many times a feature occurs.

In the current study, we adopt a *two-stage* classification approach. In the first stage (i.e., *Subjectivity*), we build a binary classifier to separate objective from subjective cases. For the second stage (i.e., *Sentiment*) we apply binary classification that distinguishes S-POS from S-NEG cases. We disregard the neutral and mixed classes for this study. SAMAR uses different feature sets, each of which is designed to address an individual research question:

4.2 Morphological Features

Word forms: In order to minimize data sparseness as a result of the morphological richness of Arabic, we tokenize the text automatically. We use AMIRA (Diab, 2009), a suite for automatic

[1] We use the term 'metadata' as an approximation, as some features are more related to social interaction phenomena.

Data set	# instances	# types	# tokens	# OBJ	# S-POS	# S-NEG	# S-MIXED	Kappa (*K*)
DAR	2,798	11,810	3,133	328	1647	726	97	0.89
MONT	3,097	82,545	20,003	576	1,101	1,027	393	0.88
TRGD	3,015	63,383	16,894	1,428	483	759	345	0.85
TRGD-MSA	1,466	31,771	9,802	960	226	186	94	0.85
TRGD-DIA	1,549	31,940	10,398	468	257	573	251	0.82
THR	3,008	49,425	10,489	1,206	652	1,014	136	0.85

Table 2: Data and inter-annotator agreement statistics.

processing of MSA, trained on Penn Arabic Treebank (Maamouri et al., 2004) data, which consists of newswire text. We experiment with two different configurations to extract base forms of words: (1) *Token* (TOK), where the stems are left as is with no further processing of the morpho-tactics that result from the segmentation of clitics; (2) *Lemma* (LEM), where the words are reduced to their lemma forms, (citation forms): for verbs, this is the 3rd person masculine singular perfective form and for nouns, this corresponds to the singular default form (typically masculine). For example, the word وبحسناتهم (*wbHsnAtHm*) is tokenized as و + ب + حسنات + هم (*w+b+HsnAt+Hm*) (note that in TOK, AMIRA does not split off the pluralizing suffix ات (*At*) from the stem حسن (*Hsn*)), while in the lemmatization step by AMIRA, the lemma rendered is حسنه (*Hsnp*). Thus, SAMAR uses the form of the word as *Hsnp* in the LEM setting, and *HsnAt* in the TOK setting.

POS tagging: Since we use only the base forms of words, the question arises whether we lose meaningful morphological information and consequently whether we could represent this information in the POS tags instead. Thus, we use two sets of POS features that are specific to Arabic: the reduced tag set (RTS) and the extended reduced tag set (ERTS) (Diab, 2009). The RTS is composed of 42 tags and reflects only number for nouns and some tense information for verbs whereas the ERTS comprises 115 tags and enriches the RTS with gender, number, and definiteness information. Diab (2007b; 2007a) shows that using the ERTS improves results for higher processing tasks such as base phrase chunking of Arabic.

4.3 Standard Features

This group includes two features that have been employed in various SSA studies.

Unique: Following Wiebe et al. (2004), we apply a UNIQUE (Q) feature: We replace low frequency words with the token "UNIQUE". Experiments showed that setting the frequency threshold to 3 yields the best results.

Polarity Lexicon (PL): The lexicon (cf. section 3) is used in two different forms for the two tasks: For subjectivity classification, we follow Bruce and Wiebe (1999; 2011b) and add a binary *has_adjective* feature indicating whether or not any of the adjectives in the sentence is part of our manually created polarity lexicon. For sentiment classification, we apply two features, *has_POS_adjective* and *has_NEG_adjective*. These binary features indicate whether a POS or NEG adjective from the lexicon occurs in a sentence.

4.4 Dialectal Arabic Features

Dialect: We apply the two gold language variety features, {*MSA, DA*}, on the Twitter data set to represent whether the tweet is in MSA or in a dialect.

4.5 Genre Specific Features

Gender: Inspired by gender variation research exploiting social media data (e.g., (Herring, 1996)), we apply three *gender* (GEN) features corresponding to the set {*MALE, FEMALE, UNKNOWN*}. Abdul-Mageed and Diab (2012a) suggest that there is a relationship between politeness strategies and sentiment expression. And gender variation research in social media shows that expression of linguistic politeness (Brown and Levinson, 1987) differs based on the gender of the user.

User ID: The *user ID* (UID) labels are inspired by research on Arabic Twitter showing that a considerable share of tweets is produced by organizations such as news agencies (Abdul-Mageed et al., 2011a) as opposed to lay users. We hence employ two features from the set {PERSON, ORGANIZATION} to classification of the Twitter data set. The assumption is that tweets by persons will have a higher correlation with expression of sentiment.

Document ID: Projecting a *document ID* (DID) feature to the paragraph level was shown to improve subjectivity classification on data from the health policy domain (Abdul-Mageed et al., 2011c). Hence, by employing DID at the instance level, we are investigating the utility of this feature for social media as well as at a finer level of analysis, i.e., the sentence level.

5 Empirical Evaluation

For each data set, we divide the data into 80% training (TRAIN), 10% for development (DEV), and 10% for testing (TEST). The classifier was optimized on the DEV set; all results that we report below are on TEST. In each case, our baseline is the majority class in the training set. We report accuracy as well as the F scores for the individual classes (objective vs. subjective and positive vs. negative).

5.1 Impact of Morphology on SSA

We run two experimental conditions: 1. A comparison of TOK to LEM (cf. sec. 4.2); 2. A combination of RTS and ERTS with TOK and LEM.

TOK vs. LEM: Table 3 shows the results for the morphological preprocessing conditions. The baseline, Base, is the majority class in the training data. For all data sets, Subjective is the majority class. For subjectivity classification we see varying performance. DAR: TOK outperforms LEM for all metrics, yet performance is below Base. TGRD: LEM preprocessing yields better accuracy results than Base. LEM is consistently better than TOK for all metrics. THR: We see the opposite performance compared to the TGRD data set where TOK outperforms LEM and also outperforming Base. Finally for MONT: the performance of LEM and TOK are exactly the same yielding the same results as in Base.

For sentiment classification, the majority class is positive for DAR and MONT and negative for TGRD and THR. We note that there are no obvious trends between TOK and LEM. DAR: we observe better performance of LEM over Base and TOK. TGRD: Both preprocessing schemes outperform Base on all metrics with TOK outperforming LEM across the board. THR: LEM outperforms TOK for all metrics of sentiment, yet they are below Base performance. MONT: TOK outperforms LEM in terms of accuracy, and positive sentiment, yet LEM slightly outperforms TOK for negative sentiment classification. Both TOK and LEM are beat by Base in terms of accuracy and positive classification. Given the observed results, we observe no clear trends for the impact for morphological preprocessing alone on performance.

		SUBJ			SENTI		
Data	**Cond.**	**Acc**	***F*-O**	***F*-S**	**Acc**	***F*-P**	***F*-N**
DAR	Base	*84.75*	0.00	*91.24*	*63.02*	*77.32*	0.00
	TOK	**83.90**	0.00	**91.24**	67.71	77.04	45.61
	LEM	83.76	0.00	91.16	**70.16**	**78.65**	**50.43**
TRGD	Base	*61.59*	0.00	*76.23*	*56.45*	0.00	*72.16*
	TOK	69.54	64.06	73.56	**65.32**	**49.41**	**73.62**
	LEM	**71.19**	**64.78**	**75.63**	62.10	41.98	71.86
THR	Base	*52.92*	0.00	*69.21*	*75.00*	0.00	*85.71*
	TOK	**58.44**	**28.09**	**70.78**	60.47	37.04	71.19
	LEM	57.79	26.97	70.32	**63.37**	**38.83**	**73.86**
MONT	Base	*83.44*	0.00	*90.97*	*86.82*	*92.94*	0.00
	TOK	83.44	0.00	90.97	**74.55**	**83.63**	42.86
	LEM	83.44	0.00	90.97	72.27	81.68	**42.99**

Table 3: SSA results with preprocessing TOK and LEM.

Adding POS tags: Table 4 shows the results of adding POS tags based on the two tagsets RTS and ERTS. Subjectivity classification: The results show that adding POS information improves accuracy and F score for all the data sets except MONT which is still at Base performance. RTS outperforms ERTS with TOK, and the opposite with LEM where ERTS outperforms RTS, however, overall TOK+RTS yields the highest performance of 91.49% F score on subjectivity classification for the DAR dataset. For the TGRD and THR data sets, we note that TOK+ERTS is equal to or outperforms the other conditions on subjectivity classification. For MONT there is no difference between experimental conditions and no impact for adding the POS tag information. In the sentiment classification task:

The sentiment task shows a different trend: here, the highest performing systems do not use POS tags. This is attributed to the variation in genre between the training data on which AMIRA is trained (MSA newswire) and the data sets we are experimenting with in this work. However in relative compari-

		SUBJ			SENTI		
Data	**Cond.**	**Acc**	***F*-O**	***F*-S**	**Acc**	***F*-P**	***F*-N**
DAR	Base	*84.75*		*91.24*	*63.02*	*77.32*	
	TOK+RTS	**84.32**	0.00	**91.49**	66.15	76.36	40.37
	TOK+ERTS	83.90	0.00	91.24	67.19	77.09	42.20
	LEM+RTS	83.47	0.00	90.99	67.71	77.21	44.64
	LEM+ERTS	83.47	0.00	90.99	**68.75**	**77.94**	**46.43**
TGRD	Base	*61.59*		*76.23*	*56.45*		*72.16*
	TOK+RTS	70.20	64.57	74.29	62.90	43.90	72.29
	TOK+ERTS	71.19	65.06	**75.49**	62.90	42.50	72.62
	LEM+RTS	70.20	64.57	74.29	62.90	46.51	71.60
	LEM+ERTS	**72.19**	**76.54**	71.19	**65.32**	**48.19**	**73.94**
THR	Base	*52.92*		*69.21*	*75.00*		*85.71*
	TOK+RTS	57.47	28.42	69.75	59.30	33.96	70.59
	TOK+ERTS	**59.42**	**28.57**	**71.66**	59.88	**38.94**	70.13
	LEM+RTS	**59.42**	**28.57**	**71.66**	59.88	33.01	**71.37**
	LEM+ERTS	58.77	25.73	71.46	**60.47**	37.04	71.19
MONT	Base	*83.44*		*90.97*	*86.82*	*92.94*	
	TOK+RTS	83.44	0.00	90.97	69.09	79.27	39.29
	TOK+ERTS	83.44	0.00	90.97	**71.82**	**81.55**	**40.38**
	LEM+RTS	83.44	0.00	90.97	70.00	80.36	36.54
	LEM+ERTS	83.44	0.00	90.97	69.55	79.64	39.64

Table 4: SSA results with different morphological preprocessing and POS features.

son between RTS and ERTS for sentiment shows that in a majority of the cases, ERTS outperforms RTS, thus indicating that the additional morphological features are helpful. One possible explanation may be that variations of some of the morphological features (e.g., existence of a gender, person, adjective feature) may correlate more frequently with positive or negative sentiment.

5.2 Standard Features for Social Media Data

RQ2 concerns the question whether standard features can be used successfully for classifying social media text characterized by the usage of dialect and by differing text lengths. We add the standard features, polarity (PL) and UNIQUE (Q), to the two tokenization schemes and the POS tag sets. We report only the best performing conditions here.

Table 5 shows the best performing settings per corpus from the previous section as well as the best performing setting given the new features. The results show that apart from THR and TGRD for sentiment, all corpora gain in accuracy for both subjectivity and sentiment. In the case of subjectivity, while considerable improvements are gained for both DAR (11.51% accuracy) and THR (32.90% accuracy), only slight improvements ($< 1\%$ accuracy) are reached for both TGRD and MONT. For sentiment classification, the improvements in accuracy are less than the case of subjectivity: 1.84% for DAR and 6.81% for MONT. The deterioration on THR is surprising and may be a result of the nature of sentiment as expressed in the THR data set: Wikipedia has a 'Neutral Point of View' policy based on which users are required to focus their contributions not on other users but content, and as such sentiment is expressed in nuanced indirect ways in THR. While the subjectivity results show that it is feasible to use the combination of the UNIQUE feature and the polarity lexicon features successfully, even for shorter texts, such as in the twitter data (TGRD), this conclusion does not always hold for sentiment classification. However, we assume that the use of the polarity lexicon would result in higher gains if the lexicon were adapted to the new domains.

5.3 SSA Given Arabic Dialects

RQ3 investigates how much the results of SSA are affected by the presence or absence of dialectal Arabic in the data. For this question, we focus on the TGRD data set because it contains a non-negligible amount (i.e., 48.62%) of tweets in dialect.

First, we investigate how our results change when we split the TGRD data set into two subsets, one containing only MSA, the other one containing only DA. We extract the 80-10-10% data split, then train and test the classifier exclusively on either MSA or dialect data. The subjectivity results for this experiment are shown in Table 6, and the sentiment re-

Data	SUBJ Best condition	Acc	*F*-O	*F*-S	SENTI Best condition	Acc	*F*-P	*F*-N
DAR	TOK+RTS	84.32	0.00	91.49	LEM+ERTS	68.75	77.94	46.43
	TOK+ERTS+PL+Q3	**95.83**	0.00	97.87	LEM+ERTS+PL+Q3	**70.59**	79.51	47.92
TGRD	LEM+ERTS	72.19	76.54	71.19	LEM+ERTS	65.32	73.94	48.19
	LEM+ERTS+PL	**72.52**	65.84	77.01	LEM+ERTS+PL	65.32	73.94	48.19
THR	L./T.+ERTS	59.42	28.57	71.66	LEM+ERTS	63.37	38.83	73.86
	TOK+ERTS +PL+Q3	**83.33**	0.00	90.91	LEM+RTS+PL+Q3	61.05	34.95	72.20
MONT	LEM+ERTS	83.44	0.00	90.97	TOK	74.55	83.63	42.86
	LEM+RTS+PL+Q3	**84.19**	3.92	91.39	TOK+PL+Q3	81.36	88.64	48.10

Table 5: SSA results with standard features. Number in bold signify improvements over the best results in section 5.1.

Cond.	TGRD Acc	TGRD *F*-O	TGRD *F*-S	TGRD-MSA Acc	TGRD-MSA *F*-O	TGRD-MSA *F*-S	TGRD-DA Acc	TGRD-DA *F*-O	TGRD-DA *F*-S
Base	61.59	0.00	76.23	51.68	68.14	0.00	78.40	0.00	87.89
TOK	69.54	64.06	73.56	**61.74**	70.16	46.73	78.40	5.41	87.80
LEM	71.19	64.78	75.63	**65.10**	72.04	53.57	**79.01**	15.00	88.03

Table 6: Dialect-specific subjectivity experiments.

sults are shown in Table 7. For both tasks, the results show considerable differences between MSA and DA: For TGRD-MSA, the results are lower than for TGRD-DA, which is a direct consequence of the difference in distribution of subjectivity between the two subcorpora. TGRD-DA is mostly subjective while TGRD-MSA is more balanced. With regard to sentiment, TGRD-DA consists of mostly negative tweets while TGRD-MSA again is more balanced. These results suggest that knowing whether a tweet is in dialect would help classification.

For subjectivity, we can see that TGRD-MSA improves by 13.5% over the baseline while for TGRD-DA, the improvement is more moderate, $< 3\%$. We assume that this is partly due to the higher skew in TGRD-DA, moreover, it is known that our preprocessing tools yield better performance on MSA data leading to better tokenization and lemmatization.

For sentiment classification on TGRD-MSA, neither tokenization nor lemmatization improve over the baseline. This is somewhat surprising since we expect AMIRA to work well on this data set and thus to lead to better classification results. However, a considerable extent of the MSA tweets are expected to come from news headlines (Abdul-Mageed et al., 2011a), and headlines usually are not loci of explicitly subjective content and hence are difficult to classify and in essence harder to preprocess since the genre is different from regular newswire even if MSA. For the TGRD-DA data set, both lemmatization and tokenization improve over the baseline.

The results for both subjectivity and sentiment on the MSA and DA sets suggest that processing errors by AMIRA trained exclusively on MSA newswire data) result in deteriorated performance. However we do not observe such trends on the TGRD-DA data sets. This is not surprising since the TGRD-DA is not very different from the newswire data on which AMIRA was trained: Twitter users discuss current events topics also discussed in newswire. There is also a considerable lexical overlap between MSA and DA. Furthermore, dialectal data may be loci for more sentiment cues like emoticons, certain punctuation marks (e.g. exclamation marks), etc. Such clues are usually absent (or less frequent) in MSA data and hence the better sentiment classification on TGRD-DA.

We also experimented with adding POS tags and standard features. These did not have any positive effect on the results with one exception, which is shown in Table 8: For sentiment, adding the RTS tagset has a positive effect on the two data sets.

In a second experiment, we used the original TGRD corpus but added the language variety (LV) (i.e., MSA and DA) features. For both subjectivity and sentiment, the best results are acquired using the LEM+PL+LV settings. However, for subjectivity, we observe a drop in accuracy from 72.52% (LEM+ERTS+PL) to 69.54%. For sentiment, we also observe a performance drop in accuracy, from 65.32% (LEM+ERTS+PL) to 64.52%. This means that knowing the language variety does not provide

Cond.	TGRD Acc	TGRD *F*-P	TGRD *F*-N	TGRD-MSA Acc	TGRD-MSA *F*-P	TGRD-MSA *F*-N	TGRD-DA Acc	TGRD-DA *F*-P	TGRD-DA *F*-N
Base	56.45	0.00	72.16	53.49	69.70	0.00	67.47	0.00	80.58
TOK	65.32	49.41	73.62	53.49	56.52	50.00	**68.67**	23.53	80.30
LEM	62.10	41.98	71.86	48.84	52.17	45.00	**73.49**	38.89	83.08
TOK+RTS	70.20	64.57	74.29	55.81	61.22	48.65	**71.08**	29.41	81.82

Table 7: Dialect-specific sentiment experiments.

Data	SUBJ Condition	SUBJ Acc	SUBJ *F*-O	SUBJ *F*-S	SENTI Condition	SENTI Acc	SENTI *F-P*	SENTI *F-N*
DAR	TOK+ERTS+PL+Q3	**95.83**	0.00	97.87	LEM+PL+GEN	**71.28**	79.86	50.00
TGRD	LEM+ERTS+PL	**72.52**	65.84	77.01	TOK+ERTS+PL+GEN+LV+UID	**65.87**	49.41	74.25
THR	TOK+ERTS+PL+Q3	**83.33**	0.00	90.91	TOK+PL+GEN+UID	**67.44**	39.13	77.78
MONT	LEM+RTS+PL+Q3	**84.19**	3.92	91.39	TOK+PL+Q3	81.36	88.64	48.10

Table 8: Overall best SAMAR performance. Numbers in bold show improvement over the baseline.

Data	Condition	Acc	*F*-O	*F*-S
DAR	TOK+ERTS+PL+GEN	84.30	0.00	91.48
TGRD	LEM+RTS+PL+UID	71.85	65.31	76.32
THR	LEM+RTS+PL+GEN+UID	66.67	0.00	80.00
MONT	LEM+RTS+PL+DID	83.17	0.00	90.81

Table 9: Subjectivity results with genre features.

Data	Condition	Acc	*F*-P	*F*-N
DAR	LEM+PL+GEN	**71.28**	79.86	50.00
TGRD	TOK+ERTS+PL+GEN+LV +UID	**65.87**	49.41	74.25
THR	TOK+PL+GEN+UID	**67.44**	39.13	77.78
MONT	LEM+PL+DID	76.82	47.42	85.13

Table 10: Sentiment results with genre features. Numbers in bold show improvement over table 5.

enough information for successfully conquering the differences between those varieties.

5.4 Leveraging Genre Specific Features

RQ4 investigates the question whether we can leverage features typical for social media for classification. We apply all GENRE features exhaustively.We report the best performance on each data set.

Table 9 shows the results of adding the genre features to the subjectivity classifier. For this task, no data sets profit from these features.

Table 10 shows the results of adding the genre features to the sentiment classifier. Here, all the data sets, with the exception of MONT, profit from the new features. In the case of DAR, adding gender information improves classification by 1.73% in accuracy. For TGRD, the combination of the gender (GN), language variety (LV), and user ID slightly (0.52%) improves classification over previous best settings. For THR, adding the gender and user ID information improves classification by 4.07%.

Our results thus show the utility of the gender, LV, and user ID features for sentiment classification. The results for both subjectivity and sentiment show that the document ID feature is not a useful feature.

6 Overall Performance

Table 8 provides the best results reached by SAMAR. For subjectivity classification, SAMAR improves on all data sets when the POS features are combined with the standard features. For sentiment classification, SAMAR also improves over the baseline on all the data sets, except MONT. The results also show that all optimal feature settings for subjectivity, except with the MONT data set, include the ERTS POS tags while the results in Section 5.1 showed that adding POS information without additional features, while helping in most cases with subjectivity, does not help with sentiment classification.

7 Conclusion and Future Work

In this paper, we presented SAMAR, an SSA system for Arabic social media. We explained the rich feature set SAMAR exploits and showed how complex morphology characteristic of Arabic can be handled in the context of SSA. For the future, we plan to carry out a detailed error analysis of SAMAR in an attempt to improve its performance, use a recently-developed wider coverage polarity lexicon (Abdul-Mageed and Diab, 2012b) together with another DA lexicon that we are currently developing.

References

Ahmed Abbasi, Hsinchun Chen, and Arab Salem. 2008. Sentiment analysis in multiple languages: Feature selection for opinion classification in Web forums. *ACM Transactions on Information Systems*, 26:1–34.

Muhammad Abdul-Mageed and Mona Diab. 2012a. *AWATIF*: A multi-genre corpus for Modern Standard Arabic subjectivity and sentiment analysis. In *Proceedings of LREC*, Istanbul, Turkey.

Muhammad Abdul-Mageed and Mona Diab. 2012b. Toward building a large-scale Arabic sentiment lexicon. In *Proceedings of the 6th International Global WordNet Conference*, Matsue, Japan.

Muhammad Abdul-Mageed, Hamdan Albogmi, Abdulrahman Gerrio, Emhamed Hamed, and Omar Aldibasi. 2011a. Tweeting in Arabic: What, how and whither. Presented at the 12th Annual Conference of the Association of Internet Researchers (Internet Research 12.0, Performance and Participation), Seattle, WA.

Muhammad Abdul-Mageed, Mona Diab, and Mohamed Korayem. 2011b. Subjectivity and sentiment analysis of Modern Standard Arabic. In *Proceedings of the 49th Annual Meeting of the Association for Computational Linguistics: Human Language Technologies*, pages 587–591, Portland, OR.

Muhammad Abdul-Mageed, Mohamed Korayem, and Ahmed YoussefAgha. 2011c. "Yes we can?": Subjectivity annotation and tagging for the health domain. In *Proceedings of RANLP2011*, Hissar, Bulgaria.

Ann Banfield. 1982. *Unspeakable Sentences: Narration and Representation in the Language of Fiction*. Routledge, Boston.

Penelope Brown and Stephen Levinson. 1987. *Politeness: Some Universals in Language Usage*. Cambridge University Press.

Rebecca Bruce and Janyce Wiebe. 1999. Recognizing subjectivity. A case study of manual tagging. *Natural Language Engineering*, 5(2):187–205.

Kushal Dave, Steve Lawrence, and David Pennock. 2003. Mining the peanut gallery: Opinion extraction and semantic classification of product reviews. In *Proceedings of the 12th International Conference on World Wide Web*, pages 519–528, Budapest, Hungary. ACM.

Mona Diab, Dan Jurafsky, and Kadri Hacioglu. 2007. Automatic processing of Modern Standard Arabic text. In Abdelhadi Soudi, Antal van den Bosch, and Günter Neumann, editors, *Arabic Computational Morphology*. Springer.

Mona Diab, Nizar Habash, Owen Rambow, Mohamed Altantawy, and Yassin Benajiba. 2010. COLABA: Arabic dialect annotation and processing. In *LREC Workshop on Semitic Language Processing*, pages 66–74, Valetta, Malta.

Mona Diab. 2007a. Improved Arabic base phrase chunking with a new enriched POS tag set. In *Proceedings of the 2007 Workshop on Computational Approaches to Semitic Languages: Common Issues and Resources*, pages 89–96, Prague, Czech Republic.

Mona Diab. 2007b. Towards an optimal POS tag set for Modern Standard Arabic processing. In *Proceedings of Recent Advances in Natural Language Processing (RANLP)*, Borovets, Bulgaria.

Mona Diab. 2009. Second generation AMIRA tools for Arabic processing: Fast and robust tokenization, POS tagging, and base phrase chunking. In *Proceedings of the Second International Conference on Arabic Language Resources and Tools*, pages 285–288, Cairo, Egypt.

Nizar Habash, Owen Rambow, and Ryan Roth. 2009. MADA+TOKAN: A toolkit for Arabic tokenization, diacritization, morphological disambiguation, POS tagging, stemming and lemmatization. In *Proceedings of the Second International Conference on Arabic Language Resources and Tools*, pages 102–109, Cairo, Egypt.

Susan Herring. 1996. Bringing familiar baggage to the new frontier: Gender differences in computer-mediated communication. In J. Selzer, editor, *Conversations*. Allyn & Bacon.

Minqing Hu and Bing Liu. 2004. Mining and summarizing customer reviews. In *Proceedings of the Tenth ACM SIGKDD International Conference on Knowledge Discovery and Data Mining*, pages 168–177, Seattle, WA.

Thorsten Joachims. 2008. Svmlight: Support vector machine. http://svmlight.joachims.org/, Cornell University, 2008.

Soo-Min Kim and Eduard Hovy. 2004. Determining the sentiment of opinions. In *Proceedings of the 20th International Conference on Computational Linguistics*, pages 1367–1373, Geneva, Switzerland.

Mohamed Maamouri, Anne Bies, Tim Buckwalter, and W. Mekki. 2004. The Penn Arabic Treebank: Building a large-scale annotated Arabic corpus. In *NEMLAR Conference on Arabic Language Resources and Tools*, pages 102–109, Cairo, Egypt.

Peter Turney. 2002. Thumbs up or thumbs down? Semantic orientation applied to unsupervised classification of reviews. In *Proceedings of the 40th Annual Meeting of the Association for Computational Linguistics (ACL'02)*, Philadelphia, PA.

Janyce Wiebe, Rebecca Bruce, and Tim O'Hara. 1999. Development and use of a gold standard data set for subjectivity classifications. In *Proceedings of the 37th*

Annual Meeting of the Association for Computational Linguistics (ACL-99), pages 246–253, University of Maryland.

Janyce Wiebe, Theresa Wilson, Rebecca Bruce, Matthew Bell, and Melanie Martin. 2004. Learning subjective language. *Computational Linguistics*, 30:227–308.

Jeonghee Yi, Tetsuya Nasukawa, Razvan Bunescu, and Wayne Niblack. 2003. Sentiment analyzer: Extracting sentiments about a given topic using natural language processing techniques. In *Proceedings of the 3rd IEEE International Conference on Data Mining*, pages 427–434, Melbourne, FL.

Hong Yu and Vasileios Hatzivassiloglou. 2003. Towards answering opinion questions: Separating facts from opinions and identifying the polarity of opinion sentences. In *Proceedings of the Conference on Empirical Methods in Natural Language Processing (EMNLP)*, Sapporo, Japan.

Opinum: statistical sentiment analysis for opinion classification

Boyan Bonev, Gema Ramírez-Sánchez, Sergio Ortiz Rojas
Prompsit Language Engineering
Avenida Universidad, s/n. Edificio Quorum III.
03202 Elche, Alicante (Spain)
{boyan,gramirez,sortiz}@prompsit.com

Abstract

The classification of opinion texts in positive and negative can be tackled by evaluating separate key words but this is a very limited approach. We propose an approach based on the order of the words without using any syntactic and semantic information. It consists of building one probabilistic model for the positive and another one for the negative opinions. Then the test opinions are compared to both models and a decision and confidence measure are calculated. In order to reduce the complexity of the training corpus we first lemmatize the texts and we replace most named-entities with wildcards. We present an accuracy above 81% for Spanish opinions in the financial products domain.

1 Introduction

Most of the texts written by humans reflect some kind of sentiment. The interpretation of these sentiments depend on the linguistic skills and emotional intelligence of both the author and the reader, but above all, this interpretation is subjective to the reader. They don't really exist in a string of characters, for they are subjective states of mind. Therefore sentiment analysis is a prediction of how most readers would react to a given text.

There are texts which intend to be objective and texts which are intentionally subjective. The latter is the case of opinion texts, in which the authors intentionally use an appropriate language to express their positive or negative sentiments about something. In this paper we work on the classification of opinions in two classes: those expressing positive sentiment (the author is in favour of something) and those expressing negative sentiment, and we will refer to them as positive opinions and negative opinions.

Sentiment analysis is possible thanks to the opinions available online. There are vast amounts of text in fora, user reviews, comments in blogs and social networks. It is valuable for marketing and sociological studies to analyse these freely available data on some definite subject or entity. Some of the texts available do include opinion information like stars, or recommend-or-not, but most of them do not. A good corpus for building sentiment analysis systems would be a set of opinions separated by domains. It should include some information about the cultural origin of authors and their job, and each opinion should be sentiment-evaluated not only by its own author, but by many other readers as well. It would also be good to have a marking of the subjective and objective parts of the text. Unfortunately this kind of corpora are not available at the moment.

In the present work we place our attention at the supervised classification of opinions in positive and negative. Our system, which we call *Opinum*[1], is trained from a corpus labeled with a value indicating whether an opinion is positive or negative. The corpus was crawled from the web and it consists of a 160MB collection of Spanish opinions about financial products. Opinum's approach is general enough and it is not limited to this corpus nor to the financial domain.

There are state-of-the-art works on sentiment

[1] An Opinum installation can be tested from a web interface at http://aplica.prompsit.com/en/opinum

analysis which care about differentiating between the objective and the subjective part of a text. For instance, in the review of a film there is an objective part and then the opinion (Raaijmakers et al., 2008). In our case we work directly with opinion texts and we do not make such difference. We have noticed that in customer reviews, even when stating objective facts, some positive or negative sentiment is usually expressed.

Many works in the literature of sentiment analysis take lexicon-based approaches (Taboada et al., 2011). For instance (Hu and Liu, 2004; Blair-Goldensohn et al., 2008) use WordNet to extend the relation of positive and negative words to other related lexical units. However the combination of which words appear together may also be important and there are comparisons of different Machine learning approaches (Pang et al., 2002) in the literature, like Support Vector Machines, k-Nearest Neighbours, Naive-Bayes, and other classifiers based on global features. In (McDonald et al., 2007) structured models are used to infer the sentiment from different levels of granularity. They score cliques of text based on a high-dimensional feature vector.

In the Opinum approach we score each sentence based on its n-gram probabilites. For a complete opinion we sum the scores of all its sentences. Thus, if an opinion has several positive sentences and it finally concludes with a negative sentence which settles the whole opinion as negative, Opinum would probably fail. The n-gram sequences are good at capturing phrasemes (multiwords), the motivation for which is stated in Section 2. Basically, there are phrasemes which bear sentiment. They may be different depending on the domain and it is recommendable to build the models with opinions belonging to the target domain, for instance, financial products, computers, airlines, etc. A study of domain adaptation for sentiment analysis is presented in (Blitzer et al., 2007). In Opinum different classifiers would be built for different domains. Building the models does not require the aid of experts, only a labeled set of opinions is necessary. Another contribution of Opinum is that it applies some simplifications on the original text of the opinions for improving the performance of the models.

In the remainder of the paper we first state the motivation of our approach in Section 2, then in Section 3 we describe in detail the Opinum approach. In Section 4 we present our experiments with Spanish financial opinions and we state some conclusions and future work in Section 5.

2 Hypothesis

When humans read an opinion, even if they do not understand it completely because of the technical details or domain-specific terminology, in most cases they can notice whether it is positive or negative. The reason for this is that the author of the opinion, consciously or not, uses nuances and structures which show a positive or negative feeling. Usually, when a user writes an opinion about a product, the intention is to communicate that subjective feeling, apart from describing the experience with the product and giving some technical details.

The hypothesis underlying the traditional keyword or lexicon-based approaches (Blair-Goldensohn et al., 2008; Hu and Liu, 2004) consist in looking for some specific positive or negative words. For instance, "great" should be positive and "disgusting" should be negative. Of course there are some exceptions like "not great", and some approaches detect negation to invert the meaning of the word. More elaborate cases are constructions like "an offer you can't refuse" or "the best way to lose your money".

There are domains in which the authors of the opinions might not use these explicit keywords. In the financial domain we can notice that many of the opinions which express the author's insecurity are actually negative, even though the words are mostly neutral. For example, "I am not sure if I would get a loan from this bank" has a negative meaning. Another difficulty is that the same words could be positive or negative depending on other words of the sentence: "A loan with high interests" is negative while "A savings account with high interests" is positive. In general more complex products have more complex and subtle opinions. The opinion about a cuddly toy would contain many keywords and would be much more explicit than the opinion about the conditions of a loan. Even so, the human readers can get the positive or negative feeling at a glance.

The hypothesis of our approach is that it is possible to classify opinions in negative and positive based on canonical (lemmatized) word sequences. Given a set of positive opinions $\mathbf{O}^p$ and a set of negative opinions $\mathbf{O}^n$, the probability distributions of their n-gram word sequences are different and can be compared to the n-grams of a new opinion in order to classify it. In terms of statistical language models, given the language models M^p and M^n obtained from $\mathbf{O}^p$ and $\mathbf{O}^n$, the probability $p_o^p = P(o|\mathbf{O}^p)$ that a new opinion would be generated by the positive model is smaller or greater than the probability $p_o^n = P(o|\mathbf{O}^N)$ that a new opinion would be generated by the negative model.

We build the models based on sequences of canonical words in order to simplify the text, as explained in the following section. We also replace some named entities like names of banks, organizations and people by wildcards so that the models do not depend on specific entities.

3 The Opinum approach

The proposed approach is based on n-gram language models. Therefore building a consistent model is the key for its success. In the field of machine translation a corpus with size of 500MB is usually enough for building a 5-gram language model, depending on the morphological complexity of the language.

In the field of sentiment analysis it is very difficult to find a big corpus of context-specific opinions. Opinions labeled with stars or a positive/negative label can be automatically downloaded from different customers' opinion websites. The sizes of the corpora collected that way range between 1MB and 20MB for both positive and negative opinions.

Such a small amount of text would be suitable for bigrams and would capture the difference between "not good" and "really good", but this is not enough for longer sequences like "offer you can't refuse". In order to build consistent 5-gram language models we need to simplify the language complexity by removing all the morphology and replacing the surface forms by their canonical forms. Therefore we make no difference between "offer you can't refuse" and "offers you couldn't refuse".

We also replace named entities by wildcards: *person_entity*, *organization_entity* and *company_entity*. Although these replacements also simplify the language models to some extent, their actual purpose is to avoid some negative constructions to be associated to concrete entities. For instance, we do not care that "do not trust John Doe Bank" is negative, instead we prefer to know that "do not trust company_entity" is negative regardless of the entity. This generality allows us to better evaluate opinions about new entities. Also, in the cases when all the opinions about some entity E1 are good and all the opinions about some other entity E2 are bad, entity replacement prevents the models from acquiring this kind of bias.

Following we detail the lemmatization process, the named entities detection and how we build and evaluate the positive and negative language models.

3.1 Lemmatization

Working with the words in their canonical form is for the sake of generality and simplification of the language model. Removing the morphological information does not change the semantics of most phrasemes (or multiwords).

There are some lexical forms for which we keep the surface form or we add some morphological information to the token. These exceptions are the subject pronouns, the object pronouns and the possessive forms. The reason for this is that for some phrasemes the personal information is the key for deciding the positive or negative sense. For instance, let us suppose that some opinions contain the sequences

$$o_t = \text{“They made money from me”},$$
$$o_i = \text{“I made money from them”}.$$

Their lemmatization, referred to as $\mathcal{L}_0(\cdot)$, would be[2]

$$\mathcal{L}_0(o_t) = \mathcal{L}_0(o_i) = \text{“SubjectPronoun make money from ObjectPronoun”},$$

Therefore we would have equally probable $P(o_t|M^p) = P(o_i|M^p)$ and $P(o_t|M^n) = P(o_i|M^n)$, which does not express the actual sentiment of the phrasemes. In order to capture this

[2]The notation we use here is for the sake of readability and it slightly differs from the one we use in Opinum.

kind of differences we prefer to have

$$\mathcal{L}_1(o_t) = \text{“SubjectPronoun\_3p make money from ObjectPronoun\_1p”},$$
$$\mathcal{L}_1(o_i) = \text{“SubjectPronoun\_1p make money from ObjectPronoun\_3p”}.$$

The probabilities still depend on how many times do these lexical sequences appear in opinions labeled as positive or negative, but with $\mathcal{L}_1(\cdot)$ we would have that

$$P(o_t|M^p) < P(o_i|M^p),$$
$$P(o_t|M^n) > P(o_i|M^n),$$

that is, o_i fits better the positive model than o_t does, and vice versa for the negative model.

In our implementation lemmatization is performed with Apertium, which is an open-source rule-based machine translation engine. Thanks to its modularized architecture (described in (Tyers et al., 2010)) we use its morphological analyser and its part-of-speech disambiguation module in order to take one lexical form as the most probable one, in case there are several possibilities for a given surface. Apertium currently has morphological analysers for 30 languages (most of them European), which allows us to adapt Opinum to other languages without much effort.

3.2 Named entities replacement

The corpora with labeled opinions are usually limited to a number of enterprises and organizations. For a generalization purpose we make the texts independent of concrete entities. We do make a difference between names of places, people and organizations/companies. We also detect dates, phone numbers, e-mails and URL/IP. We substitute them all by different wildcards. All the rest of the numbers are substituted by a “Num” wildcard. For instance, the following subsequence would have a $\mathcal{L}_2(o_e)$ lemmatization + named entity substitution:

$$o_e = \text{“Joe bought 300 shares of Acme Corp. in 2012”}$$
$$\mathcal{L}_2(o_e) = \text{“Person buy Num share of Company in Date”}$$

The named entity recognition task is integrated within the lemmatization process. We collected a list of names of people, places, companies and organizations to complete the morphological dictionary of Apertium. The morphological analysis module is still very fast, as the dictionary is first compiled and transformed to the minimal deterministic finite automaton. For the dates, phone numbers, e-mails, IP and URL we use regular expressions which are also supported by the same Apertium module.

Regarding the list of named entities, for a given language (Spanish in our experiments) we download its Wikipedia database which is a freely available resource. We heuristically search it for organizations, companies, places and people. Based on the number of references a given entity has in Wikipedia's articles, we keep the first 1.500.000 most relevant entities, which cover the entities with 4 references or more (the popular entities are referenced from tens to thousands of times).

Finally, unknown surface forms are replaced by the “Unknown” lemma (the known lemmas are lowercase). These would usually correspond to strange names of products, erroneous words and finally to words which are not covered by the monolingual dictionary of Apertium. Therefore our approach is suitable for opinions written in a rather correct language. If unknown surfaces were not replaced, the frequently misspelled words would not be excluded, which is useful in some domains. This is at the cost of increasing the complexity of the model, as all misspelled words would be included. Alternatively, the frequently misspelled words could be added to the dictionary.

3.3 Language models

The language models we build are based on n-gram word sequences. They model the likelihood of a word w_i given the sequence of $n-1$ previous words, $P(w_i|w_{i-(n-1)}, \ldots, w_{i-1})$. This kind of models assume independence between the word w_i and the words not belonging to the n-gram, w_j, $j < i - n$. This is a drawback for unbounded dependencies but we are not interested in capturing the complete grammatical relationships. We intend to capture the probabilities of smaller constructions which may hold positive/negative sentiment. Another assumption we make is independence between different sentences.

In Opinum the words are lemmas (or wildcards replacing entities), and the number of words among which we assume dependence is $n = 5$. A maximum n of 5 or 6 is common in machine translation where huge amounts of text are used for building a language model (Kohen et al., 2007). In our case we have at our disposal a small amount of data but the language is drastically simplified by removing the morphology and entities, as previously explained. We have experimentally found that $n > 5$ does not improve the classification performance of lemmatized opinions and could incur over-fitting.

In our setup we use the IRSTLM open-source library for building the language model. It performs an n-gram count for all n-grams from $n = 1$ to $n = 5$ in our case. To deal with data sparseness a redistribution of the zero-frequency probabilities is performed for those sets of words which have not been observed in the training set $\mathcal{L}(\mathbf{O})$. Relative frequencies are discounted to assign positive probabilities to every possible n-gram. Finally a smoothing method is applied. Details about the process can be found in (Federico et al., 2007). For Opinum we run IRSTLM twice during the training phase: once taking as input the opinions labeled as positive and once taking the negatives:

$$\begin{aligned} M^p &\leftarrow \text{Irstlm}\left(\mathcal{L}\left(\mathbf{O}^p\right)\right) \\ M^n &\leftarrow \text{Irstlm}\left(\mathcal{L}\left(\mathbf{O}^n\right)\right) \end{aligned}$$

These two models are further used for querying new opinions on them and deciding whether it is positive or negative, as detailed in the next subsection.

3.4 Evaluation and confidence

In the Opinum system we query the M^p, M^n models with the KenLM (Heafield, 2011) open-source library because it answers the queries very quickly and has a short loading time, which is suitable for a web application. It also has an efficient memory management which is positive for simultaneous queries to the server.

The queries are performed at sentence level. Each sentence $s \in o_t$ is assigned a score which is the log probability of the sentence being generated by the language model. The decision is taken by comparing its scores for the positive and for the negative models. For a given opinion o_t, the log-probability sums can be taken:

$$d_{o_t} = \sum_{s \in o_t} \log P(s|M^p) - \sum_{s \in o_t} \log P(s|M^n) \underset{?}{\gtrless} 0$$

If this difference is close to zero, $|d_{o_t}|/w_{o_t} < \varepsilon_0$, it can be considered that the classification is neutral. The number of words w_{o_t} is used as a normalization factor. If it is large, $|d_{o_t}|/w_{o_t} > \varepsilon_1$, it can be considered that the opinion has a very positive or very negative sentiment. Therefore Opinum classifies the opinions with qualifiers: *very/somewhat/little positive/negative* depending on the magnitude $|d_{o_t}|/w_{o_t}$ and $\text{sign}(d_{o_t})$, respectively.

The previous assessment is also accompanied by a confidence measure given by the level of agreement among the different sentences of an opinion. If all its sentences have the same positivity/negativity, measured by $\text{sign}(d_{s_j})$, $s_j \in o$, with large magnitudes then the confidence is the highest. In the opposite case in which there is the same number of positive and negative sentences with similar magnitudes the confidence is the lowest. The intermediate cases are those with sentences agreeing in sign but some of them with very low magnitude, and those with most sentences of the same sign and some with different sign. We use Shannon's entropy measure $H(\cdot)$ to quantify the amount of disagreement. For its estimation we divide the range of possible values of d in B ranges, referred to as bins:

$$H_{o_t} = \sum_{b=1}^{B} p(d_b) \log \frac{1}{p(d_b)}.$$

The number of bins should be low (less than 10), otherwise it is difficult to get a low entropy measure because of the sparse values of d_b. We set two thresholds η_0 and η_1 such that the confidence is said to be *high/normal/low* if $H_{o_t} < \eta_0$, $\eta_0 < H_{o_t} < \eta_1$ or $H_{o_t} > \eta_1$, respectively

The thresholds ε, η and the number of bins B are experimentally set. The reason for this is that they are used to tune subjective qualifiers (very/little, high/low confidence) and will usually depend on the training set and on the requirements of the application. Note that the classification in positive or negative sentiment is not affected by these parameters.

From a human point of view it is also a subjective assessment but in our setup it is looked at as a feature implicitly given by the labeled opinions of the training set.

4 Experiments and results

In our experimental setup we have a set of positive and negative opinions in Spanish, collected from a web site for user reviews and opinions. The opinions are constrained to the financial field including banks, savings accounts, loans, mortgages, investments, credit cards, and all other related topics. The authors of the opinions are not professionals, they are mainly customers. There is no structure required for their opinions, and they are free to tell their experience, their opinion or their feeling about the entity or the product. The users meant to communicate their review to other humans and they don't bear in mind any natural language processing tools. The authors decide whether their own opinion is positive or negative and this field is mandatory.

The users provide a number of stars as well: from one to five, but we have not used this information. It is interesting to note that there are 66 opinions with only one star which are marked as positive. There are also 67 opinions with five stars which are marked as negative. This is partially due to human errors, a human can notice when reading them. However we have not filtered these noisy data, as removing human errors could be regarded as biasing the data set with our own subjective criteria.

Regarding the size of the corpus, it consists of 9320 opinions about 180 different Spanish banks and financial products. From these opinions 5877 are positive and 3443 are negative. There is a total of 709741 words and the mean length of the opinions is 282 words for the positive and 300 words for the negative ones. In the experiments we present in this work, we randomly divide the data set in 75% for training and 25% for testing. We check that the distribution of positive and negative remains the same among test and train.

After the $\mathcal{L}_2(\cdot)$ lemmatization and entity substitution, the number of different words in the data set is 13067 in contrast with the 78470 different words in the original texts. In other words, the lexical complexity is reduced by 83%. Different substitutions play a different role in this simplification. The "Unknown" wildcard represents a 7,13% of the original text. Entities were detected and replaced 33858 times (7807 locations, 5409 people, 19049 companies, 502 e-mails addresses and phone numbers, 2055 URLs, 1136 dates) which is a 4,77% of the text. There are also 46780 number substitutions, a 7% of the text. The rest of complexity reduction is due to the removal of the morphology as explained in Subsection 3.1.

In our experiments, the training of Opinum consisted of lemmatizing and susbstituting entities of the 6990 opinions belonging the training set and building the language models. The positive model is built from 4403 positive opinions and the negative model is built from 2587 negative opinions. Balancing the amount of positive and negative samples does not improve the performance. Instead, it obliges us to remove an important amount of positive opinions and the classification results are decreased by approximately 2%. This is why we use all the opinions available in the training set. Both language models are n-grams with $n \in [1, 5]$. Having a 37% less samples for the negative opinions is not a problem thank to the smoothing techniques applied by IRSTLM. Nonetheless if the amount of training texts is too low we would recommend taking a lower n. A simple way to set n is to take the lowest value of n for which classification performance is improved. An unnecessarily high n could overfit the models.

The tests are performed with 2330 opinions (not involved in building the models). For measuring the accuracy we do not use the qualifiers information but only the decision about the positive or negative class. In Figure 1 we show the scores of the opinions for the positive and negative models. The score is the sum of scores of the sentences, thus it can be seen that longer opinions (bigger markers) have bigger scores. Independence of the size is not necessary for classifying in positive and negative. In the diagonal it can be seen that positive samples are close to the negative ones, this is to be expected: both positive and negative language models are built for the same language. However the small difference in their scores yields an 81,98% success rate in the classification. An improvement of this rate would be difficult to achieve taking into account that there is

Test	Original Spanish text	Meaning in English	Result
Similar words, different meaning	"Al tener la web, no pierdes el tiempo por teléfono."	As you have the website you don't waste time on the phone.	Positive
	"En el telfono os hacen perder el tiempo y no tienen web."	They waste your time on the phone and they don't have a website.	Negative
	"De todas formas me solucionaron el problema."	Anyway, they solved my problem.	Positive
	"No hay forma de que me solucionen el problema."	There is no way to make them solve my problem.	Negative
A negative opinion of several sentences	"Con XXXXXX me fue muy bien."	I was fine with XXXXXX.	Positive
	"Hasta que surgieron los problemas."	Until the problems began.	Negative
	"Por hacerme cliente me regalaban 100 euros."	They gave me 100 euros for becoming a client.	Positive
	"Pero una vez que eres cliente no te aportan nada bueno."	But once you are a client, they they do not offer anything good.	Negative
	"Estoy pensando cambiar de banco."	I am considering switching to another bank.	Negative
The complete opinion	"Con XXXXXX me fue muy [. . .] cambiar de banco."	I was fine with XXXXXX [. . .] switching to another bank.	Negative

Table 1: Some tests on Opinum for financial opinions in Spanish.

noise in the training set and that there are opinions without a clear positive or negative feeling. A larger corpus would also contribute to a better result. Even though we have placed many efforts in simplifying the text, this does not help in the cases in which a construction of words is never found in the corpus. A construction could even be present in the corpus but in the wrong class. For instance, in our corpus "no estoy satisfecho" (meaning "I am not satisfied") appears 3 times among the positive opinions and 0 times among the negative ones. This weakness of the corpus is due to sentences referring to a money back guarantee: "si no esta satisfecho le devolvemos el dinero" which are used in a positive context.

Usually in long opinions a single sentence does not change the positiveness score. For some examples see Table 4. In long opinions every sentence is prone to show the sentiment except for the cases of irony or opinions with an objective part. The performance of Opinum depending on the size of the opinions of the test set is shown in Figure 2. In Figure 3 the ROC curve of the classifier shows its stability against changing the true-positive versus false-negative rates. A comparison with other methods would be a valuable source of evaluation. It is not feasible at this moment because of the lack of free customers opinions databases and opionion classifiers as well. The success rate we obtain can be compared to the 69% baseline given by a classifier based on the frequencies of single words.

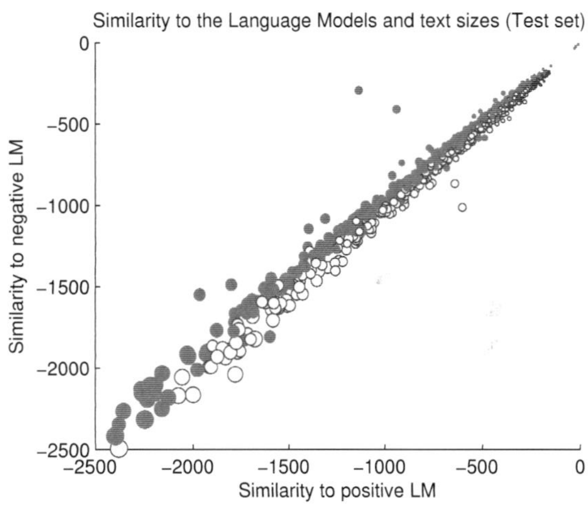

Figure 1: Relation between similarity to the models (x and y axis) and the relative size of the opinions (size of the points).

The query time of Opinum on a standard computer ranges from $1,63$ s for the shortest opinions to $1,67$ s for those with more than 1000 words. In our setup, most of the time is spent in loading the morphological dictionary, few milliseconds are spent in the morphological analysis of the opinion and the named entity substitution, and less than a millisecond is spent in querying each model. In a batch

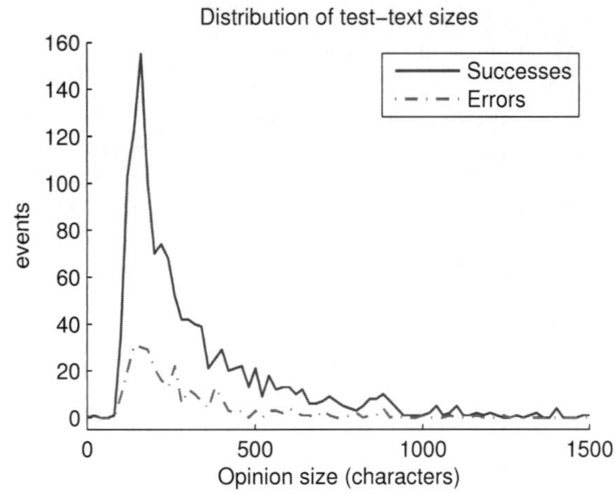

Figure 2: Number of successful and erroneous classifications (vertical axis) depending on the size of the test opinions (horizontal axis).

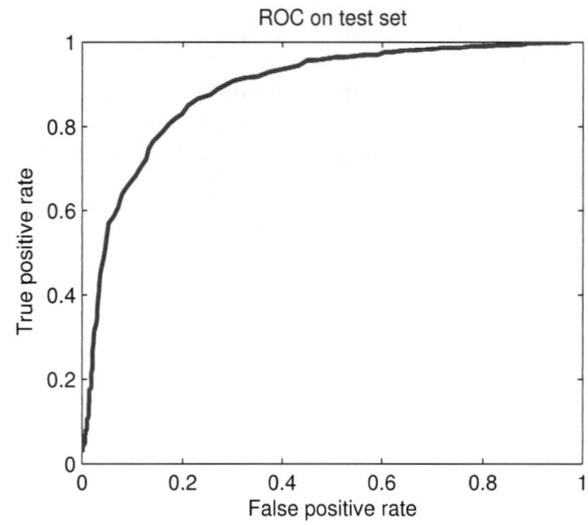

Figure 3: Receiver Operating Characteristic (ROC) curve of the Opinum classifier for financial opinions.

mode, the morphological analysis could be done for all the opinions together and thousands of them could be evaluated in seconds. In Opinum's web interface we only provide the single opinion queries and we output the decision, the qualifiers information and the confidence measure.

5 Conclusions and future work

Opinum is a sentiment analysis system designed for classifying customer opinions in positive and negative. Its approach based on morphological simplification, entity substitution and n-gram language models, makes it easily adaptable to other classification targets different from positive/negative. In this work we present experiments for Spanish in the financial domain but Opinum could easily be trained for a different language or domain. To this end an Apertium morphological analyser would be necessary (30 languages are currently available) as well as a labeled data set of opinions. Setting n for the n-gram models depends on the size of the corpus but it would usually range from 4 to 6, 5 in our case. There are other parameters which have to be experimentally tuned and they are not related to the positive or negative classification but to the subjective qualifier very/somewhat/little and to the confidence measure.

The classification performance of Opinum in our financial-domain experiments is 81,98% which would be difficult to improve because of the noise in the data and the subjectivity of the labeling in positive and negative. The next steps would be to study the possibility to classify in more than two classes by using several language models. The use of an external neutral corpus should also be considered in the future.

It is necessary to perform a deeper analysis of the impact of lexical simplification on the accuracy of the language models. It is also very important to establish the limitations of this approach for different domains. Is it equally successful for a wider domain? For instance, trying to build the models from a mixed set of opinions of the financial domain and the IT domain. Would it work for a general domain?

Regarding applications, Opinum could be trained for a given domain without expert knowledge. Its queries are very fast which makes it feasible for free on-line services. An interesting application would be to exploit the named entity recognition and associate positive/negative scores to the entities based on their surrounding text. If several domains were available, then the same entities would have different scores depending on the domain, which would be a valuable analysis.

References

Philipp Koehn, H. Hoang, A. Birch, C. Callison-Burch, M. Federico, N. Bertoldi, B. Cowan, W. Shen, C. Moran, R. Zens, C. Dyer, O. Bojar, A. Constantin and E. Herbst. 2007. Moses: open source toolkit for statistical machine translation. *Proceedings of the 45th Annual Meeting of the ACL on Interactive Poster and Demonstration Sessions*, pp. 177–180. Prague, Czech Republic, 2007.

Sasha Blair-Goldensohn, Tyler Neylon, Kerry Hannan, George A. Reis, Ryan Mcdonald and Jeff Reynar. 2008. Building a sentiment summarizer for local service reviews. *In NLP in the Information Explosion Era, NLPIX2008*, Beiging, China, April 22nd, 2008.

Hu, Minqing and Liu, Bing. 2004. Mining and summarizing customer reviews. *Proceedings of the tenth ACM SIGKDD international conference on Knowledge discovery and data mining*, Seattle, WA, USA, 2004.

Ryan McDonald, Kerry Hannan, Tyler Neylon, Mike Wells and Jeff Reynar. 2007. Structured Models for Fine-to-Coarse Sentiment Analysis. *Proceedings of the 45th Annual Meeting of the Association of Computational Linguistics*, 2007.

John Blitzer, Mark Dredze and Fernando Pereira. 2007. Biographies, bollywood, boomboxes and blenders: Domain adaptation for sentiment classification. *ACL*, 2007.

Bo Pang, Lillian Lee and Shivakumar Vaithyanathan. 2002. Thumbs up? Sentiment Classification using Machine Learning Techniques. *EMNLP*, 2002.

Maite Taboada, Julian Brooke, Milan Tofiloski, Kimberly Voll, Manfred Stede. 2011. Lexicon-based methods for sentiment analysis. *Computational Linguistics*, Vol. 37, Nr. 2, pp. 267–307, June 2011.

Stephan Raaijmakers, Khiet P. Truong and Theresa Wilson. 2008. Multimodal Subjectivity Analysis of Multiparty Conversation. *EMNLP*, 2008.

Tyers, F. M., Snchez-Martnez, F., Ortiz-Rojas, S. and Forcada, M. L. 2010. Free/open-source resources in the Apertium platform for machine translation research and development. *The Prague Bulletin of Mathematical Linguistics*, No. 93, pp. 67–76, 2010.

Marcello Federico and Mauro Cettolo. 2007. Efficient Handling of N-gram Language Models for Statistical Machine Translation. *ACL 2007 Workshop on SMT*, Prague, Czech Republic, 2007.

Kenneth Heafield. 2011. KenLM: Faster and Smaller Language Model Queries. *ACL 6th Workshop on SMT*, Edinburgh, Scotland, UK, July 30–31, 2011.

Sentimantics: Conceptual Spaces for Lexical Sentiment Polarity Representation with Contextuality

Amitava Das **Björn Gambäck**
Department of Computer and Information Science
Norwegian University of Science and Technology
Sem Sælands vei 7-9, NO-7094 Trondheim, Norway
amitava.santu@gmail.com gamback@idi.ntnu.no

Abstract

Current sentiment analysis systems rely on static (context independent) sentiment lexica with proximity based fixed-point prior polarities. However, sentiment-orientation changes with context and these lexical resources give no indication of ***which value to pick at what context.*** The general trend is to pick the highest one, but which that is may vary at context. To overcome the problems of the present proximity-based static sentiment lexicon techniques, the paper proposes a new way to represent sentiment knowledge in a Vector Space Model. This model can store dynamic prior polarity with varying contextual information. The representation of the sentiment knowledge in the Conceptual Spaces of distributional Semantics is termed ***Sentimantics.***

1 Introduction

Polarity classification is the classical problem from where the cultivation of Sentiment Analysis (SA) started. It involves sentiment / opinion classification into semantic classes such as *positive, negative or neutral* and/or other fine-grained emotional classes like *happy, sad, anger, disgust,surprise* and similar. However, for the present task we stick to the standard binary classification, i.e., positive and/or negative.

The Concept of Prior Polarity: Sentiment polarity classification ("*The text is positive or negative?*") started as a semantic orientation determination problem: by identifying the semantic orientation of adjectives, Hatzivassiloglou *et al.* (1997) proved the effectiveness of empirically building a sentiment lexicon. Turney (2002) suggested review classification by *Thumbs Up* and *Thumbs Down*, while the concept of prior polarity lexica was firmly established with the introduction of SentiWordNet (Esuli *et al.*, 2004).

More or less all sentiment analysis researchers agree that prior polarity lexica are necessary for polarity classification, and prior polarity lexicon development has been attempted for other languages than English as well, including for Chinese (He *et al.*, 2010), Japanese (Torii *et al.*, 2010), Thai (Haruechaiyasak *et al.*, 2010), and Indian languages (Das and Bandyopadhyay, 2010).

Polarity Classification Using the Lexicon: High accuracy for prior polarity identification is very hard to achieve, as prior polarity values are approximations only. Therefore the prior polarity method may not excel alone; additional techniques are required for contextual polarity disambiguation. The use of other NLP methods or machine learning techniques over human produced prior polarity lexica was pioneered by Pang *et al.* (2002). Several researches then tried syntactic-statistical techniques for polarity classification, reporting good accuracy (Seeker et al., 2009; Moilanen et al., 2010), making the ***two-step methodology*** (sentiment lexicon followed by further NLP techniques) the standard method for polarity classification.

Incorporating Human Psychology: The existing reported solutions or available systems are still far from perfect or fail to meet the satisfaction level of the end users. The main issue may be that there are many conceptual rules that govern sentiment and there are even more clues (possibly unlimited) that can convey these concepts from realization to verbalization of a human being (Liu,

2010). The most recent trends in prior polarity adopt an approach to sentiment knowledge representation which lets the mental lexicon model hold the contextual polarity, as in human mental knowledge representation.

Cambria *et al.* (2011) made an important contribution in this direction by introducing a new paradigm: *Sentic Computing*[1], in which they use an emotion representation and a Common Sense-based approach to infer affective states from short texts over the web. Grassi (2009) conceived the *Human Emotion Ontology* as a high level ontology supplying the most significant concepts and properties constituting the centerpiece for the description of human emotions.

The Proposed Sentimantics: The present paper introduces the concept of *Sentimantics* which is related to the existing prior polarity concept, but differs from it philosophically in terms of contextual dynamicity. It ideologically follows the path of Minsky (2006), Cambria *et al.* (2011) and (Grassi, 2009), but with a different notion.

Sentiment analysis research started years ago, but still the question "***What is sentiment or opinion?***" remains unanswered! It is very hard to define sentiment or opinion, and to identify the regulating or the controlling factors of sentiment; an analytic definition of opinion might even be impossible (Kim and Hovy, 2004). Moreover, no concise set of psychological forces could be defined that really affect the writers' sentiments, i.e., broadly the human sentiment.

Sentimantics tries to solve the problem with a practical necessity and to overcome the problems of the present proximity-based static sentiment lexicon techniques.

As discussed earlier, the two-step methodology is the most common one in practice. As described in Section 3, a syntactic-polarity classifier was therefore developed, to examine the impact of proposed *Sentimantics* concept, by comparing it to the standard polarity classification technique. The strategy was tested on both English and Bengali. The intension behind choosing two distinct language families is to establish the credibility of the proposed methods.

[1] http://sentic.net/sentics/

For English we choose the widely used MPQA[3] corpus, but for the Bengali we had to create our own corpus as discussed in the following section.

The remainder of the paper then concentrates on the problems with using prior polarity values only, in Section 4, while the Sentimantics concept proper is discussed in Section 5. Finally, some initial conclusions are presented in Section 6.

2 Bengali Corpus

News text can be divided into two main types: (1) news reports that aim to objectively present factual information, and (2) opinionated articles that clearly present authors' and readers' views, evaluation or judgment about some specific events or persons (and appear in sections such as 'Editorial', 'Forum' and 'Letters to the editor'). A Bengali news corpus has been acquired for the present task, based on 100 documents from the 'Reader's opinion' section ('Letters to the Editor') from the web archive of a popular Bengali newspaper.[4] In total, the corpus contains 2,235 sentences (28,805 word forms, of which 3,435 are distinct). The corpus has been annotated with positive and negative phrase polarities using Sanchay[5], the standard annotation tool for Indian languages. The annotation was done semi-automatically: a module marked the sentiment words from SentiWordNet (Bengali)[6] and then the corpus was corrected manually.

3 The Syntactic Polarity Classifier

Adhering to the standard two-step methodology (i.e., prior polarity lexicon followed by any NLP technique), a Syntactic-Statistical polarity classifier based on Support Vector Machines (SVMs) has been quickly developed using SVMTool.[7] The intension behind the development of this syntactic polarity classifier was to examine the effectiveness and the limitations of the standard two-step methodology at the same time.

The selection of an appropriate feature set is crucial when working with Machine Learning techniques such as SVM. We decided on a feature

[3] http://www.cs.pitt.edu/mpqa/

[4] http://www.anandabazar.com/

[5] http://ltrc.iiit.ac.in/nlpai_contest07/Sanchay/

[6] http://www.amitavadas.com/sentiwordnet.php

[7] http://www.lsi.upc.edu/~nlp/SVMTool/

Polarity	Precision		Recall	
	Eng.	Bng.	Eng.	Bng.
Total	76.03%	70.04%	65.8%	63.02%
Positive	58.6%	56.59%	54.0%	52.89%
Negative	76.3%	75.57%	69.4%	65.87%

Table 1: Overall and class-wise results of syntactic polarity classification

set including *Sentiment Lexicon, Negative Words, Stems, Function Words, Part of Speech and Dependency Relations*, as most previous research agree that these are the prime features to detect the sentimental polarity from text (see, e.g., Pang and Lee, 2005; Seeker et al., 2009; Moilanen et al., 2010; Liu et. al., 2005).

Sentiment Lexicon: SentiWordNet 3.0 [8] for English and SentiWordNet (Bengali) for Bengali.

Negative Words: Manually created. Contains 80 entries collected semi-automatically from both the MPQA[9] corpus and the Movie Review dataset[10] by Cornell for English. 50 negative words were collected manually for Bengali.

Stems: The Porter Stemmer[11] for English. The Bengali Shallow Parser[12] was used to extract root words (from morphological analysis output).

Function Words: Collected from the web. [13] Only personal pronouns are dropped for the present task. A list of 253 entries was collected manually from the Bengali corpus.

POS, Chunking and Dependency Relations: The Stanford Dependency parser [14] for English. The Bengali Shallow Parser was used to extract POS, chunks and dependency relations.

The results of SVM-based syntactic classification for English and Bengali are presented in Table 1, both in total and for each polarity class separately.

To understand the effects of various features on the performance of the system, we used the feature ablation method. The dictionary-based approach using only SentiWordNet gave a 50.50% precision

Features	Precision	
	Eng.	Bng.
Sentiment Lexicon	50.50%	47.60%
+Negative Words	55.10%	50.40%
+Stemming	59.30%	56.02%
+ Function Words	63.10%	58.23%
+ Part of Speech	66.56%	61.90%
+Chunking	68.66%	66.80%
+Dependency Relations	76.03%	70.04%

Table 2: Performance of the syntactic polarity classifier by feature ablation

(Eng.) and 47.60% (Bng.) which can be considered as baselines. As seen in Table 2, incremental use of other features like negative words, function words, part of speech, chunks and tools like stemming improved the precision of the system to 68.66% (Eng.) and 66.80% (Bng.). Further use of syntactic features in terms of dependency relations improved the system precision to 76.03% (Eng.) and 70.04% (Bng.). The feature ablation proves the accountability of the two-step polarity classification technique. The prior polarity lexicon (completely dictionary-based) approach gives about 50% precision; the further improvements of the system are obtained by other NLP techniques.

To support our argumentation for choosing SVM, we tested the same classification problem with another machine learning technique, Conditional Random Fields (CRF)[15] with the same data and setup. The performance of the CRF-based model is much worse than the SVM, with a precision of 70.04% and recall of 67.02% for English, resp. 61.23% precision and 55.00% recall for Bengali. The feature ablation method was also tested for the CRF model and the performance was more or less the same when the dictionary features and lexical features were used (i.e., SentiWordNet + Negative Words + Stemming + Function Words + Part of Speech). But it was difficult to increase the performance level for the CRF by using syntactic features like chunking and dependency relations. SVMs work excellent to normalize this dynamic situation.

It has previously been noticed that multi-engine based methods work well for this type of heterogeneous tagging task, e.g., in Named Entity

[8] http://sentiwordnet.isti.cnr.it/
[9] http://www.cs.pitt.edu/mpqa/
[10] http://www.cs.cornell.edu/People/pabo/movie-review-data/
[11] http://tartarus.org/martin/PorterStemmer/java.txt
[12] ltrc.iiit.ac.in/showfile.php?filename=downloads/shallow_parser.php
[13] http://www.flesl.net/Vocabulary/Single-word_Lists/function_word_list.php
[14] http://nlp.stanford.edu/software/lex-parser.shtml

[15] http://crfpp.googlecode.com/svn/trunk/doc/index.html

Recognition (Ekbal and Bandyopadhyay, 2010) and POS tagging (Shulamit et al., 2010). We have not tested with that kind of setup, but rather looked at the problem from a different perspective, questioning the basics: *Is the two-step methodology for the classification task ideal or should we look for other alternatives?*

4 What Knowledge at What Level?

In this section we address some limitations regarding the usage of prior polarity values from existing of prior polarity lexical resources. Dealing with unknown/new words is a common problem. It becomes more difficult for sentiment analysis because it is very hard to find out any contextual clue to predict the sentimental orientation of any unknown/new word. There is another problem: word sense disambiguation, which is indeed a significant subtask when applying a resource like SentiWordNet (Cem *et al.*, 2011).

A prior polarity lexicon is attached with two probabilistic values (positivity and negativity), but according to the best of our knowledge no previous research clarifies *which value to pick in what context?* – and there is no information about this in SentiWordNet. The general trend is to pick the highest one, but which may vary by context. An example may illustrate the problem better: Suppose a word "*high*" (Positivity: 0.25, Negativity: 0.125 from SentiWordNet) is attached with a positive polarity (its positivity value is higher than its negativity value) in the sentiment lexicon, but the polarity of the word may vary in any particular use.

`Sensex reaches high+.`

`Prices go high-.`

Hence further processing is required to disambiguate these types of words. Table 3 shows how many words in the SentiWordNet(s) are ambiguous and need special care. There are 6,619 (Eng.) and 7,654 (Bng.) lexicon entries in SentiWordNet(s) where both the positivity and the negativity values are greater than zero. Therefore these entries are ambiguous because there is no clue in the SentiWordNet which value to pick in what context. Similarly, there are 3,187 (Eng.) and 2,677 (Bng.) lexical entries in SentiWordNet(s) whose positivity and negativity value difference is less than 0.2. These are also ambiguous words.

Types	Eng.	Bng.
	Numbers (%) English: n/28,430 Bengali: n/30,000	
Total Token	115,424	30,000
Positivity > 0 ∨ Negativity > 0	28,430	30,000
Positivity > 0 ∧ Negativity > 0	6619 (23.28 %)	7,654 (25.51 %)
Positivity > 0 ∧ Negativity = 0	**10,484 (36.87 %)**	**8,934 (29.78 %)**
Positivity = 0 ∧ Negativity > 0	**11,327 (39.84 %)**	**11,780 (39.26 %)**
Positivity > 0 ∧ Negativity > 0 ∧ |Positivity-Negativity| ≥ 0.2	3,187 (11.20 %)	2,677 (8.92 %)

Table 3: SentiWordNet(s) statistics

The main concern of the present task is the ambiguous entries from SentiWordNet(s). The basic hypothesis is that if we can add some sort of contextual information with the prior polarity scores in the sentiment lexicon, the updated rich lexicon network will serve better than the existing one, and reduce or even remove the need for further processing to disambiguate the contextual polarity. How much contextual information would be needed and how this knowledge should be represented could be a perpetual debate. To answer these questions we introduce ***Sentimantics:*** *Distributed Semantic Lexical Models to hold the sentiment knowledge with context.*

5 Technical Solutions for Sentimantics

In order to propose a model of Sentimantics we started with existing resources such as ConceptNet [16] (Havasi *et al.*, 2007) and SentiWordNet for English, and SemanticNet (Das and Bandyopadhyay, 2010) and SentiWordNet (Bengali) for Bengali. The common sense lexica like ConceptNet and SemanticNet are developed for general purposes, and to formalize Sentimantics from these resources is problematic due to lack of dimensionality. Section 5.1 presents a more rational explanation with empirical results.

In the end we developed a Syntactic Co-Occurrence Based Vector Space Model to hold the Sentimantics from scratch by a corpus driven semi-supervised method (Section 5.2). This model performs better than the previous one and quite satisfactory. Generally extracting knowledge from

[16] http://csc.media.mit.edu/conceptnet

this kind of VSM is very expensive algorithmically because it is a very high dimensional network. Another important limitation of this type of model is that it demands very well defined processed input to extract knowledge, e.g., ***Input:*** *(high)* ***Context:*** *(sensex, share market, point)*. Philosophically, the motivation of Sentimantics is to provide a rich lexicon network which will serve better than the existing one and reduce the requirement of further language processing techniques to disambiguate the contextual polarity. This model consists of relatively fewer dimensions. The final model is the best performing lexicon network model, which could be described as the acceptable solution for the Sentimantics problem. The details of the proposed models are described in the following.

5.1 Semantic Network Overlap, SNO

We started experimentation with network overlap techniques. The network overlap technique finds overlaps of nodes between two lexical networks: namely ConceptNet-SentiWordNet for English and SemanticNet-SentiWordNet (Bengali) for Bengali. The working principle of the network overlap technique is very simple. The algorithm starts with any SentiWordNet node and finds its closest neighbours from the commonsense networks (ConceptNet or SemanticNet). If, for example, a node chosen from SentiWordNet is "long/লম্বা", the closest neighbours of this concept extracted from the commonsense networks are: "road (40%) / waiting (62%) / car (35%) / building (54%) / queue (70%) …" The association scores (as the previous example) are also extracted to understand the semantic similarity association. Hence the desired *Sentimantics* lexical network is developed by this network overlap technique. The next prime challenge is to assign contextual polarity to each association. For this a corpus-based method was used; based on the MPQA[17] corpus for English and the corpus developed by us for. The corpora are pre-processed with dependency relations and stemming using the same parsers and stemmers as in Section 3. The dependency relations are necessary to understand the relations between the evaluative expression and other modifier-modified chunks in any subjective sentence. Stemming is

[17] http://www.cs.pitt.edu/mpqa/

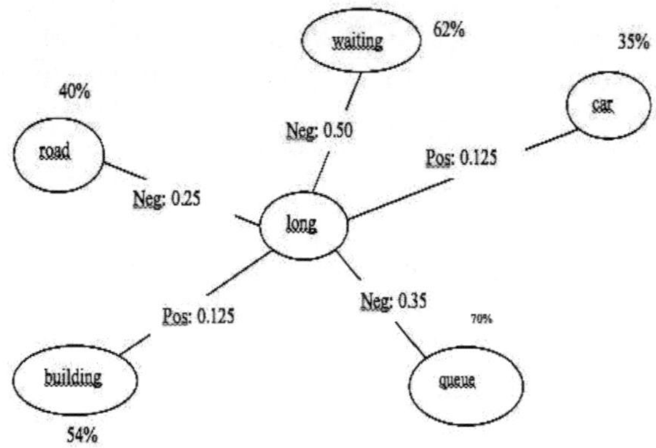

Figure 1: The Sentimantics Network

necessary to understand the root form of any word and for dictionary comparison. The corpus-driven method assigns each sentiment word in the developed lexical network a contextual prior polarity, as shown in Figure 1.

Semantic network-based polarity calculation

Once the desired lexical semantic network to hold the Sentimantics has been developed, we look further to leverage the developed knowledge for the polarity classification task. The methodology of contextual polarity extraction from the network is very simple, and only a dependency parser and stemmer are required. For example, consider the following sentence.

```
We have been waiting in a long queue.
```

To extract the contextual polarity from this sentence it must be known that *waiting-long-queue* are interconnected with dependency relations, and stemming is a necessary pre-processing step for dictionary matching. To extract contextual polarity from the developed network the desired input is (*long*) with its context (*waiting, queue*). The accumulated contextual polarity will be Neg: (0.50+0.35)=0.85. For comparison if the score was extracted from SentiWordNet (English) it would be Pos: 0.25 as this is higher than the negative score (*long*: Pos: 0.25, Neg: 0.125 in SentiWordNet).

SNO performance and limitations

An evaluation proves that the present Network Overlap technique outperforms the previous syntactic polarity classification technique. The precision scores for this technique are 62.3% for English and 59.7% for Bengali on the MPQA and

Type	Number		Solved By Semantic Overlap Technique
Positivity > 0 ∧ Negativity > 0	Eng.	6,619	2,304 (34.80 %)
	Bng.	7,654	2,450 (32 %)
|Positivity - Negativity| ≥ 0.2	Eng.	3,187	957 (30 %)
	Bng.	2,677	830 (31.5 %)

Table 4: Results of Semantic Overlap

Bengali corpora: clearly higher than the baselines based on SentiWordNet (50.5 and 47.6%; Table 2).

Still, the overall goal to "*reduce/remove the requirement to use further NLP techniques to disambiguate the contextual polarity*" could not be established empirically. To understand why, we performed an analysis of the errors and missed cases of the semantic network overlap technique: most of the errors were caused by lack of coverage. ConceptNet and SemanticNet were both developed from the news domain and for a different task. The comparative coverage of SentiWordNet (English) and MPQA is 74%, i.e., if we make a complete set of sentiment words from MPQA then altogether 74% of that set is covered by SentiWordNet, which is very good and an acceptable coverage. For Bengali the comparative coverage is 72%, which is also very good. However, the comparative coverage of SentiWordNet (English)-ConceptNet and SentiWordNet (Bengali)-SemanticNet is very low: 54% and 50% respectively: only half of the sentiment words in the SentiWordNets are covered by ConceptNet (Eng) resp. SemanticNet (Bng).

Now look at the evaluation in Table 4 which we report to support our empirical reasoning behind the question "*What knowledge to keep at what level?*" It shows how much fixed point-based static prior polarity is being resolved by the Semantic Network Overlap technique. The comparative results are noteworthy but not satisfactory: only 34% (Eng.) and 32% (Bng.) of the cases of "*Positivity* > 0 ∧ *Negativity* > 0" resp. 30% (Eng.) and 31.5 % (Bng.) of the cases of "|*Positivity* - *Negativity*| ≥ 0.2" are resolved by this technique. The results are presented in Table 4.

As a result of the error analysis, we instead decided to develop a Vector Space Model from scratch in order to solve the Sentimantics problem and to reach a satisfactory level of coverage. The experiments in this direction are reported below.

5.2 Starting from Scratch: Syntactic Co-Occurrence Network Construction

A syntactic word co-occurrence network was constructed for only the sentimental words from the corpora. The syntactic network is defined in a way similar to previous work such the Spin Model (Takamura *et al.*, 2005) and Latent Semantic Analysis to compute the association strength with seed words (Turney and Litman, 2003). The hypothesis is that all the words occurring in the syntactic territory tend to have similar semantic orientation. In order to reduce dimensionality when constructing the network, only the open word classes *noun*, *verb*, *adjective* and *adverb* are included, as those classes tend to have maximized sentiment properties. Involving fewer features generates VSMs with fewer dimensions.

For the network creation we again started with SentiWordNet 3.0 to mark the sentiment words in the MPQA corpus. As the MPQA corpus is marked at expression level, SentiWordNet was used to mark only the lexical entries of the subjective expressions in the corpus. As before, the Stanford POS tagger and the Porter Stemmer were used to get POS classes and stems of the English terms, while SentiWordNet (Bengali), the Bengali corpus and the Bengali processors were used for Bengali.

Features were extracted from a ±4 word window around the target terms. To normalize the extracted words from the corpus we used CF-IOF, concept frequency-inverse opinion frequency (Cambria *et al.*, 2011), while a Spectral Clustering technique (Dasgupta and Ng, 2009) was used for the in-depth analysis of word co-occurrence patterns and their relationships at discourse level. The clustering algorithm partitions a set of lexica into a finite number of groups or clusters in terms of their syntactic co-occurrence relatedness.

Numerical weights were assigned to the words and then the cosine similarity measure was used to calculate vector similarity:

$$s\left(\vec{q_k}, \vec{d_j}\right) = \vec{q_k} \cdot \vec{d_j} = \sum_{i=1}^{N} w_{i,k} \times w_{i,j} \quad \text{-----(1)}$$

When the lexicon collection is relatively static, it makes sense to normalize the vectors once and store them, rather than include the normalization in the similarity metric (as in Equation 2).

$$s\left(\vec{q_k}, \vec{d_j}\right) = \frac{\sum_{i=1}^{N} w_{i,k} \times w_{i,j}}{\sqrt{\sum_{i=1}^{N} w_{i,k}^2} \times \sqrt{\sum_{j=1}^{N} w_{j,k}^2}} \quad \text{-------(2)}$$

ID	Lexicon	1	2	3
1	Broker	**0.63**	0.12	0.04
1	NASDAQ	**0.58**	0.11	0.06
1	**Sensex**	**0.58**	0.12	0.03
1	*High*	**0.55**	0.14	0.08
2	India	0.11	**0.59**	0.02
2	**Population**	0.15	**0.55**	0.01
2	*High*	0.12	**0.66**	0.01
3	Market	0.13	0.05	**0.58**
3	**Petroleum**	0.05	0.01	**0.86**
3	UAE	0.12	0.04	**0.65**
3	*High*	0.03	0.01	**0.93**

Table 5: Five example cluster centroids

After calculating the similarity measures and using a predefined threshold value (experimentally set to 0.5), the lexica are classified using a standard spectral clustering technique: Starting from a set of initial cluster centers, each document is assigned to the cluster whose center is closest to the document. After all documents have been assigned, the center of each cluster is recomputed as the centroid or mean $\vec{\mu}_j$ (where $\vec{\mu}_j$ is the clustering coefficient) of its members:

$$\vec{\mu} = (1/|c_j|) \sum_{x \in c_j} \vec{x}$$

Table 5 gives an example of cluster centroids by spectral clustering. Bold words in the lexicon name column are cluster centers. Comparing two members of Cluster_2, '**India**' and '**Population**', it can be seen that '**India**' is strongly associated with Cluster_2 (p=0.59), but has some affinity with the other clusters as well (e.g., p=0.11 with Cluster_1). These non-zero values are still useful for calculating vertex weights during the contextual polarity calculation.

Polarity Calculation using the Syntactic Co-Occurrence Network

The relevance of the semantic lexicon nodes was computed by summing up the edge scores of those edges connecting a node with other nodes in the same cluster. As the cluster centers also are interconnected with weighted vertices, inter-cluster relations could be calculated in terms of weighted network distance between two nodes within two separate clusters.

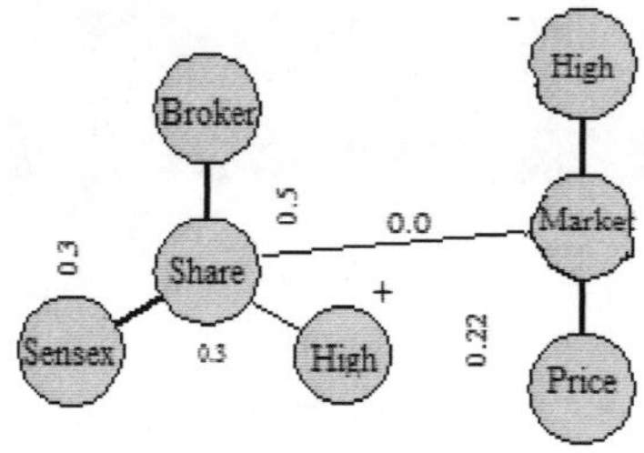

Figure 2: Semantic affinity graph for contextual prior polarity

As an example, the lexicon level semantic orientation from Figure 2 could be calculated as follows:

$$S_d(w_i, w_j) = \frac{\sum_{k=0}^{n} v_k}{k} * w_j^p \quad \text{----(3) or}$$

$$= \sum_{c=0}^{m} \frac{\sum_{k=0}^{n} v_k}{k} * \prod_{c=0}^{m} l_c * w_j^p \text{---(4)}$$

Where $S_d(w_i, w_j)$ is the semantic orientation of w_i with w_j given as context. Equations (3) and (4) are for intra-cluster and inter-cluster semantic distance measure respectively. k is the number of weighted vertices between two lexica w_i and w_j. v_k the weighted vertex between two lexica, m the number of cluster centers between them, l_c the distance between their cluster centers, and w^P_j the polarity of the known word w_j.

This network was created and used in particular to handle unknown words. For the prediction of semantic orientation of an unknown word, a bag-of-words method was adopted: the bag-of-words chain was formed with most of the known words, syntactically co-located.

A classifier based on Conditional Random Fields was then trained on the corpus with a small set of features: co-occurrence distance, ConceptNet similarity scores, known or unknown based on SentiWordNet. With the help of these very simple features, the CRF classifier identifies the most probable bag-of-words to predict the semantic orientation of an unknown word. As an example: Suppose X marks the unknown words and that the probable bag-of-words are:

```
9_11-X-Pentagon-USA-Bush
Discuss-Terrorism-X-President
Middle_East-X-Osama
```

Once the target bag-of-words has been identified, the following equation can be used to calculate the polarity of the unknown word *X*.

```
Discuss-0.012-Terrorism-0.0-X-0.23-
           President
```

The scores are extracted from ConceptNet and the equation is:

$$w_x^p = \sum_{i=0}^{n} e_i * \sum_{j=1}^{n} p_i \text{ -----(5)}$$

Where e_i is the edge distances extracted from ConceptNet and P_i is the polarity information of the lexicon in the bag-of-words.

The syntactic co-occurrence network gives reasonable performance increment over the normal linear sentiment lexicon and the Semantic Network Overlap technique, but it has some limitations: it is difficult to formulate a good equation to calculate semantic orientation within the network. The formulation we use produced a less distinguishing value for different bag of words. As example in Figure 2:

$$(\textbf{High}, \textit{Sensex}) = \frac{0.3+0.3}{2} = 0.3$$

$$(\textit{Price}, \textbf{High}) = \frac{0.22+0.35}{2} = 0.29$$

The main problem is that it is nearly impossible to predict polarity for an unknown word. Standard polarity classifiers generally degrade in performance in the presence of unknown words, but the Syntactic Co-Occurrence Network is very good at handling unknown or new words.

The performance of the syntactic co-occurrence measure on the corpora is shown in Table 6, with a 70.0% performance for English and 68.0% for Bengali; a good increment over the Semantic Network Overlap technique: about 45% (Eng.) and 41% (Bng.) of the "$Positivity > 0 \wedge Negativity > 0$" cases and 43% (Eng.) and 38% (Bng.) of the "$|Positivity - Negativity| \geq 0.2$" cases were resolved by the Syntactic co-occurrence based technique.

To better aid our understanding of the developed lexical network to hold Sentimantics we visualized this network using the Fruchterman Reingold force directed graph layout algorithm (Fruchterman and Reingold, 1991) and the NodeXL [18] network analysis tool (Smith et al., 2009).

Type	Number		Solved By Syntactic Co-Occurrence Network
Positivity>0 && Negativity>0	**Eng.**	6,619	2978 (45 %)
	Bng.	7,654	3138 (41 %)
|Positivity-Negativity|>=0.2	**Eng.**	3,187	1370 (43 %)
	Bng.	2,677	1017 (38 %)

Table 6: Results of the syntactic co-occurrence based technique

6 Conclusions

The paper has introduced *Sentimantics*, a new way to represent sentiment knowledge in the Conceptual Spaces of distributional Semantics by using in a Vector Space Model. This model can store dynamic prior polarity with varying contextual information. It is clear from the experiments presented that developing the Vector Space Model from scratch is the best solution to solving the Sentimantics problem and to reach a satisfactory level of coverage. Although it could not be claimed that the two issues "*What knowledge to keep at what level?*" and "*reduce/remove the requirement of using further NLP techniques to disambiguate the contextual polarity*" were fully solved, our experiments show that a proper treatment of Sentimantics can radically increase sentiment analysis performance. As we showed by the syntactic classification technique the lexicon model only provides 50% accuracy and further NLP techniques increase it to 70%, whereas by the VSM based technique it reaches 70% accuracy while utilizing fewer language processing resources and techniques.

To the best of our knowledge this is the first research endeavor which enlightens the necessity of using the dynamic prior polarity with context. It is an ongoing task and presently we are exploring its possible applications to multiple domains and languages. The term *Sentimantics* may or may not remain in spotlight with time, but we do believe that this is high time to move on for the dynamic prior polarity lexica.

[18] http://www.codeplex.com/NodeXL

References

Cambria Erik, Amir Hussain and Chris Eckl. 2011. Taking Refuge in Your Personal Sentic Corner. SAAIP, IJCNLP, pp. 35-43.

Cem Akkaya, Janyce Wiebe, Conrad Alexander and Mihalcea Rada. 2011. Improving the Impact of Subjectivity Word Sense Disambiguation on Contextual Opinion Analysis. CoNLL.

Das Amitava and Bandyopadhyay S. 2010. SemanticNet-Perception of Human Pragmatics. COGALEX-II, COLING, pp 2-11.

Das Amitava Bandyopadhyay S. 2010. SentiWordNet for Indian Languages. ALR, COLING, pp 56-63.

Dasgupta, Sajib and Vincent Ng. 2009. Topic-wise, Sentiment-wise, or Otherwise? Identifying the Hidden Dimension for Unsupervised Text Classification. EMNLP.

Ekbal A. and Bandyopadhyay S. 2010. Voted NER System using Appropriate Unlabeled Data. *Lingvisticae Investigationes Journal.*

Esuli Andrea and Fabrizio Sebastiani. 2006. SentiWordNet: A Publicly Available Lexical Resource for Opinion Mining. LREC, pp. 417-422.

Fruchterman Thomas M. J. and Edward M. Reingold. 1991. Graph drawing by force-directed placement. *Software: Practice and Experience*, 21(11):1129–1164.

Grassi, Marco. 2009. Developing HEO Human Emotions Ontology. Joint International Conference on Biometric ID management and Multimodal Communication, vol. 5707 of LNCS, pp 244–251.

Haruechaiyasak Choochart, Alisa Kongthon, Palingoon Pornpimon and Sangkeettrakarn Chatchawal. 2010. Constructing Thai Opinion Mining Resource: A Case Study on Hotel Reviews. ALR, pp 64–71.

Hatzivassiloglou Vasileios and Kathleen R. McKeown. 1997. Predicting the Semantic Orientation of Adjectives. ACL, pp. 174–181.

Havasi, C., Speer, R., Alonso, J. 2007. ConceptNet 3: a Flexible, Multilingual Semantic Network for Common Sense Knowledge. RANLP.

He Yulan, Alani Harith and Zhou Deyu. 2010. Exploring English Lexicon Knowledge for Chinese Sentiment Analysis. CIPS-SIGHAN, pp 28-29.

Kim Soo-Min and Eduard Hovy. 2004. Determining the Sentiment of Opinions. COLING, pp. 1367-1373.

Liu Bing. 2010. *NLP Handbook*. Chapter: Sentiment Analysis and Subjectivity, 2nd Edition.

Liu Hugo, Henry Lieberman and Ted Selker. 2003. A Model of Textual Affect Sensing using Real-World Knowledge. IUI, pp. 125-132.

Minsky Marvin. 2006. *The Emotion Machine*. Simon and Schuster, New York.

Moilanen Karo, Pulman Stephen and Zhang Yue. 2010. Packed Feelings and Ordered Sentiments: Sentiment Parsing with Quasi-compositional Polarity Sequencing and Compression. WASSA, pp. 36--43.

Ohana Bruno and Brendan Tierney. 2009. Sentiment classification of reviews using SentiWordNet. In the 9th IT&T Conference.

Pang Bo, Lillian Lee and Vaithyanathan Shivakumar. 2002. Thumbs up? Sentiment Classification using Machine Learning Techniques. EMNLP, pp 79-86.

Pang, Bo and Lillian Lee. 2005. Seeing stars: Exploiting class relationships for sentiment categorization with respect to rating scales. ACL, pp. 115-124.

Seeker Wolfgang, Adam Bermingham, Jennifer Foster and Deirdre Hogan. 2009. Exploiting Syntax in Sentiment Polarity Classification. National Centre for Language Technology Dublin City University, Ireland.

Shulamit Umansky-Pesin, Roi Reichart and Ari Rappoport. 2010. A Multi-Domain Web-Based Algorithm for POS Tagging of Unknown Words. COLING.

Smith Marc, Ben Shneiderman, Natasa Milic-Frayling, Eduarda Mendes Rodrigues, Vladimir Barash, Cody Dunne, Tony Capone, Adam Perer, and Eric Gleave. 2009. Analyzing (social media) networks with NodeXL. 4th International Conference on Communities and Technologies, pp. 255-264.

Takamura Hiroya, Inui Takashi and Okumura Manabu. 2005. Extracting Semantic Orientations of Words using Spin Model. ACL, pp. 133-140.

Torii Yoshimitsu, Das Dipankar, Bandyopadhyay Sivaji and Okumura Manabu. 2011. Developing Japanese WordNet Affect for Analyzing Emotions. WASSA, ACL, pp. 80-86

Turney Peter and Michael Littman. 2003. Measuring praise and criticism: Inference of semantic orientation from association. *ACM Transactions on Information Systems*, 21(4):315–346.

Turney Peter. 2002. Thumbs up or thumbs down? Semantic orientation applied to unsupervised classification of reviews. ACL, pp. 417–424.

Turney Peter. 2006. Similarity of Semantic Relations. *Computational Linguistics*, 32(3):379-416.

Analysis of Travel Review Data from Reader's Point of View

Maya Ando **Shun Ishizaki**
Graduate School of Media and Governance
Keio University
5322 Endo, Fujisawa-shi, Kanagawa 252-0882, Japan
maya@sfc.keio.ac.jp ishizaki@sfc.keio.ac.jp

Abstract

In the NLP field, there have been a lot of works which focus on the reviewer's point of view conducted on sentiment analyses, which ranges from trying to estimate the reviewer's score. However the reviews are used by the readers. The reviews that give a big influence to the readers should have the highest value, rather than the reviews to which was assigned the highest score by the writer. In this paper, we conducted the analyses using the reader's point of view. We asked 20 subjects to read 500 sentences in the reviews of Rakuten travel and extracted the sentences that gave a big influence to the subjects. We analyze the influential sentences from the following two points of view, 1) targets and evaluations and 2) personal tastes. We found that "room", "service", "meal" and "scenery" are important targets which are items included in the reviews, and that "features" and "human senses" are important evaluations which express sentiment or explain targets. Also we showed personal tastes appeared on "meal" and "service".

1 Introduction

Reviews are indispensable in the current e-commerce business. In the NLP field, there have been a lot of works conducted on sentiment analyses, which ranges from trying to estimate the reviewer's score or analyzing them by the aspects of reviewer's evaluations. However the reviews are used by the customers, not by the reviewers. So, the business value of the review lies on the customer's point of view, rather than the reviewer's point of view. The reviews which give a great influence to the customers should have the highest value, rather than the reviews to which were assigned the highest score by the writer. We defined customers as readers and reviewers as writers. We found the differences between the writer's view and the reader's one using scores given by reviewers. Especially the negative information is found much more influential to the readers than the positive one (Ando et al., 2012).

We conducted the analyses using the *reader's point of view*. We asked 20 subjects to read 500 review sentences in Rakuten travel reviews[1] and extract the sentences from them that gave a great influence. We analyzed the influential sentences from the following two points of view, 1) *targets* and *evaluations* (Chap. 4) and 2) Personal tastes (Chap. 5).

2 Previous Study

There have been a lot of works on sentiment analysis in the past decade. Some of them were classifying reviews into positive, negative, or neutral (Turney, 2002; Pang et al., 2002; Koppel et al., 2006; Pang, 2005; Okanohara et al., 2006; Thelwall et al., 2010). These works were conducted based on the writer's point of view, i.e. the targets are mainly assigned by the writers. In our research, we will describe reader's point of view.

---

[1] Rakuten Travel Inc.
http://travel.rakuten.co.jp/ (Japanese)

In some reviews, there is information called helpfulness which is given by readers. Ghose et al. (2007) used it as one of the features in order to rank the reviews. Passos (2010) also used it to identify authoritativeness of reviews. They didn't conduct any detailed analysis like what we conducted in this paper. So far, the usage of the helpfulness information is limited, and indeed the information is too obscure to be used in the analyses we are trying to conduct.

3 Data Preparation

We use hotel's reviews of Rakuten travel Inc. We defined influential sentences as those that influence readers to make them book the hotel. In practice, influential sentences are very sparse. So, in order to collect them efficiently, we used a heuristic that it is relatively more likely to find them in the sentences with exclamation marks ("!") located at their ends. We randomly extract 500 sentences which have more than one "!" at the end, and used for the analyses. Note that exclamation mark doesn't change the meaning of the sentence. We conducted a preliminary survey and found that our assumption works well.

We asked 20 subjects to extract influential sentences from the 500 sentences. The task is to extract sentences by which each subject thinks it influential enough to decide he/she wants to book or never to do the hotel. We asked them not to include their personal tastes. There are 84 influential sentences on which more than 4 subjects agreed. In the following sections, these 84 sentences will be called *the influential sentences* and the other sentences are regarded as *the non-influential sentences*.

4 Analysis of Target and Evaluation

We analyze classes of targets and evaluations which are most influential to the readers. Here, the targets are such as meals or locations of the hotels, and the evaluations are the reader's impressions about the targets such as good or convenient. We allow duplication of the classification, i.e. if a sentence contains more than one target or evaluation then we extract all the target or evaluation terms.

We categorized the targets into 11 classes and the evaluations into 7 classes (Table1). The table contains the Chi-square test results for each class. It indicates how significantly each class appears in the influential sentences compared to the non-influential sentences. "Less than 1%" means that the chance having the number of classes in the influential sentences and that in the non-influential sentences is less than 1%, if random distribution is assumed. "None" means there is no significant influence. The results of Chi-square test show that the three classes of target, "room", "meal" and "service" give influence to the readers (less than 1%), and "scenery" is also influential (less than 5%). Two classes of the evaluations, "human senses" and "features" are influential (less than 1%). "Features" are expressions describing the writer's view about particular targets in the hotel.

We found that some particular combinations of a target and an evaluation are influential (Table 2). "-" indicates infrequence (less than 6). We will discuss the combinations of "meal + human senses", "service + feelings" and "room/ meal/ service/ scenery + features".

In the combination of "meal + human senses", "human senses" are all about taste. The number of the influential sentences is 12, and the non-influential sentences are 19. We analyze each set of sentences, and found that the influential sentences include particular name of dish like "sukiyaki" much more often (less than 1%). Non-influential sentences include more abstract expressions, like "breakfast". The readers are influenced by particular food.

The combination of "feeling + service" appeared in influential sentences relatively more often(less than 2.5%). "Service" includes service of the hotel like "welcome fruit" or "staff's service". "Feeling" is influential only when it combines with "service" (ex. 1).

Ex. 1: ...there was happy surprise service at the dinner!!

"Features" is very frequent. Investigating the combination with targets, we found that "room", "meal" and "service" are the ones which made significant difference (less than 1%) by combining with "features". These are the key to make "features" more influential for readers. "Scenery" is a target originally created and has a significant difference less than 5%. It is a bit unexpected, but was useful information for some readers.

Table 1. Target and Evaluation with Chi-square test

Result of Chi-square test	Target	evaluation
Less than 1%	Room, meal, service	Human sense (e.g. delicious, stink), Features (e.g. marvelous, bad)
Less than 5%	Scenery	-
None	Location, staff, facility, hotel, bath, plan, price	recommendation (e.g. This is my recommendation) next visiting (e.g. I'll never use this hotel), feeling (e.g. happy) request (e.g. I want you to…), others (e.g. Thank you)

Table 2. Combination of Target and Evaluation with Chi-square test

	room	meal	bath	service	facility	scenery
features	less than 1%	less than 1%	NO	less than 1%	NO	less than 5%
feelings	NO	-	-	less than 2.5%	-	-
human senses	-	less than 1%	-	-	-	-

5 Personal tastes in the influential sentences

Although we instructed the subjects not to include particular personal tastes, we observed the selections of the influential sentences are different among the subject. 289 sentences are selected as influential sentences by at least one subject, and 94 sentences are selected by only one subject.

The personal tastes often appear on the target, so we analyzed differences of targets among the subject. We clustered the subjects based on their choice of the targets. For each subject, we create a frequency vector whose elements are including the most popular 7 targets, namely "location", "room", "meal", "bath", "service", "facility", and "scenery". Then the cosine metrics is applied to calculate the similarity between any pair of the subjects. Next, we run the hierarchical agglomerative clustering with the farthest neighbor method to form their clusters. Three figures, Figures 1 to 3, show the results of three clusters in Rader charts. Each of three clusters has a typical personal taste, namely groups who are influenced more by "service" very strongly (Fig. 1), by "meal" (Fig. 2) or by both "service" and "meal "(Fig. 3).

We analyze influential sentences by using the number of sentences including "service". Table 3 shows the numbers of sentences that were judged influential by certain numbers of subjects on "service". In this analysis, we categorize the influential sentences into positive and negative ones. For example, there were 2 positively influential sentences that were judged influential by 9 subjects. From Table 3, we can observe that the sentences can clearly be grouped into two; sentences which 7 or more subjects judged influential (we will call them as a popular group) and sentences less than 7 subjects judged influential (unpopular group).

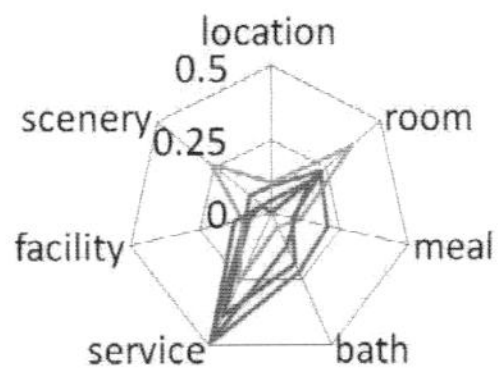

Figure 1. "Service" type

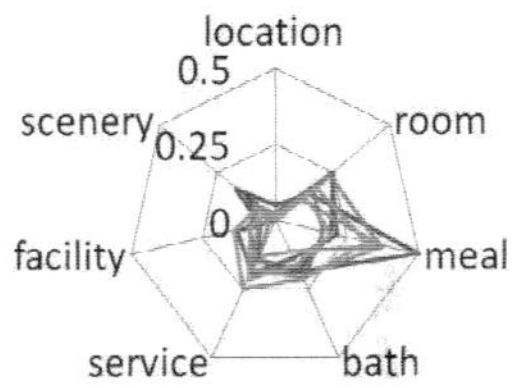

Figure 2. "Meal" type

Figure 3. "Service & meal" type

Table 3: the number of influential sentences judged by certain number of subjects on "service"

	10 or more	9	8	7	6	5	Less than 5
Positive	3	2	1	0	1	5	33
Negative	3	3	1	0	0	2	4

In the "service" target, 63 sentences are selected as influential by at least one subject. Among them, 45 sentences are positive, 13 sentences are negative and 5 sentences are classified other (i.e. neither positive nor negative). There are four sets of data by combining positive-negative axis and axis. We will analyze them one by one.

[Negative & Popular]
There are 7 sentences in this group and we found that 3 of them include "feeling" evaluation, such as "surprised" or "angry". In contrast, there is no sentence including feeling in the negative & unpopular group. Also, very unpleasant events

like "arrogant attitude of hotel staff," "lost the luggage" and "payment trouble" are found negatively influential by many subjects.

[Negative & Unpopular]

There are sentences about staff's attitude in this group, too, but it is less important compared to the ones in the popular group. For example, staff's attitude is about greetings or conversation by the hotel staff. We believe it is depending on people if they care those issues or not.

[Positive & Popular]

In this group, there are 2 sentences that show unexpected warm service (ex. 2). Also, there are sentences that express high satisfactions not only in service but also in other targets, such as meal.

> Ex. 2: ...they kept the electric carpet on because it was cold. We, with my elderly farther, were so glad and impressed!!

[Positive & Unpopular]

All sentences include some positive descriptions about services, such as "carrying the luggage" or "welcome fruit". Some subjects are influenced, but the others aren't. We believe it is because some people think that these are just usual services to be provided.

Now, we describe analyses on the "meal" target. There are 68 influential sentences selected by at least one subject. There are 58 positive sentences, 5 negative sentences and 4 sentences otherwise. We analyze the four groups, just like what we did for "service".

[Negative & Popular]

We find strong negative opinion about meal itself like "Their rice was cooked terrible", which are not found in the unpopular group. Many people are influenced when the meal is described badly.

[Negative & Unpopular]

There are 2 sentences about the situation of the restaurant, such as "crowded" or "existence of a large group of people". We believe that the most important feature of meal is taste, not the situation. Many people might know such situation happens by chance, so only some people cares about this kind of issue.

[Positive & Popular]

The sentences in both popular and unpopular groups include "delicious", but "delicious" with emphasizing adjectives, like "really delicious" were found only in the popular group.

[Positive & Unpopular]

The sentences including "cost performance" and "large portion" only appear in the unpopular group. We believe that the size might be influential to people who like to eat a lot, but people who might not be interested in them.

The analyses show that there is personal taste and we analyzed it in detail by examining the examples. It indicates that personalization is very important for the readers to find the reviews that might satisfy readers.

6 Conclusion

The main focus of our study is on the *reader's point view* to evaluate reviews, compared to the *writer's point of view* that was the major focus in the previous studies. We defined the influential sentences as those that could make the reader's decision. We analyzed the 84 influential sentences, based on the selection by the 20 subjects from the 500 sentences. We conducted the following two analyses.

1) We analyzed targets and evaluations in influential sentences. We found that "room", "service", "meal" and "scenery" are important targets, and "features" and "human senses" are important evaluations. We also analyzed combinations of the targets and evaluations. We find that some combinations make it more influential than each of them.
2) We analyzed the personal tastes. The subjects can be categorized into three clusters, which can be explained intuitively. We found that the most important targets to characterize the clusters are "service" and "meal".

There are many directions in our future work. One of the important topics is to conduct cognitive analysis on the influential sentences. We found that expressions can be very influential by adding a simple modifier ("really delicious"). Furthermore, many metaphorical expressions are found in influential sentences (this topic was not covered in this paper). We would like to conduct the cognitive analyses on these topics to clarify the characteristics of the reader's point of view. We believe it will reveal new types of information in reviews that is also useful for applications.

References

Alexandre Passos and Jacques Wainer, 2010, What do you know? A topic-model approach to authority identification, Proc. Of Computational Social Science and Wisdom of Crowds(NIP2010).

Anindya Ghose and Panagiotis G. Ipeirotis. 2007. Designing novel review ranking systems: Predicting usefulness and impact of reviews. Proc. of the International Conference on Electronic Commerce (ICEC), pp. 303-309.

Bo Pang, Lillian Lee and Shivakumar Vaithyanathan. 2002. "Thumbs up? Sentiment Classification using Machine Learning Techniques". Proceedings of the Conference on Empirical Methods in Natural Language Processing (EMNLP). pp. 79–86.

Bo Pang and Lillian Lee. 2005. "Seeing stars: Exploiting class relationships for sentiment categorization with respect to rating scales". Proceedings of the Association for Computational Linguistics (ACL). pp. 115–124.

Daisuke Okanohara and Jun'ichi Tsujii. 2007.Assigning Polarity Scores to Reviews Using Machine Learning Techniques. Journal of Natural Language Processing. 14(3). pp. 273-295.

Koppel, M. and Schler, J. 2006. "The Importance of Neutral Examples in Learning Sentiment". Computational Intelligence. 22(2). pp.100-109.

Maya Ando and Shun Ishizaki. 2012, Analysis of influencial reviews on Web(in Japanese), Proc. Of the 18th Annual Conference of the Association for Natural Language Processing, pp. 731-734.

P. Victor, C. Cornelis, M. De Cock, and A. Teredesai. 2009. "Trust- and distrustbased recommendations for controversial reviews." in Proceedings of the WebSci'09, Society On-Line.

Peter Turney. 2002. "Thumbs Up or Thumbs Down? Semantic Orientation Applied to Unsupervised Classification of Reviews". Proceedings of the Association for Computational Linguistics. pp. 417-424.

Thelwall, Mike; Buckley, Kevan; Paltoglou, Georgios; Cai, Di; Kappas, Arvid. 2010. "Sentiment strength detection in short informal text". Journal of the American Society for Information Science and Technology 61 (12). pp. 2544-2558.

Multilingual Sentiment Analysis using Machine Translation?

Alexandra Balahur and Marco Turchi
European Commission Joint Research Centre
Institute for the Protection and Security of the Citizen
Via E. Fermi 2749, Ispra, Italy
alexandra.balahur, marco.turchi@jrc.ec.europa.eu

Abstract

The past years have shown a steady growth in interest in the Natural Language Processing task of sentiment analysis. The research community in this field has actively proposed and improved methods to detect and classify the opinions and sentiments expressed in different types of text - from traditional press articles, to blogs, reviews, fora or tweets. A less explored aspect has remained, however, the issue of dealing with sentiment expressed in texts in languages other than English. To this aim, the present article deals with the problem of sentiment detection in three different languages - French, German and Spanish - using three distinct Machine Translation (MT) systems - Bing, Google and Moses. Our extensive evaluation scenarios show that SMT systems are mature enough to be reliably employed to obtain training data for languages other than English and that sentiment analysis systems can obtain comparable performances to the one obtained for English.

1 Introduction

Together with the increase in the access to technology and the Internet, the past years have shown a steady growth of the volume of user-generated contents on the Web. The diversity of topics covered by this data (mostly containing subjective and opinionated content) in the new textual types such as blogs, fora, microblogs, has been proven to be of tremendous value to a whole range of applications, in Economics, Social Science, Political Science, Marketing, to mention just a few. Notwithstanding these proven advantages, the high quantity of user-generated contents makes this information hard to access and employ without the use of automatic mechanisms. This issue motivated the rapid and steady growth in interest from the Natural Language Processing (NLP) community to develop computational methods to analyze subjectivity and sentiment in text. Different methods have been proposed to deal with these phenomena for the distinct types of text and domains, reaching satisfactory levels of performance for English. Nevertheless, for certain applications, such as news monitoring, the information in languages other than English is also highly relevant and cannot be disregarded. Additionally, systems dealing with sentiment analysis in the context of monitoring must be reliable and perform at similar levels as the ones implemented for English.

Although the most obvious solution to these issues of multilingual sentiment analysis would be to use machine translation systems, researchers in sentiment analysis have been reluctant to using such technologies due to the low performance they used to have. However, in the past years, the performance of Machine Translation systems has steadily improved. Open access solutions (e.g. Google Translate[1], Bing Translator[2]) offer more and more accurate translations for frequently used languages.

Bearing these thoughts in mind, in this article we study the manner in which sentiment analysis can be done for languages other than English, using Machine Translation. In particular, we will study

[1]http://translate.google.it/

[2]http://www.microsofttranslator.com/

this issue in three languages - French, German and Spanish - using three different Machine Translation systems - Google Translate, Bing Translator and Moses (Koehn et al., 2007).

We employ these systems to obtain training and test data for these three languages and subsequently extract features that we employ to build machine learning models using Support Vector Machines Sequential Minimal Optimization. We additionally employ meta-classifiers to test the possibility to minimize the impact of noise (incorrect translations) in the obtained data.

Our experiments show that machine translation systems are mature enough to be employed for multilingual sentiment analysis and that for some languages (for which the translation quality is high enough) the performance that can be attained is similar to that of systems implemented for English.

2 Related Work

Most of the research in subjectivity and sentiment analysis was done for English. However, there were some authors who developed methods for the mapping of subjectivity lexicons to other languages. To this aim, (Kim and Hovy, 2006) use a machine translation system and subsequently use a subjectivity analysis system that was developed for English to create subjectivity analysis resources in other languages. (Mihalcea et al., 2009) propose a method to learn multilingual subjective language via cross-language projections. They use the Opinion Finder lexicon (Wilson et al., 2005) and use two bilingual English-Romanian dictionaries to translate the words in the lexicon. Since word ambiguity can appear (Opinion Finder does not mark word senses), they filter as correct translations only the most frequent words. The problem of translating multi-word expressions is solved by translating word-by-word and filtering those translations that occur at least three times on the Web. Another approach in obtaining subjectivity lexicons for other languages than English was explored by Banea et al. (Banea et al., 2008b). To this aim, the authors perform three different experiments, obtaining promising results. In the first one, they automatically translate the annotations of the MPQA corpus and thus obtain subjectivity annotated sentences in Romanian. In the second approach, they use the automatically translated entries in the Opinion Finder lexicon to annotate a set of sentences in Romanian. In the last experiment, they reverse the direction of translation and verify the assumption that subjective language can be translated and thus new subjectivity lexicons can be obtained for languages with no such resources. Further on, another approach to building lexicons for languages with scarce resources is presented by Banea et al. (Banea et al., 2008a). In this research, the authors apply bootstrapping to build a subjectivity lexicon for Romanian, starting with a set of seed subjective entries, using electronic bilingual dictionaries and a training set of words. They start with a set of 60 words pertaining to the categories of noun, verb, adjective and adverb from the translations of words in the Opinion Finder lexicon. Translations are filtered using a measure of similarity to the original words, based on Latent Semantic Analysis (LSA) (Deerwester et al., 1990) scores. Yet another approach to mapping subjectivity lexica to other languages is proposed by Wan (2009), who uses co-training to classify un-annotated Chinese reviews using a corpus of annotated English reviews. He first translates the English reviews into Chinese and subsequently back to English. He then performs co-training using all generated corpora. (Kim et al., 2010) create a number of systems consisting of different subsystems, each classifying the subjectivity of texts in a different language. They translate a corpus annotated for subjectivity analysis (MPQA), the subjectivity clues (Opinion finder) lexicon and re-train a Nave Bayes classifier that is implemented in the Opinion Finder system using the newly generated resources for all the languages considered. Finally, (Banea et al., 2010) translate the MPQA corpus into five other languages (some with a similar ethimology, others with a very different structure). Subsequently, they expand the feature space used in a Nave Bayes classifier using the same data translated to 2 or 3 other languages. Their conclusion is that by expanding the feature space with data from other languages performs almost as well as training a classifier for just one language on a large set of training data.

Attempts of using machine translation in different natural language processing tasks have not been widely used due to poor quality of translated texts, but recent advances in Machine Translation have motivated such attempts. In Information Retrieval, (Savoy and Dolamic, 2009) proposed a comparison between Web searches using monolingual and translated queries. On average, the results show a drop in performance when translated queries are used, but it is quite limited, around 15%. For some language pairs, the average result obtained is around 10% lower than that of a monolingual search while for other pairs, the retrieval performance is clearly lower. In cross-language document summarization, (Wan et al., 2010; Boudin et al., 2010) combined the MT quality score with the informativeness score of each sentence in a set of documents to automatically produce summary in a target language using a source language texts. In (Wan et al., 2010), each sentence of the source document is ranked according both the scores, the summary is extracted and then the selected sentences translated to the target language. Differently, in (Boudin et al., 2010), sentences are first translated, then ranked and selected. Both approaches enhance the readability of the generated summaries without degrading their content.

3 Motivation and Contribution

The main motivation for the experiments we present in this article is the known lack of resources and approaches for sentiment analysos in languages other than English. Although, as we have seen in the Related Work section, a few attempts were made to build systems that deal with sentiment analysis in other languages, they mostly employed bilingual dictionaries and used unsupervised approaches. The very few that employed supervised learning using translated data have, in change, concentrated only on the issue of sentiment classification and have disregarded the impact of the translation quality and the difference that the use of distinct translation systems can make in this settings. Moreover, such approaches have usually employed only simple machine learning algorithms. No attempt has been made to study the use of meta-classifiers to enhance the performance of the classification through the removal of noise in the data.

Our main contribution in this article is the comparative study of multilingual sentiment analysis performance using distinct machine translation systems, with varying levels of translation quality. In this sense, we employ three different systems - Bing Translator, Google Translate and Moses to translate data from English to three languages - French, German and Spanish. We subsequently study the performance of classifying sentiment from the translated data and different methods to minimize the effect of noise in the data.

Our comparative results show, on the one hand, that machine translation can be reliably used for multilingual sentiment analysis and, on the other hand, which are the main characteristics of the data for such approaches to be successfully employed.

4 Dataset Presentation and Analysis

For our experiments, we employed the data provided for English in the NTCIR 8 Multilingual Opinion Analysis Task (MOAT)[3]. In this task, the organizers provided the participants with a set of 20 topics (questions) and a set of documents in which sentences relevant to these questions could be found, taken from the New York Times Text (2002-2005) corpus. The documents were given in two different forms, which had to be used correspondingly, depending on the task to which they participated. The first variant contained the documents split into sentences (6165 in total) and had to be used for the task of opinionatedness, relevance and answerness. In the second form, the sentences were also split into opinion units (6223 in total) for the opinion polarity and the opinion holder and target tasks. For each of the sentences, the participants had to provide judgments on the opinionatedness (whether they contained opinions), relevance (whether they are relevant to the topic). For the task of polarity classification, the participants had to employ the dataset containing the sentences that were also split into opinion units (i.e. one sentences could contain two/more opinions, on two/more different targets or from two/more different opinion holders).

For our experiments, we employed the latter representation. From this set, we randomly chose 600 opinion units, to serve as test set. The rest of opinion units will be employed as training set. Subsequently, we employed the Google Translate, Bing

[3]http://research.nii.ac.jp/ntcir/ntcir-ws8/permission/ntcir8xinhua-nyt-moat.html

Translator and Moses systems to translate, on the one hand, the training set and on the other hand the test set, to French, German and Spanish. Additionally, we employed the Yahoo system to translate only the test set into these three languages. Further on, this translation of the test set by the Yahoo service has been corrected by a person for all the languages. This corrected data serves as Gold Standard[4]. Most of these sentences, however, contained no opinion (were neutral). Due to the fact that the neutral examples are majoritary and can produce a large bias when classifying, we decided to eliminate these examples and employ only the positive and negative sentences in both the training, as well as the test sets. After this elimination, the training set contains 943 examples (333 positive and 610 negative) and the test set and Gold Standard contain 357 examples (107 positive and 250 negative).

5 Machine Translation

During the 1990's the research community on Machine Translation proposed a new approach that made use of statistical tools based on a noisy channel model originally developed for speech recognition (Brown et al., 1994). In the simplest form, Statistical Machine Translation (SMT) can be formulated as follows. Given a source sentence written in a foreign language f, the Bayes rule is applied to reformulate the probability of translating f into a sentence e written in a target language:

$$e_{best} = arg \max_e p(e|f) = arg \max_e p(f|e) p_{LM}(e)$$

where $p(f|e)$ is the probability of translating e to f and $p_{LM}(e)$ is the probability of producing a fluent sentence e. For a full description of the model see (Koehn, 2010).

The noisy channel model was extended in different directions. In this work, we analyse the most popular class of SMT systems: PBSMT. It is an extension of the noisy channel model using phrases rather than words. A source sentence f is segmented into a sequence of I phrases $f^I = \{f_1, f_2, \dots f_I\}$ and the same is done for the target sentence e, where the notion of phrase is not related to any grammatical assumption; a phrase is an n-gram. The best translation e_{best} of f is obtained by:

$$\begin{aligned} e_{best} &= arg \max_e p(e|f) = arg \max_e p(f|e) p_{LM}(e) \\ &= arg \max_e \prod_{i=1}^{I} \phi(f_i|e_i)^{\lambda_\phi} d(a_i - b_{i-1})^{\lambda_d} \\ & \prod_{i=1}^{|e|} p_{LM}(e_i|e_1 \dots e_{i-1})^{\lambda_{LM}} \end{aligned}$$

where $\phi(f_i|e_i)$ is the probability of translating a phrase e_i into a phrase f_i. $d(a_i - b_{i-1})$ is the distance-based reordering model that drives the system to penalise significant reorderings of words during translation, while allowing some flexibility. In the reordering model, a_i denotes the start position of the source phrase that is translated into the ith target phrase, and b_{i-1} denotes the end position of the source phrase translated into the $(i-1)$th target phrase. $p_{LM}(e_i|e_1 \dots e_{i-1})$ is the language model probability that is based on the Markov's chain assumption. It assigns a higher probability to fluent/grammatical sentences. λ_ϕ, λ_{LM} and λ_d are used to give a different weight to each element. For more details see (Koehn et al., 2003).

Three different SMT systems were used to translate the human annotated sentences: two existing online services such as *Google Translate* and *Bing Translator*[5] and an instance of the open source phrase-based statistical machine translation toolkit Moses (Koehn et al., 2007).

To train our models based on Moses we used the freely available corpora: Europarl (Koehn, 2005), JRC-Acquis (Steinberger et al., 2006), Opus (Tiedemann, 2009), News Corpus (Callison-Burch et al., 2009). This results in 2.7 million sentence pairs for English-French, 3.8 for German and 4.1 for Spanish. All the modes are optimized running the MERT algorithm (Och, 2003) on the development part of the News Corpus. The translated sentences are recased and detokonized (for more details on the system, please see (Turchi et al., 2012).

[4]Please note that each sentence may contain more than one opinion unit. In order to ensure a contextual translation, we translated the whole sentences, not the opinion units separately. In the end, we eliminate duplicates of sentences (due to the fact that they contained multiple opinion units), resulting in around 400 sentences in the test and Gold Standard sets and 5700 sentences in the training set

[5]`http://translate.google.com/` and `http://www.microsofttranslator.com/`

Performances of a SMT system are automatically evaluated comparing the output of the system against human produced translations. Bleu score (Papineni et al., 2001) is the most used metric and it is based on averaging n-gram precisions, combined with a length penalty which penalizes short translations containing only sure words. It ranges between 0 and 1, and larger value identifies better translation.

6 Sentiment Analysis

In the field of sentiment analysis, most work has concentrated on creating and evaluating methods, tools and resources to discover whether a specific "target"or "object" (person, product, organization, event, etc.) is "regarded" in a positive or negative manner by a specific "holder" or "source" (i.e. a person, an organization, a community, people in general, etc.). This task has been given many names, from opinion mining, to sentiment analysis, review mining, attitude analysis, appraisal extraction and many others.

The issue of extracting and classifying sentiment in text has been approached using different methods, depending on the type of text, the domain and the language considered. Broadly speaking, the methods employed can be classified into unsupervised (knowledge-based), supervised and semi-supervised methods. The first usually employ lexica or dictionaries of words with associated polarities (and values - e.g. 1, -1) and a set of rules to compute the final result. The second category of approaches employ statistical methods to learn classification models from training data, based on which the test data is then classified. Finally, semi-supervised methods employ knowledge-based approaches to classify an initial set of examples, after which they use different machine learning methods to bootstrap new training examples, which they subsequently use with supervised methods.

The main issue with the first approach is that obtaining large-enough lexica to deal with the variability of language is very expensive (if it is done manually) and generally not reliable (if it is done automatically). Additionally, the main problem of such approaches is that words outside contexts are highly ambiguous. Semi-supervised approaches, on the other hand, highly depend on the performance of the initial set of examples that is classified. If we are to employ machine translation, the errors in translating this small initial set would have a high negative impact on the subsequently learned examples. The challenge of using statistical methods is that they require training data (e.g. annotated corpora) and that this data must be reliable (i.e. not contain mistakes or "noise"). However, the larger this dataset is, the less influence the translation errors have.

Since we want to study whether machine translation can be employed to perform sentiment analysis for different languages, we employed statistical methods in our experiments. More specifically, we used Support Vector Machines Sequential Minimal Optimization (SVM SMO) since the literature in the field has confirmed it as the most appropriate machine learning algorithm for this task.

In the case of statistical methods, the most important aspect to take into consideration is the manner in which texts are represented - i.e. the features that are extracted from it. For our experiments, we represented the sentences based on the unigrams and the bigrams that were found in the training data. Although there is an ongoing debate on whether bigrams are useful in the context of sentiment classification, we considered that the quality of the translation can also be best quantified in the process by using these features (because they give us a measure of the translation correctness, both regarding words, as well as word order). Higher level n-grams, on the other hand, would only produce more sparse feature vectors, due to the high language variability and the mistakes in the traslation.

7 Experiments

In order to test the performance of sentiment classification when using translated data, we performed a series of experiments:

- In the first set of experiments, we trained an SVM SMO classifier on the training data obtained for each language, with each of the three machine translations, separately (i.e. we generated a model for each of the languages considered, for each of the machine translation systems employed). Subsequently, we tested the models thus obtained on the corresponding test set (e.g. training on the Spanish training set obtained using Google Translate and testing on the Spanish test set obtained using Google Translate) and on the Gold Standard for the corresponding language (e.g. training on the Spanish training set obtained using Google Translate and testing on the Spanish Gold Standard). Additionally, in order to study the manner in which the noise in the training data can be removed, we employed two meta-classifiers - AdaBoost and Bagging (with varying sizes of the bag).

- In the second set of experiments, we combined the translated data from all three machine translation systems for the same language and created a model based on the unigram and bigram features extracted from this data (e.g. we created a Spanish training model using the unigrams and bigrams present in the training sets generated by the translation of the training set to Spanish by Google Translate, Bing Translator and Moses). We subsequently tested the performance of the sentiment classification using the Gold Standard for the corresponding language, represented using the features of this model.

Table 1 presents the number of unigram and bigram features employed in each of the cases.

In the following subsections, we present the results of these experiments.

7.1 Individual Training with Translated Data

In the first experiment, we translated the training and test data from English to all the three other languages considered, using each of the three machine translation systems. Subsequently, we represented, for each of the languages and translation systems, the sentences as vectors, whose features marked the presence/absence (1 or 0) of the unigrams and bigrams contained in the corresponding trainig set (e.g. we obtained the unigrams and bigrams in all the sentences in the training set obtained by translating the English training data to Spanish using Google and subsequently represented each sentence in this training set, as well as the test set obtained by translating the test data in English to Spanish using Google marking the presence of the unigram and bigram features). In order to test the approach on the Gold Standard (for each language), we represented this set using the corresponding unigram and bigram features extracted from the corresponding training set (for the example given, we represented each sentence in the Gold Standard by marking the presence/absence of the unigrams and bigrams from the training data for Spanish using Google Translate).

The results of these experiments are presented in Table 2, in terms of weighted F1 measure.

7.2 Joint Training with Translated Data

In the second set of experiments, we added together all the translations of the training data obtained for the same language, with the three different MT systems. Subsequently, we represented, for each language in part, each of the sentences in the joint training corpus as vectors, whose features represented the presence/absence of the unigrams and bigrams contained in this corpus. In order to test the performance of the sentiment classification, we employed the Gold Standard for the corresponding language, representing each sentence it contains according to the presence or absence of the unigrams and bigrams in the corresponding joint training corpus for that language. Finally, we applied SVM SMO to classify the sentences according to the polarity of the sentiment they contained. Additionally, we applied the AdaBoost and Bagging meta-classifiers to test the possibilities to minimize the impact of noise in the data. The results are presented in Tables 3 and 4, again, in terms of weighter F1 measure.

Language	SMO	AdaBoost M1	Bagging
To German	0.565*	0.563*	0.565*
To Spanish	0.419	0.494	0.511
To French	0.25	0.255	0.23

Table 3: For each language, each classifier has been trained merging the translated data coming form different SMT systems, and tested using the Gold Standard. *Classifier is not able to discriminate between positive and negative classes, and assigns most of the test points to one class, and zero to the other.

8 Results and Discussion

Generally speaking, from our experiments using SVM, we could see that incorrect translations imply

	Bing	Google T.	Moses
To German	0.57*	0.572*	0.562*
To Spanish	0.392	0.511	0.448
To French	0.612*	0.571*	0.575*

Table 4: For each language, the SMO classifiers have been trained merging the translated data coming form different SMT systems, and tested using independently the translated test sets. *Classifier is not able to discriminate between positive and negative classes, and assigns most of the test points to one class, and zero to the other.

an increment of the features, sparseness and more difficulties in identifying a hyperplane which separates the positive and negative examples in the training phase. Therefore, a low quality of the translation leads to a drop in performance, as the features extracted are not informative enough to allow for the classifier to learn.

From Table 2, we can see that:
a) There is a small difference between performances of the sentiment analysis system using the English and translated data, respectively. In the worst case, there is a maximum drop of 8 percentages.
b) Adaboost is sensitive to noisy data, and it is evident in our experiments where in general it does not modify the SMO performances or there is a drop. Vice versa, Bagging, reducing the variance in the estimated models, produces a positive effect on the performances increasing the F-score. These improvements are larger using the German data, this is due to the poor quality of the translated data, which increases the variance in the data.

Looking at the results in Tables 3 and 4, we can see that:
a) Adding all the translated training data together drastically increases the noise level in the training data, creating harmful effects in terms of classification performance: each classifier loses its discriminative capability.
b) At language level, clearly the results depend on the translation performance. Only for Spanish (for which we have the highest Bleu score), each classifies is able to properly learn from the training data and try to properly assign the test samples. For the other languages, translated data are so noisy that the classifier is not able to properly learn the correct information for the positive and the negative classes, this results in the assignment of most of the test points to one class and zero to the other. In Table 3, for the French language we have significant drop in performance, but the classifier is still able to learn something from the training and assign the test points to both the classes.
c) The results for Spanish presented in Table 3 confirm the capability of Bagging to reduce the model variance and increase the performance in classification.
d) At system level in Table 4, there is no evidence that better translated test set allows better classification performance.

9 Conclusions and Future Work

In this work we propose an extensive evaluation of the use of translated data in the context of sentiment analysis. Our findings show that SMT systems are mature enough to produce reliably training data for languages other than English. The gap in classification performance between systems trained on English and translated data is minimal, with a maximum of 8

Working with translated data implies an increment number of features, sparseness and noise in the data points in the classification task. To limit these problems, we test three different classification approaches showing that bagging has a positive impact in the results.

In future work, we plan to investigate different document representations, in particular we believe that the projection of our documents in space where the features belong to a sentiment lexical and include syntax information can reduce the impact of the translation errors. As well we are interested to evaluate different term weights such as tf-idf.

Acknowledgments

The authors would like to thank Ivano Azzini, from the BriLeMa Artificial Intelligence Studies, for the advice and support on using meta-classifiers. We would also like to thank the reviewers for their useful comments and suggestions on the paper.

References

Turchi, M. and Atkinson, M. and Wilcox, A. and Crawley, B. and Bucci, S. and Steinberger, R. and Van der Goot, E. 2012. *ONTS: "Optima" News Translation System.*. Proceedings of EACL 2012.

Banea, C., Mihalcea, R., and Wiebe, J. 2008. *A bootstrapping method for building subjectivity lexicons for languages with scarce resources.*. Proceedings of the Conference on Language Resources and Evaluations (LREC 2008), Maraakesh, Marocco.

Banea, C., Mihalcea, R., Wiebe, J., and Hassan, S. 2008. *Multilingual subjectivity analysis using machine translation.* Proceedings of the Conference on Empirical Methods in Natural Language Processing (EMNLP 2008), 127-135, Honolulu, Hawaii.

Banea, C., Mihalcea, R. and Wiebe, J. 2010. *Multilingual subjectivity: are more languages better?*. Proceedings of the International Conference on Computational Linguistics (COLING 2010), p. 28-36, Beijing, China.

Boudin, F. and Huet, S. and Torres-Moreno, J.M. and Torres-Moreno, J.M. 2010. *A Graph-based Approach to Cross-language Multi-document Summarization.* Research journal on Computer science and computer engineering with applications (Polibits), 43:113–118.

P. F. Brown, S. Della Pietra, V. J. Della Pietra and R. L. Mercer. 1994. *The Mathematics of Statistical Machine Translation: Parameter Estimation*, Computational Linguistics 19:263–311.

C. Callison-Burch, and P. Koehn and C. Monz and J. Schroeder. 2009. *Findings of the 2009 Workshop on Statistical Machine Translation.* Proceedings of the Fourth Workshop on Statistical Machine Translation, pages 1–28. Athens, Greece.

Deerwester, S., Dumais, S., Furnas, G. W., Landauer, T. K., and Harshman, R. 1990. *Indexing by latent semantic analysis.* Journal of the American Society for Information Science, 3(41).

Kim, S.-M. and Hovy, E. 2006. *Automatic identification of pro and con reasons in online reviews.* Proceedings of the COLING/ACL Main Conference Poster Sessions, pages 483490.

Kim, J., Li, J.-J. and Lee, J.-H. 2006. *Evaluating Multilanguage-Comparability of Subjectivity Analysis Systems.* Proceedings of the 48th Annual Meeting of the Association for Computational Linguistics, pages 595603, Uppsala, Sweden, 11-16 July 2010.

P. Koehn. 2005. *Europarl: A Parallel Corpus for Statistical Machine Translation.* Proceedings of the Machine Translation Summit X, pages 79-86. Phuket, Thailand.

P. Koehn. 2010. *Statistical Machine Translation.* Cambridge University Press.

P. Koehn and F. J. Och and D. Marcu. 2003. *Statistical Phrase-Based Translation*, Proceedings of the North America Meeting on Association for Computational Linguistics, 48–54.

P. Koehn and H. Hoang and A. Birch and C. Callison-Burch and M. Federico and N. Bertoldi and B. Cowan and W. Shen and C. Moran and R. Zens and C. Dyer and O. Bojar and A. Constantin and E. Herbst 2007. *Moses: Open source toolkit for statistical machine translation.* Proceedings of the Annual Meeting of the Association for Computational Linguistics, demonstration session, pages 177–180. Columbus, Oh, USA.

Mihalcea, R., Banea, C., and Wiebe, J. 2009. *Learning multilingual subjective language via cross-lingual projections.* Proceedings of the Conference of the Annual Meeting of the Association for Computational Linguistics 2007, pp.976-983, Prague, Czech Republic.

F. J. Och 2003. *Minimum error rate training in statistical machine translation.* Proceedings of the 41st Annual Meeting on Association for Computational Linguistics, pages 160–167. Sapporo, Japan.

K. Papineni and S. Roukos and T. Ward and W. J. Zhu 2001. *BLEU: a method for automatic evaluation of machine translation.* Proceedings of the 40th Annual Meeting on Association for Computational Linguistics, pages 311–318. Philadelphia, Pennsylvania.

J. Savoy, and L. Dolamic. 2009. *How effective is Google's translation service in search?*. Communications of the ACM, 52(10):139–143.

R. Steinberger and B. Pouliquen and A. Widiger and C. Ignat and T. Erjavec and D. Tufiş and D. Varga. 2006. *The JRC-Acquis: A multilingual aligned parallel corpus with 20+ languages.* Proceedings of the 5th International Conference on Language Resources and Evaluation, pages 2142–2147. Genova, Italy.

J. Tiedemann. 2009. *News from OPUS-A Collection of Multilingual Parallel Corpora with Tools and Interfaces.* Recent advances in natural language processing V: selected papers from RANLP 2007, pages 309:237.

Wan, X. and Li, H. and Xiao, J. 2010. *Cross-language document summarization based on machine translation quality prediction.* Proceedings of the 48th Annual Meeting of the Association for Computational Linguistics, pages 917–926.

Wilson, T., Wiebe, J., and Hoffmann, P. 2005. *Recognizing contextual polarity in phrase-level sentiment analysis.* Proceedings of HLT-EMNLP 2005, pp.347-354, Vancouver, Canada.

Language	SMT system	Nr. of unigrams	Nr. of bigrams
French	Bing	7441	17870
	Google	7540	18448
	Moses	6938	18814
	Bing+Google+Moses	9082	40977
German	Bing	7817	16216
	Google	7900	16078
	Moses	7429	16078
	Bing+Google+Moses	9371	36556
Spanish	Bing	7388	17579
	Google	7803	18895
	Moses	7528	18354
	Bing+Google+Moses	8993	39034

Table 1: Features employed.

Language	SMT	Test Set	SMO	AdaBoost M1	Bagging	Bleu Score
English		GS	0.685	0.685	0.686	
To German	Bing	GS	0.641	0.631	0.648	
		Tr	0.658	0.636	0.662	0.227
To German	Google T.	GS	0.646	0.623	0.674	
		Tr	0.687	0.645	0.661	0.209
To German	Moses	GS	0.644	0.644	0.676	
		Tr	0.667	0.667	0.674	0.17
To Spanish	Bing	GS	0.656	0.658	0.646	
		Tr	0.633	0.633	0.633	0.316
To Spanish	Google T.	GS	0.653	0.653	0.665	
		Tr	0.636	0.667	0.636	0.341
To Spanish	Moses	GS	0.664	0.664	0.671	
		Tr	0.649	0.649	0.663	0.298
To French	Bing	GS	0.644	0.645	0.664	
		Tr	0.644	0.649	0.652	0.243
To French	Google T.	GS	0.64	0.64	0.659	
		Tr	0.652	0.652	0.678	0.274
To French	Moses	GS	0.633	0.633	0.645	
		Tr	0.666	0.666	0.674	0.227

Table 2: Results obtained using the individual training sets obtained by translating with each of the three considered MT systems, to each of the three languages considered.

Unifying Local and Global Agreement and Disagreement Classification in Online Debates

Jie Yin
CSIRO ICT Centre
NSW, Australia
jie.yin@csiro.au

Nalin Narang
University of New South Wales
NSW, Australia
nalinnarang@gmail.com

Paul Thomas
CSIRO ICT Centre
ACT, Australia
paul.thomas@csiro.au

Cecile Paris
CSIRO ICT Centre
NSW, Australia
cecile.paris@csiro.au

Abstract

Online debate forums provide a powerful communication platform for individual users to share information, exchange ideas and express opinions on a variety of topics. Understanding people's opinions in such forums is an important task as its results can be used in many ways. It is, however, a challenging task because of the informal language use and the dynamic nature of online conversations. In this paper, we propose a new method for identifying participants' agreement or disagreement on an issue by exploiting information contained in each of the posts. Our proposed method first regards each post in its local context, then aggregates posts to estimate a participant's overall position. We have explored the use of sentiment, emotional and durational features to improve the accuracy of automatic agreement and disagreement classification. Our experimental results have shown that aggregating local positions over posts yields better performance than non-aggregation baselines when identifying users' global positions on an issue.

1 Introduction

With their increasing popularity, social media applications provide a powerful communication channel for individuals to share information, exchange ideas and express their opinions on a wide variety of topics. An online debate is an open forum where a participant starts a discussion by posting his opinion on a particular topic, such as regional politics, health or the military, while other participants state their support or opposition by posting their opinions. Understanding participants' opinions in online debates has become an increasingly important task as its results can be used in many ways. For example, by analysing customers' online discussions, companies can better understand customers' reviews about their products or services. For government agencies, it could help gather public opinions about policies, legislation, laws, or elections. For social science, it can assist scientists to understand a breadth of social phenomena from online observations of large numbers of individuals.

Despite the potentially wide range of applications, understanding participants' positions in online debates remains a difficult task. One reason is that online conversations are very dynamic in nature. Unlike spoken conversations (Thomas et al., 2006; Wang et al., 2011), users in online debates are not guaranteed to participate in a discussion at all times. They may enter or exit the online discussion at any point, so it is not appropriate to use models assuming continued conversation. In addition, most discussions in online debates are essentially dialogic; participants could choose to implicitly respond to a previous post, or explicitly quote some content from an earlier post and make a response. Therefore, an assumption has to be made about what a participant's post is in response to, particularly when an explicit quote is not present; in most cases, a post is assumed to be in response to the most recent post in the thread (Murakami and Raymond, 2010).

In this paper, we address the problem of detecting users' positions with respect to the main topic in online debates; we call this the *global* position of users on an issue. It is inappropriate to identify each user's global position with respect to a main topic directly, because most expressions of opinion are made not for the main topic but for posts in a *local* context. This poses a difficulty in directly building a global classifier for agreement and disagreement. We illustrate this with the example below. Here, the topic of the thread is "Beijing starts gating, locking migrant villages" and the discussion is started with a seed post criticising the Chinese government[1].

> **Seed post:** I'm most sure there will be some China sympathisers here justifying these actions imposed by the Communist Chinese government. ...
>
> **Reply 1:** Not really seeing a problem there. From you article. They can come and go. People in my country pay hundreds of thousands of pounds for security like that in their gated communities..
>
> **Reply 2:** So, you are OK with living in a Police State? ...

The author of Reply 1 argues that the Chinese policy is not as presented, and is in fact defensible. This opposes the seed post, so that the author's global position for the main topic is "disagree". The opinion expressed in Reply 2, however, is not a response to the seed post: it relates to Reply 1. It indicates that the author of Reply 2 disagrees with the opinion made in Reply 1, and thus indirectly implies agreement with the seed post. From this example, we can see that it is hard to infer the global position of Reply 2's author only from the text of their post. However, we can exploit information in the local context, such as the relationship between Replies 1 and 2, to indirectly infer the author's opinion with regard to the seed post.

Motivated by this observation, we propose a three-step method for detecting participants' global agreement or disagreement positions by exploiting local information in the posts within the debate. First, we build a local classifier to determine whether a pair of posts agree with each other or not. Second, we aggregate over posts for each pair of participants in one discussion to determine whether they agree with each other. Third, we infer the global positions of participants with respect to the main topic, so that participants can be classified into two classes: agree and disagree. The advantage of our proposed method is that it builds a unified framework which enables the classification of participants' local and global positions in online debates; the aggregation of local estimates also tends to reduce error in the global classification.

In order to evaluate the performance of our method, we have conducted experiments on data sets collected from two online debate forums. We have explored the use of sentiment, emotional and durational features for automatic agreement and disagreement classification, and our feature analysis suggests that they can significantly improve the performance of baselines using only word features. Experimental results have also demonstrated that aggregating local positions over posts yields better performance for identifying users' global positions on an issue.

The rest of the paper is organised as follows. Section 2 discusses previous work on agreement and disagreement classification. Section 3 presents our proposed method for both local and global position classification, which we validate in Section 4 with experiments on two real-world data sets. Section 5 concludes the paper and discusses possible directions for future work.

2 Related Work

Previous work in automatic identification of agreement and disagreement has mainly focused on analysing conversational speech. Thomas et al. (2006) presented a method based on support vector machines to determine whether the speeches made by participants represent support or opposition to proposed legislation, using transcripts of U.S. congressional floor debates. This method showed that the classification of participants' positions can be improved by introducing the constraint that a single speaker retains the same position during one debate. Wang et al. (2011) presented a conditional random field based approach for detecting agreement/disagreement between speakers in English broadcast conversations. Galley et al. (2004) proposed the use of Bayesian networks to model pragmatic dependencies of previous agreement or disagreement on the current utterance. These differ from our work in that the speakers are assumed to

[1] Spelling of the posts is per original on the website.

be present all the time during the conversation, and therefore, user speech models can be built, and their dependencies can be explored to facilitate agreement and disagreement classification. Our aggregation technique does, however, presuppose consistency of opinions, in a similar way to Thomas et al. (2006).

There has been other related work which aims to analyse informal texts for opinion mining and (dis)agreement classification in online discussions. Agrawal et al. (2003) described an observation that reply-to activities always show disagreement with previous authors in newsgroup discussions, and presented a clustering approach to group users into two parties: support and opposition, based on reply-to graphs between users. Murakami and Raymond (2010) proposed a method for deriving simple rules to extract opinion expressions from the content of posts and then applied a similar graph clustering algorithm for partitioning participants into supporting and opposing parties. By combining both text and link information, this approach was demonstrated to outperform the method proposed by Agrawal et al. (2003). Due to the nature of clustering mechanisms, the output of these methods are two user parties, in each of which users most agree or disagree with each other. However, users' positions in the two parties do not necessarily correspond to the global position with respect to the main issue in a debate, which is our interest here. Balasubramanyan and Cohen (2011) proposed a computational method to classify sentiment polarity in blog comments and predict the polarity based on the topics discussed in a blog post. Finally, Somasundaran and Wiebe (2010) explored the utility of sentiment and arguing opinions in ideological debates and applied a support vector machine based approach for classifying stances of individual posts. In our work, we focus on classifying people's global positions on a main issue by exploiting and aggregating local positions expressed in individual posts.

3 Our Proposed Method

To infer support or opposition positions with respect to the seed post, we propose a three-step method. First, we consider each post in its local context and build a local classifier to classify each pair of posts as agreeing with each other or not. Second, we aggregate over posts for each pair of participants in one discussion to determine whether they agree with each other. Third, we infer global positions of participants with respect to the seed post based on the thread structure.

3.1 Classifying Local Positions between Posts

To classify local positions between posts, we need to extract the reply-to pairs of posts from the threading structure. The web forums we work with tend not to present thread structure, so we consider two types of reply-to relationships between individual posts. When a post explicitly quotes the content from an earlier post, we create an *explicit* link between the post and the quoted post. When a post does not contain a quote, we assume that it is a reply to the preceding post, and thus create an *implicit* link between the two adjacent posts. After obtaining explicit/implicit links, we build a classifier to classify each pair of posts as agreeing or disagreeing with each other.

3.1.1 Features

To build a classifier for identifying local agreement and disagreement, we explored different types of features from individual posts with the aim to understand which have predictive power for our agreement/disagreement classification task.

Words We extract unigram and bigram features to capture the lexical information from each post. Since many words are topic related and might be used by both parties in a debate, we mainly use unigrams for *adjectives*, *verbs* and *adverbs* because they have been demonstrated to possess discriminative power for sentiment classification (Benamara et al., 2007; Subrahmanian and Regorgiato, 2008). Typical examples of such unigrams include "agree", "glad", "indeed", and "wrong". In addition, we extract bigrams to capture phrases expressing arguments, for example, "don't think" and "how odd" could indicate disagreement, while "I concur" could indicate agreement.

Sentiment features In order to detect sentiment opinions, we use a sentiment lexicon referred to as SentiWordNet (Baccianella et al., 2010). This lexicon assigns a positive and negative score to a large number of words in WordNet. For example, the

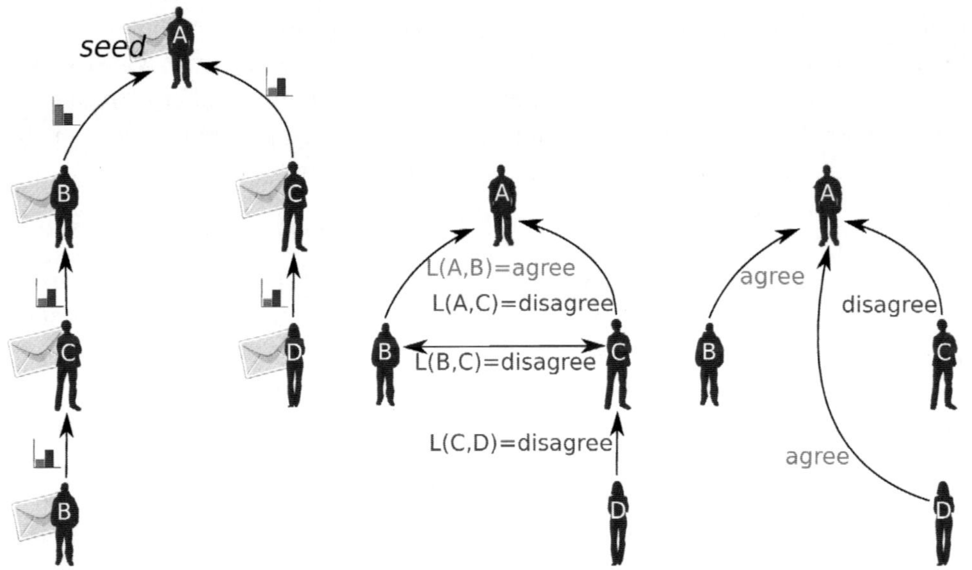

(a) Estimate $P(y|x)$ for each post

(b) Aggregate these over pairs of users to get local agreement $L(m, n)$

(c) Infer the global position of each user by walking the tree

Figure 1: Local agreement/disagreement and participants' global positions. We first estimate $P(y|x_i, x_j)$, the probability of two posts x_i and x_j being in agreement or disagreement with each other, then aggregate over posts to determine $L(m, n)$, the position between two users. Finally, we infer the global position for any user by walking this graph back to the seed.

word "odd" has a positive score of 1.125, and a negative score of 1.625. To aggregate the sentiment polarity of each post, we calculate the overall positive and negative scores for all the words that can be found in SentiWordNet, and use these two sums as two features for each post.

Emotional features We observe that personal emotions could be a good indicator of agreement/disagreement expression in online debates. Therefore, we include a set of emotional features, including occurrences of emoticons, number of capital letters, number of foul words, number of exclamation marks, and number of question marks contained in a post. Intuitively, use of foul words might be linked to emotion in a visceral way, which if used, could be a sign of strong argument and disagreement. The presence of question marks could be indicative of disagreement, and the use of exclamation marks and capital letters could be an emphasis placed on opinions.

Durational features Inspired by conversation analysis (Galley et al., 2004; Wang et al., 2011), we extract durational features, such as the length of a post in words and in characters. These features are analogous to the ones used to capture the duration of a speech for conversation analysis. Intuitively, people tend to respond with a short post if they agree with a previous opinion. Otherwise, when there is a strong argument, people tend to use a longer post to state and defend their own opinions. Moreover, we also consider the time difference between adjacent posts as additional features. Presumably, when a debate is controversial, participants would be actively involved in the discussions, and the thread would unfold quickly over time. Thus, the time difference between adjacent posts would be smaller in the debate.

3.1.2 Classification Model

We use logistic regression as the basic classifier for local position classification because it has been demonstrated to provide good predictive performance across a range of text classification tasks, such as document classification and sentiment analysis (Zhang and Oles, 2001; Pan et al., 2010). In addition to the predicted class, logistic regression can also generate probabilities of class memberships, which are quite useful in our case for aggregating local positions between participants.

Formally, logistic regression estimates the conditional probability of y given $\mathbf{x}$ in the form of

$$P_{\mathbf{w}}(y = \pm 1|\mathbf{x}) = \frac{1}{1 + e^{-y\mathbf{w}^T\mathbf{x}}}, \quad (1)$$

where $\mathbf{x}$ is the feature vector, y is the class label, and $\mathbf{w} \in R^n$ is the weight vector. Given the training data $\{\mathbf{x}_i, y_i\}_{i=1}^l$, $\mathbf{x}_i \in R^n$, $y_i \in \{1, -1\}$, we consider the following form of regularised logistic regression

$$\min_{\mathbf{w}} f(\mathbf{w}) = \frac{1}{2}\mathbf{w}^T\mathbf{w} + C\sum_{i=1}^{l} \log\left(1 + e^{-y_i\mathbf{w}^T\mathbf{x}_i}\right), \quad (2)$$

which aims to minimise the regularised negative log-likelihood of the training data. Above, $\mathbf{w}^T\mathbf{w}/2$ is used as a regularisation term to achieve good generalisation abilities. Parameter $C > 0$ is a penalty factor which controls the balance of the two terms in Equation 2. The above optimisation problem can be solved using different iterative methods, such as conjugate gradient and Newton methods (Lin et al., 2008). As a result, an optimal estimate of $\mathbf{w}$ can be obtained.

Given a representation of a post $\mathbf{x}_m$, we can use Equation 1 to estimate its membership probability of belonging to each class, $P(agree|\mathbf{x}_m)$ and $P(disagree|\mathbf{x}_m)$, respectively.

3.2 Estimating Local Positions between Participants

After obtaining local position between posts, this step aims to aggregate over posts to determine whether each pair of participants agree with each other. The intuition is that, in one threaded discussion, most of the participants tend to retain their positions in the course of their arguments. This assumption holds for the ground-truth annotations we have obtained in our data sets. Given local predictions obtained from the previous step, we adopt the weighted voting scheme to determine the local position for each pair of participants. Specifically, given a pair of users i and j, we aggregate over all the reply-to posts between them to calculate the overall agreement score $r(i, j)$ as follows:

$$r(i,j) = \sum_{k=1}^{N(i,j)} P(agree|\mathbf{x}_k) - \sum_{k=1}^{N(i,j)} P(disagree|\mathbf{x}_k). \quad (3)$$

Here, $N(i, j)$ denotes the number of post exchanges between users i and j, and $r(i, j)$ indicates the degree of agreement between users i and j. Let $L(i, j)$ denote the local position between two users i and j. If $r(i, j) > 0$, we have $L(i, j) = agree$, that is, user i agrees with user j. Otherwise, if $r(i, j) \leq 0$, we have $L(i, j) = disagree$, that is, user i disagrees with user j.

Let us consider the example in Figure 1(a) and 1(b). There are two posts exchanged between users B and C. For each of these posts, two probabilities of class membership can be obtained:

$$P(agree|\mathbf{x}_1) = 0.1, \; P(disagree|\mathbf{x}_1) = 0.9,$$
$$P(agree|\mathbf{x}_2) = 0.3, \; P(disagree|\mathbf{x}_2) = 0.7.$$

Then we can calculate the agreement score $r(B, C)$ between users B and C by aggregating over two posts, that is, $r(B, C) = (0.1+0.3) - (0.9+0.7) = -1.2 < 0$. We can conclude that user B disagrees with user C in the threaded discussion and that $L(B, C) = disagree$.

3.3 Identifying Participants' Global Positions

After estimating local positions between participants, we now can infer a participant's global support or opposition position with regards to the seed post. For this purpose, a thread structure must be considered. A thread begins with a seed post, which is further followed by other response posts. Of these responses, many employ a quote mechanism to explicitly state which post they reply to, whereas others are assumed to be in response to the most recent post in the thread. We construct a tree-like thread structure by examining all the posts in a thread and determining the parent of each post. Then, traversing through the thread structure from top to bottom allows us to infer the global position of each user with respect to the seed post. When there is more than one path from the seed to a user, the shortest path is used to infer the user's global position on the main issue.

We illustrate this inference process using Figure 1, an example thread with four users and six posts.

Let $L(m, n)$ denote the local position between two users m and n. In the figure, the local position between user B and user A (the author of the seed post), $L(A, B)$, is in agreement, while users B and C, A and C, as well as C and D each disagree. Walking the shortest path between D and the seed in Figure 1(a), we have $L(C, D) =$ *disagree* and $L(A, C) =$ *disagree*, so we can infer that the global position between user D and user A is in agreement. That is, user D agrees with the seed post. Had the local position between user A and user C, $L(A, C)$, been in agreement, then we would have concluded that user D disagrees with the seed post.

4 Experiments

In this section, we describe our experiments on two real-world data sets and report our experimental results for local and global (dis)agreement classification.

4.1 Data Sets

We used two data sets to evaluate our proposed method in our experiments. They were crawled from the U.S. Message Board (`www.usmessageboard.com`) and the Political Forum (`www.politicalforum.com`). The two data sets are referred to as **usmb** and **pf**, respectively, in our discussion. The detailed characteristics of the two data sets are given in Table 1.

Table 1: Characteristics of data sets

	usmb	**pf**
# of threads	88	33
# of posts	818	170
# of participants	270	103
Mean # of posts per thread	9.3	5.2
Mean # of participants per thread	3.1	3.1
Mean # of posts per participant	3.0	1.7

For the evaluation, each post was labelled with two annotations. The first was a global annotation with respect to the thread's seed post, and the other was a local annotation with respect to the immediate parent. Seed posts themselves were not annotated, nor were they classified by our algorithms.

Global annotations were made by two postgraduate students. Each was instructed to read all the posts in a thread, then label each post with *agree* if the author agreed with the seed post; *disagree* if they disagreed; or *neutral* if opinions were mixed or unclear. The annotators used training data until they reached 85% agreement, then annotated posts separately. At no time were they allowed to confer. Local annotations were reverse-engineered from these global annotations. The ratio of posts annotated as *agree* to those as *disagree* is about 2 to 1 on both datasets.

For our proposed three-stage method, local annotations were taken as input to train the classifier and then used as ground truth to evaluate the performance of local agreement/disagreement classification, while the global annotations were only used to evaluate our final accuracy of global agreement/disagreement identification. In contrast, the baseline classifiers that we compare against for global classification were directly trained and evaluated using global annotations.

4.2 Evaluation Metrics

We used two evaluation metrics to evaluate the performance of agreement/disagreement classification. The first metric is accuracy, which is computed as the percentage of correctly classified examples over all the test data:

$$\text{accuracy} = \frac{|\{\mathbf{x} : \mathbf{x} \in \mathcal{D}_{test} \bigcap h(x) = y\}|}{|\mathcal{D}_{test}|},$$

where $\mathcal{D}_{test}$ denotes the test data, y is the ground truth annotation label and $h(\mathbf{x})$ is the predicted class label.

Accuracy can be biased in situations with uneven division between classes, so we also evaluate our classifiers with the F-measure. For each class $i \in \{\text{agree}, \text{disagree}\}$, we first calculate precision $P(i)$ and recall $R(i)$, and the F-measure is computed as

$$F1(i) = \frac{2P(i)R(i)}{P(i) + R(i)}.$$

For our binary task, we report the average F-measure over both classes.

4.3 Local Agree/Disagree Classification

In our experiments, we used the implementation of L2-regularised logistic regression in Fan et al. (2008) as our local classifier. For each data set,

Table 2: Classification performance for local (dis)agreement

	usmb		**pf**	
	Accuracy	F-measure	Accuracy	F-measure
Naive Bayes, all features	0.46	0.42	0.52	0.51
SVM, all features	0.56	0.60	0.55	0.52
Logistic regression, all features	0.62	0.65	0.68	0.77

Table 3: Feature analysis for local (dis)agreement using logistic regression

	usmb		**pf**	
	Accuracy	F-measure	Accuracy	F-measure
words	0.50	0.55	0.55	0.63
words, sentiment	0.53	0.59	0.61	0.71
words, sentiment, emotional	0.54	0.51	0.55	0.65
words, sentiment, durational	0.58	0.61	0.64	0.72
words, sentiment, emotional, durational	0.62	0.65	0.68	0.77

we used 70% of posts as training and the other 30% were held out for testing. We compared regularised logistic regression against two baselines: naive Bayes and support vector machines (SVMs), which have been used for (dis)agreement classification in previous works (Thomas et al., 2006; Somasundaran and Wiebe, 2010). For SVMs, we used the toolbox LIBSVM in Chang and Lin (2011) to implement the classification and probability estimation. We tuned the parameter C in regularised logistic regression and SVM, using cross-validation on the training data, and thereafter the optimal C was used on the test data for evaluation.

Table 2 compares the local classification accuracy of the three methods on data sets **usmb** and **pf**, respectively. We can see from the table that logistic regression outperforms naive Bayes and SVM on the two evaluation metrics for local classification. Although logistic regression and SVM have been shown to yield comparable performance on some text categorisation tasks Li and Yang (2003), in our problem, regularised logistic regression was observed to outperform SVM for local (dis)agreement classification.

Experiments were also carried out to investigate how the performance of local classification would be changed by using different types of features. Table 3 shows the classification accuracy of logistic regression using different types of features on the two data sets. We can see from the table that using both words and sentiment features can improve the performance as compared to using only words features. On the **usmb** dataset, adding emotional features slightly improves the accuracy but degrades F-measure, while on the **pf** dataset, it degrades on accuracy and F-measure. In addition, durational features substantially improve the classification performance on the two metrics. Overall, the highest classification accuracy and F-measure can be achieved by using all four types of features.

4.4 Global Support/Opposition Identification

We also conducted experiments to validate the effectiveness of our proposed method for global position identification. Table 4 reports the performance of global classification using the three methods on the two data sets. Classifiers "without aggregation" were trained directly on global annotations, without considering local positions at all; those "with aggregation" were developed with our three-stage method, estimating global positions by aggregating local positions $L(m, n)$.

As before, logistic regression generally outperforms SVM or naive Bayes classifiers, although SVM does well on **usmb** when aggregation (via $L(m, n)$) is used. Although SVM scores well for

Table 4: Classification performance for global (dis)agreement

	usmb		pf	
	Accuracy	F-measure	Accuracy	F-measure
Without aggregation				
Naive Bayes, all features	0.42	0.41	0.48	0.47
SVM, all features	0.62	0.46	0.68	0.40
Logistic regression, all features	0.60	0.63	0.65	0.77
With aggregation				
Naive Bayes, all features	0.54	0.67	0.65	0.70
SVM, all features	0.64	0.77	0.48	0.60
Logistic regression, all features	0.64	0.77	0.68	0.76

classification accuracy without aggregation, it has degraded and classifies everything as the majority class in these cases. The F-measure is correspondingly poor due to a low recall. This observation is consistent with the findings reported in Agrawal et al. (2003).

In all cases — bar logistic regression on the **pf** set — aggregation of local classifications improves the performance of global classification. This is more marked in the **usmb** data set, which has slightly more exchanges between each pair of users (mean 1.33 per pair per topic, vs. 1.19 for the **pf** data set) and therefore more potential for aggregation. We believe that this improvement is because local classification is sometimes error prone, especially when opinions are not expressed clearly in individual posts. If so, and assuming that users tend to retain their stances within a debate, aggregation can "wash out" local classification errors.

5 Conclusion and Future Work

In this paper, we have proposed a new method for identifying participants' agreement or disagreement on an issue by exploiting local information contained in individual posts. Our proposed method builds a unified framework which enables the classification of participants' local and global positions in online debates. To evaluate the performance of our proposed method, we conducted experiments on two real-world data sets collected from two online debate forums. Our experiments have shown that regularised logistic regression is useful for this type of task; it has a built-in automatic feature selection by assigning a coefficient to each specific feature, and directly estimates probabilities of class memberships, which is quite useful for aggregating local positions between users. Our feature analysis has suggested that using sentiment, emotional and durational features can significantly improve the performance over only using word features. Experimental results have also shown that, for identifying users' global positions on an issue, aggregating local positions over posts results in better performance than no-aggregation baselines and that more benefit seems to accrue as users exchange more posts.

We consider extending this work along several directions. First, we would like to examine what other factors would have predictive power in online debates and thus could be utilised to improve the performance of agreement/disagreement classification. Second, we have so far focused on classifying users' positions into two categories: agree and disagree. However, there do exist a portion of posts falling into the neutral category; that means posts/users do not express any position towards an issue. We will explore how to extend our computational framework to classify the neutral class. Finally, in online debates, it is not uncommon to have off-topic or topic-drift posts, especially for long threaded discussions. Off-topic posts are the ones totally irrelevant to the main issue being discussed, and topic-drift posts usually exist when the topic of a debate has shifted over time. Taking these posts into consideration would increase the difficulty of automatic agreement and disagreement classification, and therefore it is another important issue we plan to investigate.

References

Rakesh Agrawal, Sridhar Rajagopalan, Ramakrishnan Srikant, and Yirong Xu. 2003. Mining newsgroups using networks arising from social bahavior. In *Proceedings of the 12th International World Wide Web Conference*, pages 529–535, Budapest, Hungary, May.

Stefano Baccianella, Andrea Esuli, , and Fabrizio Sebastiani. 2010. SENTIWORDNET 3.0: An enhanced lexical resource for sentiment analysis and opinion mining. In *Proceedings of the 7th Conference on International Language Resources and Evaluation*, pages 2200–2204, Valletta, Malta, May.

Ramnath Balasubramanyan and William W. Cohen. 2011. What pushes their buttons? Predicting comment polarity from the content of political blog posts. In *Proceedings of the ACL Workshop on Language in Social Media*, pages 12–19, Porland, Oregon, USA, June.

Farah Benamara, Carmine Cesarano, Antonio Picariello, Diego Reforgiato, and V. S. Subrahmanian. 2007. Sentiment analysis: Adjectives and adverbs are better than adjectives alone. In *Proceedings of the International AAAI Conference on Weblogs and Social Media*, Boulder, CO, USA, March.

Chih-Chung Chang and Chih-Jen Lin. 2011. LIBSVM: A library for support vector machines. *ACM Transactions on Intelligent Systems and Technology*, 2(27):1–27.

Rong-En Fan, Kai-Wei Chang, Cho-Jui Hsieh, Xiang-Rui Wang, and Chih-Jen Lin. 2008. LIBLINEAR: A library for large linear classification. *Journal of Machine Learning Research*, 9:1871–1874.

Michel Galley, Kathleen McKeown, Julia Hirschberg, and Elizabeth Shriberg. 2004. Identifying agreement and disagreement in conversational speech: Use of Bayesian networks to model pragmatic dependencies. In *Proceedings of the 42nd Meeting of the Association for Computational Linguistics*, pages 669–676, Barcelona, Spain, July.

Fan Li and Yiming Yang. 2003. A loss function analysis for classification methods in text categorisation. In *Proceedings of the 20th International Conference on Machine Learning*, pages 472–479, Washington, DC, USA, July.

Chih-Jen Lin, Ruby C. Weng, and S. Sathiya Keerthi. 2008. Trust region Newton method for large-scale logistic regression. *Journal of Machine Learning Research*, 9:627–650.

Akiko Murakami and Rudy Raymond. 2010. Support or oppose? Classifying positions in online debates from reply activities and opinion expressions. In *Proceedings of the 23rd International Conference on Computational Linguistics*, pages 869–875, Beijing, China, August.

Sinno Jialin Pan, Xiaochuan Ni, Jian-Tao Sun, Qiang Yang, and Zheng Chen. 2010. Cross-domain sentiment classification via spectral feature alignment. In *Proceedings of the 19th International World Wide Web Conference*, pages 751–760, Raleigh, NC, USA, April.

Swapna Somasundaran and Janyce Wiebe. 2010. Recognizing stances in ideological on-line debates. In *Proceedings of the NAACL HLT 2010 Workshop on Computational Approaches to Analysis and Generation of Emotion in Text*, pages 116–124, Los Angeles, CA, USA, June.

V. S. Subrahmanian and Diego Regorgiato. 2008. AVA: Adjective-verb-adverb combinations for sentiment analysis. *Intelligent Systems*, 23(4):43–50.

Matt Thomas, Bo Pang, and Lillian Lee. 2006. Get out the vote: Determining support or opposition from congressional floor-debate transcripts. In *Proceedings of the Conference on Empirical Methods in Natural Language Processing*, pages 327–335, Sydney, Australia, July.

Wen Wang, Sibel Yaman, Kristin Precoda, Colleen Richey, and Geoffrey Raymond. 2011. Detection of agreement and disagreement in broadcast conversations. In *Proceedings of the 49th Annual Meeting of the Association for Computational Linguistics*, pages 374–378, Porland, Oregon, USA, June.

Tong Zhang and Frank J. Oles. 2001. Text categorisation based on regularised linear classification methods. *Information Retrieval*, 4(1):5–31.

Prior versus Contextual Emotion of a Word in a Sentence

Diman Ghazi
EECS, University of Ottawa
dghaz038@uottawa.ca

Diana Inkpen
EECS, University of Ottawa
diana@eecs.uottawa.ca

Stan Szpakowicz
EECS, University of Ottawa &
ICS, Polish Academy of Sciences
szpak@eecs.uottawa.ca

Abstract

A set of words labelled with their prior emotion is an obvious place to start on the automatic discovery of the emotion of a sentence, but it is clear that context must also be considered. No simple function of the labels on the individual words may capture the overall emotion of the sentence; words are interrelated and they mutually influence their affect-related interpretation. We present a method which enables us to take the contextual emotion of a word and the syntactic structure of the sentence into account to classify sentences by emotion classes. We show that this promising method outperforms both a method based on a *Bag-of-Words* representation and a system based only on the prior emotions of words. The goal of this work is to distinguish automatically between prior and contextual emotion, with a focus on exploring features important for this task.

1 Introduction

Recognition, interpretation and representation of affect have been investigated by researchers in the field of affective computing (Picard 1997). They consider a wide range of modalities such as affect in speech, facial display, posture and physiological activity. It is only recently that there has been a growing interest in automatic identification and extraction of sentiment, opinions and emotions in text.

Sentiment analysis is the task of identifying positive and negative opinions, emotions and evaluations (Wilson, Wiebe, and Hoffmann, 2005). Most of the current work in sentiment analysis has focused on determining the presence of sentiment in the given text, and on determining its polarity – the positive or negative orientation. The applications of sentiment analysis range from classifying positive and negative movie reviews (Pang, Lee, and Vaithyanathan, 2002; Turney, 2002) to opinion question-answering (Yu and Hatzivassiloglou, 2003; Stoyanov, Cardie, and Wiebe, 2005). The analysis of sentiment must, however, go beyond differentiating positive from negative emotions to give a systematic account of the qualitative differences among individual emotion (Ortony, Collins, and Clore, 1988).

In this work, we deal with assigning fine-grained emotion classes to sentences in text. It might seem that these two tasks are strongly tied, but the higher level of classification in emotion recognition task and the presence of certain degrees of similarities between some emotion labels make categorization into distinct emotion classes more challenging and difficult. Particularly notable in this regard are two classes, anger and disgust, which human annotators often find hard to distinguish (Aman and Szpakowicz, 2007). In order to recognize and analyze affect in written text – seldom explicitly marked for emotions – NLP researchers have come up with a variety of techniques, including the use of machine learning, rule-based methods and the lexical approach (Neviarouskaya, Prendinger, and Ishizuka, 2011).

There has been previous work using statistical methods and supervised machine learning applied to corpus-based features, mainly unigrams, combined with lexical features (Alm, Roth, and Sproat, 2005; Aman and Szpakowicz, 2007; Katz, Singleton, and Wicentowski, 2007). The weakness of such methods is that they neglect negation, syntactic relations and semantic dependencies. They also require large (annotated) corpora for meaningful statistics and good performance. Processing may take time, and annotation effort is inevitably high. Rule-based methods (Chaumartin, 2007; Neviarouskaya, Prendinger, and Ishizuka, 2011) require manual creation of rules. That is an expensive process with weak guarantee of consistency and coverage, and likely very task-dependent; the set of rules of rule-based affect analysis task (Neviarouskaya, Prendinger, and Ishizuka, 2011) can differ drastically from what underlies other tasks such as rule-based part-of-speech tagger, discourse parsers, word sense disambiguation and machine translation.

The study of emotions in lexical semantics was the theme of a SemEval 2007 task (Strapparava and Mihalcea, 2007), carried out in an unsupervised setting (Strapparava and Mihalcea, 2008; Chaumartin, 2007; Kozareva et al., 2007; Katz, Singleton, and Wicentowski, 2007). The participants were encouraged to work with *WordNet-Affect* (Strapparava and Valitutti, 2004) and *SentiWordNet* (Esuli and Sebastiani, 2006). Word-level analysis, however, will not suffice when affect is expressed by phrases which require complex phrase- and sentence-level analyses: words are interrelated and they mutually influence their affect-related interpretation. On the other hand, words can have more than one sense, and they can only be disambiguated in context. Consequently, the emotion conveyed by a word in a sentence can differ drastically from the emotion of the word on its own. For example, according to the *WordNet-Affect* lexicon, the word "afraid" is listed in the "fear" category, but in the sentence "I am afraid it is going to rain." the word "afraid" does not convey fear.

We refer to the emotion listed for a word in an emotion lexicon as the word's *prior* emotion. A word's *contextual* emotion is the emotion of the sentence in which that word appears, taking the context into account.

Our method combines several way of tackling the problem. First, we find keywords listed in *WordNet-Affect* and select the sentences which include emotional words from that lexicon. Next, we study the syntactic structure and semantic relations in the text surrounding the emotional word. We explore features important in emotion recognition, and we consider their effect on the emotion expressed by the sentence. Finally, we use machine learning to classify the sentences, represented by the chosen features, by their contextual emotion.

happiness	sadness	anger	disgust	surprise	fear	total
398	201	252	53	71	141	1116

Table 1: The distribution of labels in the *WordNet-Affect* Lexicon.

We categorize sentences into six basic emotions defined by Ekman (1992); that has been the choice of most of previous related work. These emotions are happiness, sadness, fear, anger, disgust and surprise. There also may, naturally, be no emotion in a sentence; that is tagged as neutral/non-emotional.

We evaluate our results by comparing our method applied to our set of features with Support Vector Machine (SVM) applied to *Bag-of-Words*, which was found to give the best performance among supervised methods (Yang and Liu, 1999; Pang, Lee, and Vaithyanathan, 2002; Aman and Szpakowicz, 2007; Ghazi, Inkpen, and Szpakowicz, 2010). We show that our method is promising and that it outperforms both a system which works only with prior emotions of words, ignoring context, and a system which applies SVM to *Bag-of-Words*.

Section 2 of this paper describes the dataset and resources used. Section 3 discusses the features which we use for recognizing contextual emotion. Experiments and results are presented in Section 4. In Section 5, we conclude and discuss future work.

2 Dataset and Resources

Supervised statistical methods typically require training data and test data, manually annotated with respect to each language-processing task to be learned. In this section, we explain the dataset and lexicons used in our experiments.

***WordNet-Affect* Lexicon** (Strapparava and Valitutti, 2004). The first resource we require is an emotional lexicon, a set of words which indicate the presence of a particular emotion. In our experiments, we use *WordNet-Affect*, which contains six lists of words corresponding to the six basic emotion categories. It is the result of assigning a variety

Neutral	Negative	Positive	Both
6.9%	59.7%	31.1%	0.3%

Table 2: The distribution of labels in the Prior-Polarity Lexicon.

hp	sd	ag	dg	sr	fr	ne	total
536	173	179	172	115	115	800	2090

Table 3: The distribution of labels in Aman's modified dataset. The labels are *happiness, sadness, anger, disgust, surprise, fear, no emotion*.

of affect labels to each synset in *WordNet*. Table 1 shows the distribution of words in *WordNet-Affect*.

Prior-Polarity Lexicon (Wilson, Wiebe, and Hoffmann, 2009). The prior-polarity subjectivity lexicon contains over 8000 subjectivity clues collected from a number of sources. To create this lexicon, the authors began with the list of subjectivity clues extracted by Riloff (2003). The list was expanded using a dictionary and a thesaurus, and adding positive and negative word lists from the General Inquirer.[1] Words are grouped into strong subjective and weak subjective clues; Table 2 presents the distribution of their polarity.

Intensifier Lexicon (Neviarouskaya, Prendinger, and Ishizuka, 2010). It is a list of 112 modifiers (adverbs). Two annotators gave coefficients for intensity degree – strengthening or weakening, from 0.0 to 2.0 – and the result was averaged.

Emotion Dataset (Aman and Szpakowicz, 2007). The main consideration in the selection of data for emotional classification task is that the data should be rich in emotion expressions. That is why we chose for our experiments a corpus of blog sentences annotated with emotion labels, discussed by Aman and Szpakowicz (2007). Each sentence is tagged by its dominant emotion, or as non-emotional if it does not include any emotion. The annotation is based on Ekman's six emotions at the sentence level. The dataset contains 4090 annotated sentences, 68% of which were marked as non-emotional. The highly unbalanced dataset with non-emotional sentences as by far the largest class, and merely 3% in the fear and surprise classes, prompted us to remove 2000 of the non-emotional sentences. We lowered the number of non-emotional sentences to 38% of all the sentences, and thus reduced the imbalance. Table 3 shows the details of the chosen dataset.

[1]www.wjh.harvard.edu/~inquirer/

3 Features

The features used in our experiments were motivated both by the literature (Wilson, Wiebe, and Hoffmann, 2009; Choi et al., 2005) and by the exploration of contextual emotion of words in the annotated data. All of the features are counted based on the emotional word from the lexicon which occurs in the sentence. For ease of description, we group the features into four distinct sets: emotion-word features, part-of-speech features, sentence features and dependency-tree features.

Emotion-word features. This set of features are based on the emotion-word itself.

- The emotion of a word according to *WordNet-Affect* (Strapparava and Valitutti, 2004).
- The polarity of a word according to the prior-polarity lexicon (Wilson, Wiebe, and Hoffmann, 2009).
- The presence of a word in a small list of modifiers (Neviarouskaya, Prendinger, and Ishizuka, 2010).

Part-of-speech features. Based on the Stanford tagger's output (Toutanova et al., 2003), every word in a sentence gets one of the Penn Treebank tags.

- The part-of-speech of the emotional word itself, both according to the emotion lexicon and Stanford tagger.
- The POS of neighbouring words in the same sentence. We choose a window of [-2,2], as it is usually suggested by the literature (Choi et al., 2005).

Sentence features. For now we only consider the number of words in the sentence.

Dependency-tree features. For each emotional word, we create features based on the parse tree and its dependencies produced by the Stanford parser (Marneffe, Maccartney, and Manning, 2006). The dependencies are all binary relations: a grammatical relation holds between a governor (head) and a dependent (modifier).

According to Mohammad and Turney (2010),[2] adverbs and adjectives are some of the most emotion-inspiring terms. This is not surprising considering that they are used to qualify a noun or a verb; therefore to keep the number of features small, among all the 52 different type of dependencies, we only chose the negation, adverb and adjective modifier dependencies.

After parsing the sentence and getting the dependencies, we count the following dependency-tree Boolean features for the emotional word.

- Whether the word is in a "neg" dependency (negation modifier): true when there is a negation word which modifies the emotional word.
- Whether the word is in a "amod" dependency (adjectival modifier): true if the emotional word is (i) a noun modified by an adjective or (ii) an adjective modifying a noun.
- Whether the word is in a "advmod" dependency (adverbial modifier): true if the emotional word (i) is a non-clausal adverb or adverbial phrase which serves to modify the meaning of a word, or (ii) has been modified by an adverb.

We also have several modification features based on the dependency tree. These Boolean features capture different types of relationships involving the cue word.[3] We list the feature name and the condition on the cue word w which makes the feature true.

- Modifies-positive: w modifies a positive word from the prior-polarity lexicon.
- Modifies-negative: w modifies a negative word from the prior-polarity lexicon.
- Modified-by-positive: w is the head of the dependency, which is modified by a positive word from the prior-polarity lexicon.
- Modified-by-negative: w is the head of the dependency, which is modified by a negative word from the prior-polarity lexicon.

[2]In their paper, they also explain how they created an emotion lexicon by crowd-sourcing, but – to the best of our knowledge – it is not publicly available yet.

[3]The terms "emotional word" and "cue word" are used interchangeably.

	hp	sd	ag	dg	sr	fr	ne	total
part 1	196	64	64	63	36	52	150	625
part 2	51	18	22	18	9	14	26	158
part 1+ part 2	247	82	86	81	45	66	176	783

Table 4: The distribution of labels in the portions of Aman's dataset used in our experiments, named part 1, part 2 and part 1+part 2. The labels are *happiness, sadness, anger, disgust, surprise, fear, no emotion.*

- Modifies-intensifier-strengthen: w modifies a strengthening intensifier from the intensifier lexicon.
- Modifies-intensifier-weaken: w modifies a weakening intensifier from the intensifier lexicon.
- Modified-by-intensifier-strengthen: w is the head of the dependency, which is modified by a strengthening intensifier from the intensifier lexicon.
- Modified-by-intensifier-weaken: w is the head of the dependency, which is modified by a weakening intensifier from the intensifiers lexicon.

4 Experiments

In the experiments, we use the emotion dataset presented in Section 2. Our main consideration is to classify a sentence based on the contextual emotion of the words (known as emotional in the lexicon). That is why in the dataset we only choose sentences which contain at least one emotional word according to *WordNet-Affect*. As a result, the number of sentences chosen from the dataset will decrease to 783 sentences, 625 of which contain only one emotional word and 158 sentences which contain more than one emotional word. Their details are shown in Table 4.

Next, we represent the data with the features presented in Section 3. Those features, however, were defined for each emotional word based on their context, so we will proceed differently for sentences with one emotional word and sentences with more than one emotional word.

- In sentences with one emotional word, we assume the contextual emotion of the emotional word is the same as the emotion assigned to the sentence by the human annotators; therefore all the 625 sentences with one emotional word are represented with the set of features presented in Section 3 and the sentence's emotion will be considered as their contextual emotion.

- For sentences with more than one emotional word, the emotion of the sentence depends on all emotional words and their syntactic and semantic relations. We have 158 sentences where no emotion can be assigned to the contextual emotion of their emotional words, and all we know is the dominant emotion of the sentence.

We will, therefore, have two different sets of experiments. For the first set of sentences, the data are all annotated, so we will take a supervised approach. For the second set of sentences, we combine supervised and unsupervised learning. We train a classifier on the first set of data and we use the model to classify the emotional words into their contextual emotion in the second set of data. Finally, we propose an unsupervised method to combine the contextual emotion of all the emotional words in a sentence and calculate the emotion of the sentence.

For evaluation, we report precision, recall, F-measure and accuracy to compare the results. We also define two baselines for each set of experiments to compare our results with. The experiments are presented in the next two subsections.

4.1 Experiments on sentences with one emotional word

In these experiments, we explain first the baselines and then the results of our experiments on the sentences with only one emotional word.

Baseline

We develop two baseline systems to assess the difficulty of our task. The first baseline labels the sentences the same as the most frequent class's emotion, which is a typical baseline in machine learning tasks (Aman and Szpakowicz, 2007; Alm, Roth, and Sproat, 2005). This baseline will result in 31% accuracy.

The second baseline labels the emotion of the sentence the same as the prior emotion of the only emotional word in the sentence. The accuracy of this experiment is 51%, remarkably higher than the first baseline's accuracy. The second baseline is particularly designed to address the emotion of the sentence only based on the prior emotion of the emotional words; therefore it will allow us to assess the difference between the emotion of the sentence based on the prior emotion of the words in the sentence versus the case when we consider the context and its effect on the emotion of the sentence.

		Precision	Recall	F
SVM + *Bag-of-Words*	Happiness	0.59	0.67	0.63
	Sadness	0.38	0.45	0.41
	Anger	0.40	0.31	0.35
	Surprise	0.41	0.33	0.37
	Disgust	0.51	0.43	0.47
	Fear	0.55	0.50	0.52
	Non-emo	0.49	0.48	0.48
Accuracy	50.72%			
SVM + our features	Happiness	0.68	0.78	0.73
	Sadness	0.49	0.58	0.53
	Anger	0.66	0.48	0.56
	Surprise	0.61	0.31	0.41
	Disgust	0.43	0.38	0.40
	Fear	0.67	0.63	0.65
	Non-emo	0.51	0.53	0.52
Accuracy	58.88%			
Logistic Regression + our features	Happiness	0.78	0.82	0.80
	Sadness	0.53	0.64	0.58
	Anger	0.69	0.62	0.66
	Surprise	0.89	0.47	0.62
	Disgust	0.81	0.41	0.55
	Fear	0.71	0.71	0.71
	Non-emo	0.53	0.64	0.58
Accuracy	66.88%			

Table 5: Classification experiments on the dataset with one emotional word in each sentence. Each experiment is marked by the method and the feature set.

Learning Experiments

In this part, we use two classification algorithms, Support Vector Machines (SVM) and Logistic Regression (LR), and two different set of features, the set of features from Section 3 and *Bag-of-Words* (unigram). Unigram models have been widely used in text classification and shown to provide good results in sentiment classification tasks.

In general, SVM has long been a method of choice for sentiment recognition in text. SVM has been shown to give good performance in text classification experiments as it scales well to the large numbers of features (Yang and Liu, 1999; Pang, Lee, and Vaithyanathan, 2002; Aman and Szpakowicz, 2007). For the classification, we use the SMO algorithm (Platt, 1998) from Weka (Hall et al., 2009), setting *10-fold cross validation* as a testing option. We compare applying SMO to two sets of features, (i) *Bag-of-Words*, which are binary features defining whether a unigram exists in a sentence and (ii) our set of features. In our experiments we use unigrams from the corpus, selected using feature selection methods from Weka.

We also compare those two results with the third experiment: apply SimpleLogistic (Sumner, Frank, and Hall, 2005) from Weka to our set of features, again setting *10-fold cross validation* as a testing option. Logistic regression is a discriminative probabilistic classification model which operates over real-valued vector inputs. It is relatively slow to train compared to the other classifiers. It also requires extensive tuning in the form of feature selection and implementation to achieve state-of-the-art classification performance. Logistic regression models with large numbers of features and limited amounts of training data are highly prone to over-fitting (Alias-i, 2008). Besides, logistic regression is really slow and it is known to only work on data represented by a small set of features. That is why we do not apply SimpleLogistic to *Bag-of-Words* features. On the other hand, the number of our features is relatively low, so we find logistic regression to be a good choice of classifier for our representation method. The classification results are shown in Table 5.

We note consistent improvement. The results of both experiments using our set of features significantly outperform (on the basis of a paired t-test, p=0.005) both the baselines and SVM applied to *Bag-of-Words* features. We get the best result, however, by applying logistic regression to our feature set. The number of our features and the nature of the features we introduce make them an appropriate choice of data representation for logistic regression methods.

4.2 Experiments on sentences with more than one emotional word

In these experiments, we combine supervised and unsupervised learning. We train a classifier on the first set of data, which is annotated, and we use the model to classify the emotional words in the second group of sentences. We propose an unsupervised method to combine the contextual emotion of the emotional words and calculate the emotion of the sentence.

Baseline

We develop two baseline systems. The first baseline labels all the sentences the same: as the emotion of the most frequent class, giving 32% accuracy. The second baseline labels the emotion of the sentence the same as the most frequently occurring prior-emotion of the emotional words in the sentence. In the case of a tie, we randomly pick one of the emotions. The accuracy of this experiment is 45%. Again, as a second baseline we choose a baseline that is based on the prior emotion of the emotional words so that we can compare it with the results based on contextual emotion of the emotional words in the sentence.

Learning Experiments

For sentences with more than one emotional word, we represent each emotional word and its context by the set of features explained in section 3. We do not have the contextual emotion label for each emotional word, so we cannot train the classifier on these data. Consequently, we train the classifier on the part of the dataset which only includes sentences with one emotional word. In these sentences, each emotional word is labeled with their contextual emotion – the same as the sentence's emotion.

Once we have the classifier model, we get the probability distribution of emotional classes for each emotional word (calculated by the logistic regression function learned from the annotated data). We add up the probabilities of each class for all emotional words. Finally, we select the class with the maximum probability. The result, shown in Table 6, is compared using supervised learning, SVM, with *Bag-of-Words* features, explained in previous section, with setting *10-fold cross validation* as a testing

		Precision	Recall	F
SVM + *Bag-of-Words*	Happiness	0.52	0.60	0.54
	Sadness	0.35	0.33	0.34
	Anger	0.30	0.27	0.29
	Surprise	0.14	0.11	0.12
	Disgust	0.30	0.17	0.21
	Fear	0.44	0.29	0.35
	Non-emo	0.23	0.35	0.28
Accuracy	36.71%			
Logistic Regression + unsupervised + our features	Happiness	0.63	0.71	0.67
	Sadness	0.67	0.44	0.53
	Anger	0.50	0.41	0.45
	Surprise	1.00	0.22	0.36
	Disgust	0.80	0.22	0.34
	Fear	0.60	0.64	0.62
	Non-emo	0.37	0.69	0.48
Accuracy	54.43%			

Table 6: Classification experiments on the dataset with more than one emotional word in each sentence. Each experiment is marked by the method and the feature set.

option.[4]

By comparing the results in Table 6, we can see that the result of learning applied to our set of features significantly outperforms (on the basis of a paired t-test, p=0.005) both baselines and the result of SVM algorithm applied to *Bag-of-Words* features.

4.3 Discussion

We cannot directly compare our results with the previous results achieved by Aman and Szpakowicz (2007), because the datasets differ. F-measure, precision and recall for each class are reported on the whole dataset, but we only used part of that dataset. To show how hard this task is, and to see where we stand, the best result from (Aman and Szpakowicz, 2007) is shown in Table 7.

In our experiments, we showed that our approach and our features significantly outperform the baselines and the SVM result applied to *Bag-of-Words*. For the final conclusion, we add one more comparison. As we can see from Table 6, the accuracy result of applying SVM to *Bag-of-Words* is really low. Because supervised methods scale well on large datasets, one reason could be the size of the data we use in this experiment; therefore we try to compare

[4]Since SVM does not return a distribution probability, we cannot apply SVM to our features in this set of experiments.

	Precision	Recall	F
Happiness	0.813	0.698	0.751
Sadness	0.605	0.416	0.493
Anger	0.650	0.436	0.522
Surprise	0.723	0.409	0.522
Disgust	0.672	0.488	0.566
Fear	0.868	0.513	0.645
Non-emo	0.587	0.625	0.605

Table 7: Aman's best result on the dataset explained in Section 2.

the results of the two experiments on all 758 sentences with at least one emotional word.

For this comparison, we apply SVM with *Bag-of-Words* features to all of 758 sentences and we get an accuracy of 55.17%. Considering our features and methodology, we cannot apply logistic regression with our features to the whole dataset; therefore we calculate its accuracy by counting the percentage of correctly classified instances in both parts of the dataset, used in the two experiments, and we get an accuracy of 64.36%. We also compare the results with the baselines. The first baseline, which is the percentage of most frequent class (happiness in this case), results in 31.5% accuracy. The second baseline based on the prior emotion of the emotional words results in 50.13% accuracy. It is notable that the result of applying LR to our set of features is still significantly better than the result of applying SVM to *Bag-of-Words* and both baselines; this supports our earlier conclusion. It is hard to compare the results mentioned thus far, so we have combined all the results in Figure 1, which displays the accuracy obtained by each experiment.

We also looked into our results and assessed the cases where the contextual emotion is different from the prior emotion of the emotional word. Consider the sentence "Joe said it does not happen that often so it does not bother him." Based on the emotion lexicon, the word "bother" is classified as angry; so is the emotion of the sentence if we only consider the prior emotion of words. In our set of features, however, we consider the negation in the sentence, so the sentence is classified as non-emotional rather than angry. Another interesting sentence is the rather simple "You look like her I guess." Based on the lexicon, the word "like" is in the happy category, while

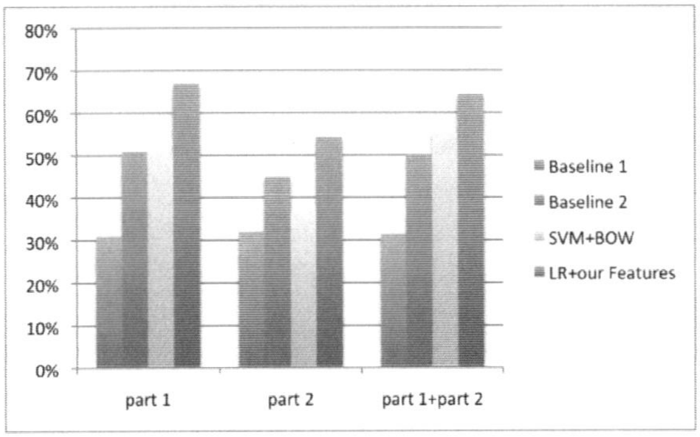

Figure 1: The comparison of accuracy results of all experiments for sentences with one emotional word (part 1), sentences with more than one emotional words (part 2), and sentences with at least one emotional word (part 1+part 2).

the sentence is non-emotional. In this case, the part-of-speech features play an important role and they catch the fact that "like" is not a verb here; it does not convey a happy emotion and the sentence is classified as non-emotional.

We also analyzed the errors, and we found some common errors due to:

- complex sentences or unstructured sentences which will cause the parser to fail or return incorrect data, resulting in incorrect dependency-tree information;
- limited coverage of the emotion lexicon.

These are some of the issues which we would like to address in our future work.

5 Conclusion and Future Directions

The focus of this study was a comparison of prior emotion of a word with its contextual emotion, and their effect on the emotion expressed by the sentence. We also studied features important in recognizing contextual emotion. We experimented with a wide variety of linguistically-motivated features, and we evaluated the performance of these features using logistic regression. We showed that our approach and features significantly outperform the baseline and the SVM result applied to *Bag-of-Words*.

Even though the features we presented did quite well on the chosen dataset, in the future we would like to show the robustness of these features by applying them to different datasets.

Another direction for future work will be to expand our emotion lexicon using existing techniques for automatically acquiring the prior emotion of words. Based on the number of instances in each emotion class, we noticed there is a tight relation between the number of words in each emotion list in the emotion lexicon and the number of sentences that are derived for each emotion class. It follows that a larger lexicon will have a greater coverage of emotional expressions.

Last but not least, one of the weaknesses of our approach was the fact that we could not use all the instances in the dataset. Again, the main reason was the low coverage of the emotion lexicon that was used. The other reason was the limitation of our method: we had to only choose the sentences that have one or more emotional words. As future work, we would like to relax the restriction by using the root of the sentence (based on the dependency tree result) as a cue word rather than the emotional word from the lexicon. So, for sentences with no emotional word, we can calculate all the features regarding the root word rather than the emotional word.

References

Alias-i. 2008. Lingpipe 4.1.0., October.

Alm, Cecilia Ovesdotter, Dan Roth, and Richard Sproat. 2005. Emotions from Text: Machine Learning for Text-based Emotion Prediction. In *HLT/EMNLP*.

Aman, Saima and Stan Szpakowicz. 2007. Identifying expressions of emotion in text. In *Proc. 10th International Conf. Text, Speech and Dialogue*, pages 196–205. Springer-Verlag.

Chaumartin, François-Regis. 2007. UPAR7: a knowledge-based system for headline sentiment tagging. In *Proc. 4th International Workshop on Semantic Evaluations*, SemEval '07, pages 422–425.

Choi, Yejin, Claire Cardie, Ellen Riloff, and Siddharth Patwardhan. 2005. Identifying sources of opinions with conditional random fields and extraction patterns. In *Proc. Human Language Technology and Empirical Methods in Natural Language Processing*, HLT '05, pages 355–362.

Ekman, Paul. 1992. An argument for basic emotions. *Cognition & Emotion*, 6(3):169–200.

Esuli, Andrea and Fabrizio Sebastiani. 2006. SENTI-WORDNET: A Publicly Available Lexical Resource for Opinion Mining. In *Proc. 5th Conf. on Language Resources and Evaluation LREC 2006*, pages 417–422.

Ghazi, Diman, Diana Inkpen, and Stan Szpakowicz. 2010. Hierarchical approach to emotion recognition and classification in texts. In *Canadian Conference on AI*, pages 40–50.

Hall, Mark, Eibe Frank, Geoffrey Holmes, Bernhard Pfahringer, Peter Reutemann, and Ian H. Witten. 2009. The WEKA data mining software: an update. *SIGKDD Explor. Newsl.*, 11:10–18, November.

Katz, Phil, Matthew Singleton, and Richard Wicentowski. 2007. SWAT-MP: the SemEval-2007 systems for task 5 and task 14. In *Proc. 4th International Workshop on Semantic Evaluations*, SemEval '07, pages 308–313.

Kozareva, Zornitsa, Borja Navarro, Sonia Vázquez, and Andrés Montoyo. 2007. UA-ZBSA: a headline emotion classification through web information. In *Proc. 4th International Workshop on Semantic Evaluations*, SemEval '07, pages 334–337.

Marneffe, Marie-Catherine De, Bill Maccartney, and Christopher D. Manning. 2006. Generating typed dependency parses from phrase structure parses. In *Proc. LREC 2006*.

Mohammad, Saif M. and Peter D. Turney. 2010. Emotions evoked by common words and phrases: using mechanical turk to create an emotion lexicon. In *Proc. NAACL HLT 2010 Workshop on Computational Approaches to Analysis and Generation of Emotion in Text*, CAAGET '10, pages 26–34.

Neviarouskaya, Alena, Helmut Prendinger, and Mitsuru Ishizuka. 2010. AM: textual attitude analysis model. In *Proc. NAACL HLT 2010 Workshop on Computational Approaches to Analysis and Generation of Emotion in Text*, pages 80–88.

Neviarouskaya, Alena, Helmut Prendinger, and Mitsuru Ishizuka. 2011. Affect Analysis Model: novel rule-based approach to affect sensing from text. *Natural Language Engineering*, 17(1):95–135.

Ortony, Andrew, Allan Collins, and Gerald L. Clore. 1988. *The cognitive structure of emotions*. Cambridge University Press.

Pang, Bo, Lillian Lee, and Shivakumar Vaithyanathan. 2002. Thumbs up?: sentiment classification using machine learning techniques. In *Proc. ACL-02 conference on Empirical methods in natural language processing - Volume 10*, EMNLP '02, pages 79–86.

Platt, John C. 1998. Sequential Minimal Optimization: A Fast Algorithm for Training Support Vector Machines.

Riloff, Ellen. 2003. Learning extraction patterns for subjective expressions. In *Proc. 2003 Conf. on Empirical Methods in Natural Language Processing*, pages 105–112.

Stoyanov, Veselin, Claire Cardie, and Janyce Wiebe. 2005. Multi-perspective question answering using the opqa corpus. In *Proc. Conference on Human Language Technology and Empirical Methods in Natural Language Processing*, HLT '05, pages 923–930.

Strapparava, Carlo and Rada Mihalcea. 2007. SemEval-2007 Task 14: Affective Text. In *Proc. Fourth International Workshop on Semantic Evaluations (SemEval-2007)*, pages 70–74, Prague, Czech Republic, June.

Strapparava, Carlo and Rada Mihalcea. 2008. Learning to identify emotions in text. In *Proc. 2008 ACM symposium on Applied computing*, SAC '08, pages 1556–1560.

Strapparava, Carlo and Alessandro Valitutti. 2004. WordNet-Affect: an Affective Extension of WordNet. In *Proc. 4th International Conf. on Language Resources and Evaluation*, pages 1083–1086.

Sumner, Marc, Eibe Frank, and Mark A. Hall. 2005. Speeding Up Logistic Model Tree Induction. In *Proc. 9th European Conference on Principles and Practice of Knowledge Discovery in Databases*, pages 675–683.

Toutanova, Kristina, Dan Klein, Christopher D. Manning, and Yoram Singer. 2003. Feature-Rich Part-of-Speech Tagging with a Cyclic Dependency Network. In *Proc. HLT-NAACL*, pages 252–259.

Turney, Peter D. 2002. Thumbs up or thumbs down?: semantic orientation applied to unsupervised classification of reviews. In *Proc. 40th Annual Meeting on Association for Computational Linguistics*, ACL '02, pages 417–424.

Wilson, Theresa, Janyce Wiebe, and Paul Hoffmann. 2005. Recognizing contextual polarity in phrase-level sentiment analysis. In *Proc. HLT-EMNLP*, pages 347–354.

Wilson, Theresa, Janyce Wiebe, and Paul Hoffmann. 2009. Recognizing Contextual Polarity: An Exploration of Features for Phrase-Level Sentiment Analysis. *Computational Linguistics*, 35(3):399–433.

Yang, Yiming and Xin Liu. 1999. A re-examination of text categorization methods. In *Proc. 22nd annual international ACM SIGIR conference on Research and development in information retrieval*, SIGIR '99, pages 42–49.

Yu, Hong and Vasileios Hatzivassiloglou. 2003. Towards answering opinion questions: separating facts from opinions and identifying the polarity of opinion sentences. In *Proc. 2003 conference on Empirical methods in natural language processing*, EMNLP '03, pages 129–136.

Cross-discourse Development of Supervised Sentiment Analysis in the Clinical Domain

Phillip Smith
School of Computer Science
University of Birmingham
pxs697@cs.bham.ac.uk

Mark Lee
School of Computer Science
University of Birmingham
M.G.Lee@cs.bham.ac.uk

Abstract

Current approaches to sentiment analysis assume that the sole discourse function of sentiment-bearing texts is expressivity. However, the persuasive discourse function also utilises expressive language. In this work, we present the results of training supervised classifiers on a new corpus of clinical texts that contain documents with an expressive discourse function, and we test the learned models on a subset of the same corpus containing persuasive texts. The results of this indicate that despite the difference in discourse function, the learned models perform favourably.

1 Introduction

Examining the role that discourse function holds is a critical part of an in-depth analysis into the capabilities of supervised sentiment classification techniques. However, it is a field that has not been comprehensively examined within the domain of sentiment analysis due to the lack of suitable cross-discourse corpora to train and test various machine learning methods upon.

In order to carry out such an investigation, this study will focus on the relationship between sentiment classification and two types of discourse function: *Expressive* and *Persuasive*. The expressive function denotes the feelings or attitudes of the author of a document. This is demonstrated in the following examples:

1. *"I didn't like the attitude of the nursing staff."*
2. *"The doctors treated me with such care."*

Intuitively, the associated polarity of each example is trivial to determine in these explicit examples. However, expressive statements do not operate in isolation of other respective discourse functions. As Biber (1988) notes, a persuasive statement incorporates elements of the expressive function in order to advise an external party of a proposed action that should be taken. The following example shows how persuasive statements make use of expressive functions:

1. *"The clumsy nurse who wrongly diagnosed me should be fired."*

The role of a persuasive statement is to incite an action in the target, dependent upon the intention that the author communicates. By using plain, sentiment-neutral language, the reader may misinterpret why the request for action is being given, and in the worst-case scenario not carry it out. Through the incorporation of expressive language, the weight of the persuasive statement is increased. This enables the speaker to emphasise the underlying sentiment of their statement, thereby increasing the likelihood of the intended action being undertaken, and their goals being accomplished. In the above example, the intention communicated by the author is the firing of the nurse. This in itself holds negative connotations, but through the use of the word 'clumsy', the negative sentiment of the statement becomes clearer to understand.

The inclusion of expressive aspects in the language of the persuasive discourse function, enables us to identify the sentiment of a persuasive comment. As there is this cross-over in the language of the two discourse functions, we can hypothesise that if we train a supervised classifier on an expressive corpus, a learned model will be created that when applied to a corpus of persuasive documents, will classify these texts to an adequate standard.

As the corpus that we developed is in the clinical domain, it is worth noting the important role that sentiment analysis can play for health practitioners, which unfortunately has not received a great deal of attention. In assessing the effectiveness of treatments given by the health service for a condition which is curable, the results themselves indicate the effectiveness of such a process. However, for palliative treatments which merely alleviate the symptoms of an illness or relieve pain, it is vital to discover the extent to which these are effective. Feedback has progressed from the filling in of paper forms to the ability to give feedback through web pages and mobile phones. Text is stored in a highly accessible way, and is now able to be efficiently processed by sentiment classification algorithms to determine the opinions that patients are expressing. This in turn should enable health services to make informed decisions about the palliative care which they provide.

2 Patient Feedback Corpus

NHS Choices[1] is a website run by the National Health Service (NHS), which acts as an extensive knowledge base for any health-related queries. This website not only provides comprehensive articles about various ailments, but also gives the users of the site the option to rate and comment on the services that are provided to them at hospitals and GP surgeries. This user feedback provides an excellent basis for the sentiment classification experiments of this work.

The reviews that are submitted are typically provided by a patient or close relative who has experienced the healthcare system within a hospital. When submitting feedback, the user is asked to split their feedback into various fields, as opposed to submitting a single documents detailing all the comments of the user. During corpus compilation, each comment was extracted verbatim, so spelling mistakes remain in the developed corpus. All punctuation also remains in order to enable future experiments to be carried out on either the sentence or phrase level within each comment.

[1]http://nhs.uk

Corpus	D	W	$D_{avglength}$	V
Expressive				
Positive	1152	75052	65.15	6107
Negative	1108	76062	68.65	6791
Persuasive				
Positive	768	46642	60.73	4679
Negative	864	113632	131.52	7943

Table 1: Persuasive & expressive corpus statistics.

In developing the corpus, we leverage the fact that the data was separated into subfields, as opposed to one long review, where the all data is merged into a single document. We extracted comments which came under three categories in the NHS Patient Feedback dataset: *Likes*, *Dislikes* and *Advice*. The *Likes* were assumed to express positive sentiment and highlight elements of the health service that patients appreciated. Conversely, the documents given under the *Dislikes* header were assumed to convey a negative sentiment. These two subsets make up the *Expressive* subset of the compiled corpus. The *Advice* documents did not have an initial sentiment associated with them, so each comment was labelled by two independent annotators at the document level as being either a positive or negative comment. These *Advice* comments contributed to the *Persuasive* subcorpus. In compiling the persuasive document sets, we automatically discarded those comments that contained the term *"N/A "* or any of its derivative forms.

3 Method

The aim in this work was to examine the effect of training a supervised classifier on a corpus whose discourse function differs to that of the training set. We experimented with three standard supervised machine learning algorithms: standard Naïve Bayes (NB), multinomial Naïve Bayes (MN NB) and Support Vector Machines (SVM) classification. Each has proven to be effective in previous sentiment analysis studies (Pang et al. , 2002), so as this experiment is rooted in sentiment classification, these methods were also assumed to perform well in this cross-discourse setting.

For the cross-discourse sentiment classification

experiments, two variants of the Naïve Bayes algorithm are used. The difference between the standard NB and MN NB is the way in which the features for classification, the words, are modelled. In the standard NB learning method, a binary presence approached is taken in modelling the words of the training documents. This differs to the MN NB classifier, which takes into account term frequency when modelling the documents. Each has proven to be a high performing classifier across various sentiment analysis domains, but no distinction has been given as to which is the preferable method to use. Therefore in this paper, both were implemented.

In the literature, results from the use of SVMs in classification based experiments have outperformed other algorithms (Joachims, 1998; Pang et al. , 2002). For these cross-discourse experiments we use the Sequential Minimal Optimization training algorithm (Platt, 1998), in order to achieve the maximal hyperplane, and maximise the potential of the created classifier. Traditionally SVMs have performed well in text classification, but across discourse domains the results of such classification has not been examined.

Each document in the corpus was modelled as a bag of words. Features used within this representation were unigrams, bigrams and bigrams augmented with part-of-speech information. Due to this, and observing the results of preliminary experimentation that included rare features, it was decided to remove any feature that did not occur more than 5 times throughout the training set. A stopword list and stemmer were also used.

Each supervised classification technique was then trained using a random sample of 1,100 documents from both the positive and negative subsections of the expressive corpus. Following this we tested the classifiers on a set of 1,500 randomly selected persuasive documents, using 750 documents from each of the positive and negative subcorpora.

The results of cross-validation (Table 2) suggested that unigram features may outperform both bigram and part-of-speech augmented bigrams for all learning methods. In particular, the accuracy results produced by the NB algorithm surpassed the results of other classifiers in the tenfold cross-validation. This suggests that within a single discourse domain, presence based features are preferable to considering the frequency of a term when generating a machine learning model.

Features	NB	Multinomial NB	SVM
Unigrams	**79.65**	**78.14**	**76.11**
Bigrams	57.79	60.84	63.36
Bigrams + POS	74.25	75.71	72.83

Table 2: Average tenfold cross-validation accuracies on only the expressive corpus. Boldface: best performance for a given classifier.

4 Results

Table 3 shows the classification accuracies achieved in all experiments. For each classifier, with each feature set, if we take the most basic baseline for the two-class (positive/negative) problem to be the random baseline of 50% classification accuracy, then this is clearly exceeded. However if we take the results of the tenfold cross-validation as a baseline for each classifier in the experiments, then only the results given by the MN NB classifier with unigram and bigram features are able to surpass this.

The results given from the NB and the MN NB classifier imply that using frequency based features are preferable to using presence based features when performing cross-discourse sentiment classification. The MN NB is one of the few classifiers tested that exceeds the results of the cross-validated model. These results support experiments carried out for topic based classification using Bayesian classifiers by McCallum and Nigam (1998), but differs from sentiment classification results from Pang et al. (2002) that suggest that term-based models perform better than the frequency-based alternative. This also differs to the results that were returned during the cross-validation of the classifiers, where presence based features produced the greatest classification accuracy.

In our tests, the feature set which yielded the highest degree of classification accuracy across all classifiers is the unigram bag of words model. Tan et al. (2002) suggest that using bigrams enhances text classification, but as sentiment classification goes beyond this task, the assumption does not hold, as the results here show. The difference in discourse function could also contribute to bigrams yielding

		Positive			Negative		
	Accuracy	Precision	Recall	F_1	Precision	Recall	F_1
NB Uni	76.07	78.29	72.13	75.09	74.17	80.00	76.97
NB Bi	58.93	55.19	**94.93**	69.80	81.90	22.93	35.83
NB Bi + POS	65.00	71.84	49.33	58.50	61.42	80.67	69.74
MN NB Uni	**83.53**	**82.04**	85.87	**83.91**	**85.17**	81.20	**83.14**
MN NB Bi	57.00	63.78	32.40	42.97	54.69	**81.60**	65.49
MN NB Bi + POS	69.97	69.59	69.87	69.73	69.75	69.47	69.61
SVM Uni	69.00	68.43	70.53	69.47	69.60	67.47	68.52
SVM Bi	55.40	60.98	30.00	40.21	53.58	80.80	64.43
SVM Bi + POS	63.27	63.11	63.87	63.49	63.43	62.67	63.04

Table 3: Results of experimentation, with the expressive corpus as the training set, and the persuasive corpus as the test set. Boldface indicates the best performance for each metric.

the lowest accuracy results. Bigrams model quite specific language patterns, but as the expressive and persuasive language differs in structure and content, then the patterns learnt in one domain do not accurately map to another domain. Bigrams contribute the least to sentiment classification in this cross-discourse scenario, and only when they are augmented with part of speech information does the accuracy sufficiently pass the random baseline. However for good recall, using bigram based features produces excellent results, at the sacrifice of adequate precision, which suggests that bigram models overfit when they are used as features in such a learned model.

The SVM classifier with a variety of features does not perform as well as the multinomial Naïve Bayes classifier. Joachims (1998) suggests that for text categorization, the SVM algorithm regularly outperforms other classifiers, but unfortunately the outcome of our experiments do not correlate with these results. This suggests that SVMs struggle with text classification when the discourse function between the training and test domains differ.

5 Discussion

The results produced through training supervised machine learning methods on an expressive corpus, and testing on a corpus which contains documents with a persuasive discourse function indicate that cross-discourse sentiment classification is feasible.

The best performance occurred when the classifier took frequency based features into account, as opposed to solely presence based features. The reasoning for this could be attributed to the way that patients were asked to submit their feedback. Instead of asking a patient to submit a single comment on their experience with the health service, they were asked to submit three distinct comments on what they liked, disliked and any advice that they had. This gave the user the opportunity to separate their sentiments, and clearly communicate their thoughts.

It is of interest to note that the cross-discourse accuracy should surpass the cross-validation accuracy on the training set. This was not to be expected, due to the differences in discourse function, and therefore features used. However, where just the presence of a particular word may have made the difference in a single domain, across domains, taking into account the frequency of a word in the learned model is effective in correctly classifying a comment by its sentiment. Unigram features outperform both the bigram and bigrams augmented with part-of-speech features in our experiments. By using single tokens as features, each word is taken out of the context that its neighbours provide. In doing so the language contributing to the relative sentiment is generalised enough to form a robust model which can then be applied across discourse domains.

6 Related Work

A number of studies (Cambria at al. , 2011; Xia et al. , 2009) have used patient feedback as the domain for their sentiment classification experiments. However our work differs to these studies as we consider the effect that cross-discourse evaluation has on the classification outcome. Other work that has considered different discourse functions in sentiment analysis, have experimented on detecting arguments (Somasundaran et al. , 2007) and the stance of political debates (Thomas et al. , 2006).

Machine learning approaches to text classification have typically performed well when using a Support Vector Machine (Joachims, 1998) classifier or a Naïve Bayes (McCallum and Nigam, 1998) based classifier. Pang et al. (2002) applied these classifiers to the movie review domain, which produced good results. However the difference in domain, and singularity of discourse function differentiates the scope of this work from theirs.

7 Conclusion & Future Work

In this study we focused on the cross-discourse development of supervised machine learning algorithms in the clinical domain, that trained and tested across the expressive and persuasive discourse functions. We demonstrated that despite the differences in function of a corpus of patient feedback, the greatest classification accuracy was achieved when considering word frequency in the features of the learned model.

This study centred on the expressive and persuasive discourse functions, but it would be interesting to examine other such functions that convey a sentiment, such as argumentation. Another interesting avenue of investigation for this work would be to explore the lexical semantics of the different discourse functions, that could be used in sentiment classification, and factor this into the evaluation of the overall sentiment of persuasive documents within a corpus.

References

Douglas Biber. 1988. *Variation Across Speech and Writing.* Cambridge University Press.

John Blitzer, Mark Dredze and Fernando Pereira. 2007. Biographies, Bollywood, Boom-boxes, and Blenders: Domain Adaptation for Sentiment Classification. In *Proceedings of the 45th Annual Meeting of the Association of Computational Linguistics*, pp. 440–447.

Erik Cambria, Amir Hussain and Chris Eckl. 2011. Bridging the Gap between Structured and Unstructured Health-Care Data through Semantics and Sentics. In *Proceedings of ACM WebSci*, Koblenz.

Andrea Esuli and Fabrizio Sebastiani. 2006. SentiWordNet: A Publicly Available Lexical Resource for Opinion Mining In *Proceedings of Language Resources and Evaluation (LREC)*, pp 417–422.

Thorsten Joachims. 1998. Text categorization with support vector machines: learning with many relevant features. In *Proceedings of ECML-98, 10th European Conference on Machine Learning*, pp. 137–142.

Andrew McCallum and Kamal Nigam. 1998. A Comparison of Event Models for Naive Bayes Text Classification. In *Proceedings of the AAAI/ICML-98 Workshop on Learning for Text Categorization*, pp. 41–48.

Bo Pang, Lillian Lee and Shivakumar Vaithyanathan. 2002. Thumbs up? Sentiment Classification using Machine Learning Techniques. In *Proceedings of the 2002 Conference on Empirical Methods in Natural Language Processing (EMNLP)*, pp. 79–87.

John Platt. Sequential Minimal Optimization: A Fast Algorithm for Training Support Vector Machines. In *Advances in Kernel Methods - Support Vector Learning.*

Swapna Somasudaran and Josef Ruppenhofer and Janyce Wiebe. 2007. Detecting Arguing and Sentiment in Meetings. In *Proceedings of the SIGdial Workshop on Discourse and Dialogue*, pp.26–34.

Chade-Meng Tan, Yuan-Fang Wang and Chan-Do Lee. 2002. The use of bigrams to enhance text categorization. In *Information Processing & Management*, 38(4) pp. 529–546.

Matt Thomas, Bo Pang and Lillian Lee. 2006. Get out the vote: Determining support or opposition from Congressional floor-debate transcripts. In *Proceeding of the 2006 Conference on Emperical Methods in Natural Language Processing (EMNLP)*, pp.327–335.

Lei Xia, Anna Lisa Gentile, James Munro and José Iria. 2009. Improving Patient Opinion Mining through Multi-step Classification. In *Proceedings of the 12th International Conference on Text, Speech and Dialogue (TSD'09)*, pp. 70–76.

POLITICAL-ADS: An annotated corpus of event-level evaluativity

Kevin Reschke
Department of Computer Science
Stanford University
Palo Alto, CA 94305 USA
reschkek@gmail.com

Pranav Anand
Department of Linguistics
University of California, Santa Cruz
Santa Cruz, CA 95064 USA
panand@ucsc.edu

Abstract

This paper presents a corpus targeting evaluative meaning as it pertains to descriptions of events. The corpus, POLITICAL-ADS is drawn from 141 television ads from the 2008 U.S. presidential race and contains 3945 NPs and 1549 VPs annotated for scalar sentiment from three different perspectives: the narrator, the annotator, and general society. We show that annotators can distinguish these perspectives reliably and that correlation between the annotator's own perspective and that of a generic individual is higher than those with the narrator. Finally, as a sample application, we demonstrate that a simple compositional model built off of lexical resources outperforms a lexical baseline.

1 Introduction

In the past decade, the semantics of evaluative language has received renewed attention in both formal and computational linguistics (Martin and White, 2005; Potts, 2005; Pang and Lee, 2008; Jackendoff, 2007). This work has focused on evaluativity at either the lexical level or the phrasal/event level stance, without bridging between the two. A parallel tradition of compositional event polarity ((Nasukawa and Yi, 2003; Moilanen and Pulman, 2007; Choi and Cardie, 2008; Neviarouskaya et al., 2010)) has grown up analogous to approaches to compositionality in formal semantics: event predicates are not of constant polarity, but provide functions from the polarities of their arguments to event polarities. Little work exists assessing the relative advantages of a compositional account, in part because no resource annotating both NP level polarity and event-level polarity in context exists. This paper introduces such a corpus, POLITICAL-ADS, a collection of 2008 U.S. presidential race television ads with scalar sentiment annotations at the NP and VP level. After describing the corpus creation and characteristics in sections 3 and 4, in section 5, we show that a compositional system achieves an accuracy of 84.2%, above a lexical baseline of 65.1%.

2 Background

While many sentiment models handle negation quasi-compositionally (Pang and Lee, 2008; Polanyi and Zaenen, 2005), Nasukawa & Yi (Nasukawa and Yi, 2003) first noted that predicates like *prevent* are "flippers", conveying that their subject and object have opposite polarity – since *trouble* is negative, something that *prevents trouble* is good. Recent work has expanded that idea into a fully compositional system (Moilanen and Pulman, 2007; Neviarouskaya et al., 2010). Moilanen and Pulman construct a system of compositional rules that builds polarityin terms of a hand-built lexicon of predicates as flippers or preservers. However, this system conflates two different assessment perspectives, that of the Narrator and of some mentioned NP (NP-to-NP perspective). The latter include psychological predicates such as *love* and *hate*, and those of admiration or censure (e.g., *admonish*, *praise*). Thus, they would mark *John dislikes scary movies* as negative, a correct NP-to-NP claim, but not necessarily correct for the Narrator. Recognizing this, Neviarouskaya et al. (Neviarouskaya et al., 2010) develop a pair of

Announcer: In tough times, who will help Michigan's auto industry? Barack Obama favors loan guarantees to help Detroit retool and revitalize. But John McCain refused to support loan guarantees for the auto industry. Now he's just paying lip service. Not talking straight. And McCain voted repeatedly for tax breaks for companies that ship jobs overseas, selling out American annotators. We just can't afford more of the same.

Figure 1: Transcript of POLITICAL-ADS ad #57

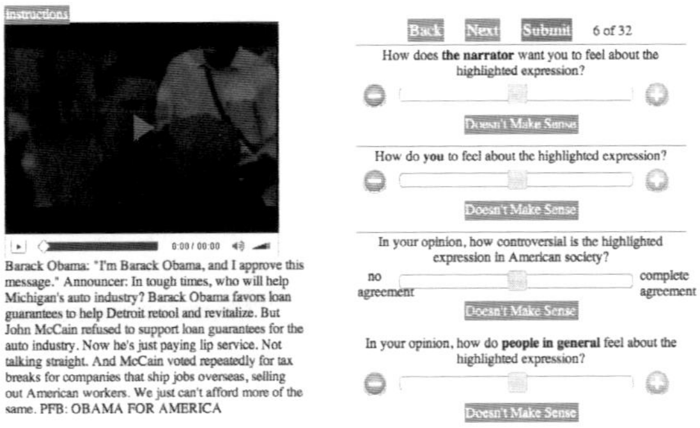

Figure 2: POLITICAL-ADS annotation interface

compositional rules over both perspectives. Importantly, neither of these approaches have been validated against a sufficiently nuanced dataset. Mailanen and Pulman test against the SemEval-07 Headlines Corpus, which asks annotators to give an overall impression of sentiment. This approach allows a headline such as *Outcry in N Korea 'nuclear test'* to be marked negative, even though outcry over military provocations is arguably good. Similarly, Neviarouskaya et al. evaluate only against NP-to-NP data as well. While the MPQA corpus (Wiebe et al., 2005), which annotates the source of each sentiment annotation, separates these two sentiment sources, work trained on it has not (Choi and Cardie, 2008; Moilanen et al., 2010). In addition, existing annotation schemes are not designed to tease apart perspectival differences. For example, MPQA includes a notion of Narrator-oriented evaluativity, but it does not include the perspectives of you and the general public.

3 The corpus

POLITICAL-ADS, is drawn from politics, a rich and recently evolving domain for evaluativity research that we hypothesized would involve a high volume of sentiment claims subject to perspectival differences. POLITICAL-ADS is a collection of 141 television ads that ran during the 2008 U.S. presidential race between Democratic candidate Barack Obama and Republican candidate John McCain. The collection consists of 81 ads from Democratic side and 60 ads from Republican side. Figure 1 provides a sample transcript.

Each transcript was parsed using the Stanford Parser and all NPs and VPs excluding those headed by auxiliaries were extracted. VP annotations were assumed to represent phrasal/event-level polarity and NP ones argument-level polarity. The annotation interface is shown in Figure 2. Annotators were shown a transcript and a movie clip, and navigated through the NPs and VPs within the document. At each point they were asked to rate their response on a [-1,1] scale for the following four questions about the highlighted expression: 1) how the narrator wants them to feel; 2) how they feel; 3) how people in general feel; 4) how controversial the issue is (included to test the whether sense of controversy yields sharper differences between the various assessment perspectives). Finally, because phrases were not prefiltered, a 'Doesn't Make Sense' button was provided for each question.

206 annotators on Mechanical Turk completed 985 transcripts at \$0.40 per transcript; each transcript was annotated by an average of 4.8 different annotators living in the U.S. We then filtered annotators by 200 phrases we deemed relatively uncontroversial in 20 randomly selected transcripts. To do this, we scored each annotator in terms of the absolute difference between their mean response and the median (each annotator's scores were first normalized by mean absolute value) in the Narrator question. We found when we thresholded annotators at a score above 0.5, agreement with our gold standard was 83.5% and dropped substantially afterwards. This threshold excluded 74 annotators, leaving 132 high-quality, or HQ, annotators (the full data is available in the corpus).

The corpus consists of 5494 phrases (1549 VPs and 3945 NPs) annotated 6.3 times on average, for a total of 34,692 annotations (9800 VP and 24892 NP). Each phrase was annotated by at least 3 HQ annotators (average 3.9 annotators), and such annotators contributed 5960 VP and 15238 NP annotations. Of these, 12.1% HQ NP and 5.4% of HQ VP responses were marked as 'Doesn't Make Sense' (DMS) for the narrator question. In general, controversy and narrator questions had the highest and lowest rates of DMS, respectively; NPs showed higher response rates than VPs; and HQ annotators had higher rates of button presses.[1] In sections 4 and 5, we will ignore the DMS responses.

4 Corpus Findings

Table 1 provides summary statistics for the corpus. Across the board, the three perspective questions averaged close to 0, and in general HQ annotators are closer to 0 (non-HQ annotators tended to provide positive responses). VPs had slightly higher variance than NPs, at marginal probability ($p < .04$), suggesting that VP responses were more extreme than NP ones. You and Generic assessments are highly correlated (Pearson's $\rho = 0.85$), but Narrator is less so ($\rho = .76/.74$). All three are weakly correlated with Controversy ($\rho = .25/.26/.29$ for Narr., You, Gen., respectively). Narrator has the highest standard deviations for the raw data, but the lowest for the normed data. In the raw data, many annotators recognized the narrators intensely partisan views and rated accordingly ($|x| > 0.8$), but were more tempered when providing their perspective ($|x| \sim 0.35$), leading to lower σ. This intensity difference is factored out in normalization, yielding the opposite pattern.

The response data was collected from our annotators in scalar form, but applications (e.g., evaluative polarity classification) it is the polarity of the response that matters. Ignoring magnitude, Table 3 shows the polarity breakdown for all HQ phrasal annotations. Positive responses are the dominant class across the board. Neutral responses are less frequent for Narrator than for the other types. NPs have fewer negatives and more neutrals than VPs.

Table 2 shows average standard deviations (i.e., agreement) by worker, question, and XP type. Note both that NPs show less variance than VPs and that non-HQ annotators less than HQ annotators (non-HQ annotators gave more 0 responses).

COND	ALL	HQ ONLY	
	RAW	RAW	NORMED
Narr.	.10 (.45)	.05 (.62)	.08 (.87)
You	.10 (.34)	.06 (.46)	.09 (.85)
Gen.	.10 (.33)	.05 (.45)	.08 (.86)
Contr.	.17 (.22)	.13 (.30)	.17 (.60)

Table 1: Mean response by category and worker type

COND	HQ ANNOTATORS					
	RAW			NORMED		
	ALL	VP	NP	ALL	VP	NP
Narr.	.69	.75	.67	.96	1.06	.93
You	.57	.63	.55	.99	1.12	.94
Gen.	.53	.58	.51	.99	1.13	.94
Contr.	.53	.58	.51	1.01	1.15	.96
	ALL ANNOTATORS					
	ALL	VP	NP			
Narr.	.63	.68	.62			
You	.54	.59	.53			
Gen.	.52	.56	.51			
Contr.	.54	.56				

Table 2: Average Standard Deviations For HQ and all annotators

5 Comparing lexical and compositional treatments

While compositional models of event-level evaluativity are logically defensible, the extent to which these models apply in the wild is an open question. Because other compositional lexicons are not freely available, we used the system described in (Reschke and Anand, 2011), which induces flippers and preservers from the MPQA subjectivity lexicon and FrameNet (Ruppenhofer et al., 2005). The MPQA lexicon is a collection of over 8,000 words marked for polarity. Our functor lexicon uses the following heuristic: verbs marked positive in MPQA are preservers; verbs marked negative are flippers. For example, *dislike* has negative MPQA polarity; therefore, it is marked as a flipper in our lexicon. This gives us 1249 predicates: 869 flippers and 380 preservers. 329 additional verbs were added from FrameNet according to their membership in five en-

[1] In a QUESTION + PHRASE TYPE + QUESTION + ANNOTATOR TYPE linear model with annotator as a random effect, all of the above effects are significant. This was the simplest model according to χ^w model comparison.

COND	POL	VP	NP
Narr.	+	2874 (51%)	6877 (51%)
	-	2654 (47%)	5590 (42%)
	0	111 (2%)	932 (7%)
You	+	2714 (49%)	6573 (50%)
	-	2466 (45%)	4967 (38%)
	0	337 (6%)	1575 (12%)
Gen.	+	2615 (48%)	6350 (49%)
	-	2541 (48%)	5125 (39%)
	0	332 (6%)	1558 (12%)
Contr.	+	3095 (57%)	6522 (51%)
	-	1755 (32%)	4159 (33%)
	0	558 (10%)	2051 (16%)

Table 3: Polarity breakdowns for HQ annotations

tailment classes (Reschke and Anand, 2011): verbs of injury/destruction, lacking, benefit, creation, and having. 124 frames across these classes were identified, and then verbs of benefit, creation, and having (*aid, generate, have*) were marked as preservers and the complement set (*forget, arrest, lack*) as flippers. As a lexical baseline, the MPQA polarity of each verb was used – flippers correspond to baseline negative events and preservers to positive ones.

A 635 VP test subset of POLITICAL-ADS was constructed by omitting intransitive VPs and VPs with non-NP complements. Gold standard labels were determined from average normed HQ annotator data. This yielded 329 positive, 284 negative, and 2 neutral events. NPs, determined similarly, divided into 393 positive, 230 negative, and 12 neutral. Of the 635 VPs in the test set, only 272 (43.5%) are in our FrameNet/MPQA lexicon and we hence compare the two systems on this subset. On this subset, the compositional system has an accuracy of 84.2%, while the lexical baseline has an accuracy of 65.1%; there were 72 instances where the compositional model outperformed the lexical baseline and 22 where the lexical outperformed the compositional. Typical examples where the compositional system won involve MPQA negatives like *break*, *cut*, and *hate* and positives like *want* and *trust*. The lexical model marks VPs like *breaks the grip of foreign oil* and *want a massive government* as negative and positive, respectively – because the NPs in question are negative, the answers should be reversed. In contrast, the lexical model wins on cases like *grow the economy* and *reform Wall Street* correct. These exemplify a robust pattern in the errors: cases where the event is marked positive while the NP is marked negative. In examples like *grow Washington*, the idea that *grow* is a preserver is reasonable. However, in *grow the economy*, the negativity of the economy is arguably measuring the state of some constant entity. While *reform* is marked positive in MPQA, it is arguably a reverser; this shows the problems with our lexicon induction.

At an intuitive level, we expect agent evaluativity to mirror event-level evaluativity because positive/negative entities tend to commit positive/negative acts, and this is borne out. For flippers or preservers, the average VP evaluativity is correlated with the average subject evaluativity. For flippers the correlation is 0.57; for preservers it is 0.52. Although our model ignored subject evaluativity, we performed a generalized linear regression with subject and object evaluativity as predictors and event-level evaluativity as outcome. For flippers the regression coefficients were 0.52 for subject ($p < 4e-4$) and -0.52 for object ($p < 1e-5$). For preservers the coefficients were 0.27 ($p < 1e-5$) for subject and 0.93 for object ($p < 2e-7$). Thus, subject polarity is an important factor for flipper events (e.g., *the hero/villain defeated the enemy*, but less so for preservers (e.g. *the hero/villain helped the enemy.*).

6 Conclusion

In this paper we have presented POLITICAL-ADS, a new resource for investigating the relationships between NP sentiment and VP sentiment systematically. We have demonstrated that annotators can reliably annotate political data with sentiment at the phrasal level from multiple perspectives. We have also shown that in the present data set that self-reporting and judging generic positions are highly correlated, while correlation with narrators is appreciably weaker, as narrators are seen as more extreme. We have also shown that the controversy of a phrase does not correlate with annotators' disagreements with the narrator. Finally, as a sample application, we demonstrated that a simple compositional model built off of lexical resources outperforms a purely lexical baseline.

References

Y. Choi and C Cardie. 2008. Learning with compositional semantics as structural inference for subsentential sentiment analysis. In *Proceedings of EMNLP 2008*.

Ray Jackendoff. 2007. *Language, consciousness, culture*. MIT Press.

J. R. Martin and P. R. R. White. 2005. *Language of Evaluation: Appraisal in English*. Palgrave Macmillan.

Karo Moilanen and Stephen Pulman. 2007. Sentiment composition. In *Proceedings of RANLP 2007*.

K. Moilanen, S. Pulman, and Y Zhang. 2010. Packed feelings and ordered sentiments: Sentiment parsing with quasi-compositional polarity sequencing and compression. In *Proceedings of WASSA 2010, EACI 2010*.

T. Nasukawa and J. Yi. 2003. Sentiment analysis: Capturing favorability using natural language processing. In *Proceedings of the 2nd international conference on Knowledge capture*.

A. Neviarouskaya, H. Prendinger, , and M. Ishizuka. 2010. Recognition of affect, judgment, and appreciation in text. In *Proceedings of COLING 2010*.

Bo Pang and Lillian Lee. 2008. Opinion mining and sentiment analysis. *Foundations and Trends in Information Retrieval*, 2(1-2):1–135.

L. Polanyi and A. Zaenen. 2005. Contextual valence shifters. in computing attitude and affect in text. In Janyce Wiebe James G. Shanahan, Yan Qu, editor, *Computing Attitude and Affect in Text: Theory and Application*. Springer Verlag, Dordrecht, The Netherlands.

Chris Potts. 2005. *The Logic of Conventional Implicature*. Oxford University Press.

K. Reschke and P. Anand. 2011. Extracting contextual evaluativity. In *Proceedings of ICWS 2011*.

Josef Ruppenhofer, Michael Ellsworth, Miriam R. L. Petruck, and Christopher R. Johnson. 2005. Framenet ii: Extended theory and practice. Technical report, ICSI Technical Report.

J. Wiebe, T. Wilson, and C. Cardie. 2005. Annotating expressions of opinions and emotions in language. In *Proceedings of LREC 2005*.

Automatically Annotating A Five-Billion-Word Corpus of Japanese Blogs for Affect and Sentiment Analysis

Michal Ptaszynski † **Rafal Rzepka ‡** **Kenji Araki ‡** **Yoshio Momouchi §**

† JSPS Research Fellow / High-Tech Research Center, Hokkai-Gakuen University
ptaszynski@hgu.jp

‡ Graduate School of Information Science and Technology, Hokkaido University
{kabura,araki}@media.eng.hokudai.ac.jp

§ Department of Electronics and Information Engineering, Faculty of Engineering, Hokkai-Gakuen University
momouchi@eli.hokkai-s-u.ac.jp

Abstract

This paper presents our research on automatic annotation of a five-billion-word corpus of Japanese blogs with information on affect and sentiment. We first perform a study in emotion blog corpora to discover that there has been no large scale emotion corpus available for the Japanese language. We choose the largest blog corpus for the language and annotate it with the use of two systems for affect analysis: ML-Ask for word- and sentence-level affect analysis and CAO for detailed analysis of emoticons. The annotated information includes affective features like sentence subjectivity (emotive/non-emotive) or emotion classes (joy, sadness, etc.), useful in affect analysis. The annotations are also generalized on a 2-dimensional model of affect to obtain information on sentence valence/polarity (positive/negative) useful in sentiment analysis. The annotations are evaluated in several ways. Firstly, on a test set of a thousand sentences extracted randomly and evaluated by over forty respondents. Secondly, the statistics of annotations are compared to other existing emotion blog corpora. Finally, the corpus is applied in several tasks, such as generation of emotion object ontology or retrieval of emotional and moral consequences of actions.

1 Introduction

There is a lack of large corpora for Japanese applicable in sentiment and affect analysis. Although there are large corpora of newspaper articles, like Mainichi Shinbun Corpus[1], or corpora of classic literature, like Aozora Bunko[2], they are usually unsuitable for research on emotions since spontaneous emotive expressions either appear rarely in these kinds of texts (newspapers), or the vocabulary is not up to date (classic literature). Although there exist speech corpora, such as Corpus of Spontaneous Japanese[3], which could become suitable for this kind of research, due to the difficulties with compilation of such corpora they are relatively small. In research such as the one by Abbasi and Chen (2007) it was proved that public Internet services, such as forums or blogs, are a good material for affect analysis because of their richness in evaluative and emotive information. One kind of these services are blogs, open diaries in which people encapsulate their own experiences, opinions and feelings to be read and commented by other people. Recently blogs have come into the focus of opinion mining or sentiment and affect analysis (Aman and Szpakowicz, 2007; Quan and Ren, 2010). Therefore creating a large blog-based emotion corpus could help overcome both problems: the lack in quantity of corpora and their applicability in sentiment and affect analysis. There have been only a few small Japanese emotion corpora developed so far (Hashimoto et al., 2011). On the other hand, although there exist large Web-based corpora (Erjavec et al., 2008; Baroni and Ueyama, 2006), access to them is usually allowed only from the Web interface, which makes additional annotations with affective information difficult. In this paper we present the first attempt to automatically annotate affect on YACIS, a large scale corpus of Japanese blogs. To do that we use two systems for affect analysis of Japanese, one for word- and sentence-level affect analysis and another especially for detailed analysis of emoticons, to annotate on the corpus different kinds of affective information (emotive expressions, emotion classes, etc.).

[1] http://www.nichigai.co.jp/sales/mainichi/mainichi-data.html

[2] http://www.aozora.gr.jp/

[3] http://www.ninjal.ac.jp/products-k/katsudo/seika/corpus/public/

The outline of the paper is as follows. Section 2 describes the related research in emotion corpora. Section 3 presents our choice of the corpus for annotation of affect- and sentiment-related information. Section 4 describes tools used in annotation. Section 5 presents detailed data and evaluation of the annotations. Section 6 presents tasks in which the corpus has already been applied. Finally the paper is concluded and future applications are discussed.

2 Emotion Corpora

Research on Affect Analysis has resulted in a number of systems developed within several years (Aman and Szpakowicz, 2007; Ptaszynski et al., 2009c; Matsumoto et al., 2011). Unfortunately, most of such research ends in proposing and evaluating a system. The real world application that would be desirable, such as annotating affective information on linguistic data is limited to processing a usually small test sample in the evaluation. The small number of annotated emotion corpora that exist are mostly of limited scale and are annotated manually. Below we describe and compare some of the most notable emotion corpora. Interestingly, six out of eight emotion corpora described below are created from blogs. The comparison is summarized in Table 1. We also included information on the work described in this paper for better comparison (YACIS).

Quan and Ren (2010) created a Chinese emotion blog corpus **Ren-CECps1.0**. They collected 500 blog articles from various Chinese blog services, such as sina blog (http://blog.sina.com.cn/), qq blog (http://blog.qq.com/), etc., and annotated them with a large variety of information, such as emotion class, emotive expressions or polarity level. Although syntactic annotations were simplified to tokenization and POS tagging, this corpus can be considered a state-of-the-art emotion blog corpus. The motivation for Quan and Ren is also similar to ours - dealing with the lack of large corpora for sentiment analysis in Chinese (in our case - Japanese).

Wiebe et al. (2005) report on creating the **MPQA** corpus of news articles. The corpus contains 10,657 sentences in 535 documents[4]. The annotation schema includes a variety of emotion-related information, such as emotive expressions, emotion valence, intensity, etc. However, Wiebe et al. focused on detecting subjective (emotive) sentences, which do not necessarily convey emotions, and classifying them into positive and negative. Thus their annotation schema, although one of the richest, does not include emotion classes.

A corpus of Japanese blogs, called **KNB**, rich in the amount and diversification of annotated information was developed by Hashimoto et al. (2011). It contains 67 thousand words in 249 blog articles. Although it is not a small scale corpus, it developed a certain standard for preparing corpora, especially blog corpora for sentiment and affect-related studies in Japan. The corpus contains all relevant grammatical annotations, including POS tagging, dependency parsing or Named Entity Recognition. It also contains sentiment-related information. Words and phrases expressing emotional attitude were annotated by laypeople as either positive or negative. One disadvantage of the corpus, apart from its small scale, is the way it was created. Eighty one students were employed to write blogs about different topics especially for the need of this research. It could be argued that since the students knew their blogs will be read mostly by their teachers, they selected their words more carefully than they would in private.

Aman and Szpakowicz (2007) constructed a small-scale English blog corpus. They did not include any grammatical information, but focused on affect-related annotations. As an interesting remark, they were some of the first to recognize the task of distinguishing between emotive and non-emotive sentences. This problem is usually one of the most difficult in text-based Affect Analysis and is therefore often omitted in such research. In our research we applied a system proved to deal with this task with high accuracy for Japanese.

Das and Bandyopadhyay (2010) constructed an emotion annotated corpus of blogs in Bengali. The corpus contains 12,149 sentences within 123 blog posts extracted from Bengali web blog archive (http://www.amarblog.com/). It is annotated with face recognition annotation standard (Ekman, 1992).

Matsumoto et al. (2011) created ***Wakamono Kotoba*** (Slang of the Youth) corpus. It contains unrelated sentences extracted manually from Yahoo! blogs (http://blog-search.yahoo.co.jp/). Each sen-

[4]The new MPQA Opinion Corpus version 2.0 contains additional 157 documents, 692 documents in total.

Table 1: Comparison of emotion corpora ordered by the amount of annotations (abbreviations: T=tokenization, POS=part-of-speech tagging, L=lemmatization, DP=dependency parsing, NER=Named Entity Recognition).

corpus name	scale (in sentences / docs)	language	annotated affective information						syntactic annotations
			emotion class standard	emotive expressions	emotive/ non-emot.	valence/ activation	emotion intensity	emotion objects	
YACIS	354 mil. /13 mil.	Japanese	10 (language and culture based)	○	○	○/○	○	○	T,POS,L,DP,NER;
Ren-CECps1.0	12,724/500	Chinese	8 (Yahoo! news)	○	○	○/×	○	○	T,POS;
MPQA	10,657/535	English	none (no standard)	○	○	○/×	○	○	T,POS;
KNB	4,186/249	Japanese	none (no standard)	○	×	○/×	×	○	T,POS,L,DP,NER;
Minato et al.	1,191sent.	Japanese	8 (chosen subjectively)	○	○	×/×	×	×	POS;
Aman&Szpak.	5,205/173	English	6 (face recognition)	○	○	×/×	○	×	×
Das&Bandyo.	12,149/123	Bengali	6 (face recognition)	○	×	×/×	○	×	×
Wakamono Kotoba	4773sentences	Japanese	9 (face recognition + 3 added subjectively)	○	×	×/×	×	×	×
Mishne	?/815,494	English	132 (LiveJournal)	×	×	×/×	×	×	×

tence contains at least one word from a slang lexicon and one word from an emotion lexicon, with additional emotion class tags added per sentence. The emotion class set used for annotation was chosen subjectively, by applying the 6 class face recognition standard and adding 3 classes of their choice.

Mishne (2005) collected a corpus of English blogs from LiveJournal (http://www.livejournal.com/) blogs. The corpus contains 815,494 blog posts, from which many are annotated with emotions (moods) by the blog authors themselves. The LiveJournal service offers an option for its users to annotate their mood while writing the blog. The list of 132 moods include words like "amused", or "angry". The LiveJournal mood annotation standard offers a rich vocabulary to describe the writer's mood. However, this richness has been considered troublesome to generalize the data in a meaningful manner (Quan and Ren, 2010).

Finally, Minato et al. (2006) collected a 14,195 word, 1,191 sentence corpus. The corpus was a collection of sentence examples from a dictionary of emotional expressions (Hiejima, 1995). The dictionary was created for the need of Japanese language learners. Differently to the dictionary applied in our research (Nakamura, 1993), in Hiejima (1995) sentence examples were mostly written by the author of the dictionary himself. The dictionary also does not propose any coherent emotion class list, but rather the emotion concepts are chosen subjectively. Although the corpus by Minato et al. is the smallest of all mentioned above, its statistics is described in detail. Therefore in this paper we use it as one of the Japanese emotion corpora to compare our work to.

All of the above corpora were annotated manually or semi-automatically. In this research we performed the first attempt to annotate a large scale blog corpus (YACIS) with affective information fully automatically. We did this with systems based on positively evaluated affect annotation schema, performance, and standardized emotion class typology.

3 Choice of Blog Corpus

Although Japanese is a well recognized and described world language, there have been only few large corpora for this language. For example, Erjavec et al. (2008) gathered a 400-million-word scale Web corpus **JpWaC**, or Baroni and Ueyama (2006) developed a medium-sized corpus of Japanese blogs **jBlogs** containing 62 million words. However, both research faced several problems, such as character encoding, or web page metadata extraction, such as the page title or author which differ between domains. Apart from the above mentioned medium sized corpora at present the largest Web based blog corpus available for Japanese is **YACIS** or **Y**et **A**nother **C**orpus of **I**nternet **S**entences. We chose this corpus for the annotation of affective information for several reasons. It was collected automatically by Maciejewski et al. (2010) from the pages of Ameba blog service. It contains 5.6 billion words within 350 million sentences. Maciejewski et al. were able to extract only pages containing Japanese posts (pages with legal disclaimers or written in languages other than Japanese were omitted). In the initial phase they provided their crawler, optimized to crawl only Ameba blog service, with 1000 links

```
<doc url="http://ameblo.jp/blog-name/entry-000001.html"
time="2009-12-05 21:11:46" id="2000001">
    <post>
        <s>今日から十月です。</s>
        [Its October from today.]
        <s>なんか、九月はいつもよりアッという間に過ぎたような気がするなぁ。</s>
        [I have a strange feeling September passed faster than usual.]
        ...
    </post>
    <comments>
        <cmt>
                <s>色々と忙しいですね～！</s>
                [Oh, you've been busy, weren't you?]
                ...
        </cmt>
        <cmt>
                <s>お疲れサマです(^0^)</s>
                [Well done! Cheers for good work (^o^)]
                ...
        </cmt>
    </comments>
</doc>
```

Figure 1: The example of YACIS XML structure.

Table 2: General Statistics of YACIS.

# of web pages	12,938,606
# of unique bloggers	60,658
average # of pages/blogger	213.3
# of pages with comments	6,421,577
# of comments	50,560,024
average # of comment/page	7.873
# of words	5,600,597,095
# of all sentences	354,288,529
# of words per sentence (average)	15
# of characters per sentence (average)	77

taken from Google (response to one simple query: 'site:ameblo.jp'). They saved all pages to disk as raw HTML files (each page in a separate file) and afterward extracted all the posts and comments and divided them into sentences. The original structure (blog post and comments) was preserved, thanks to which semantic relations between posts and comments were retained. The blog service from which the corpus was extracted (Ameba) is encoded by default in Unicode, thus there was no problem with character encoding. It also has a clear and stable HTML meta-structure, thanks to which they managed to extract metadata such as blog title and author. The corpus was first presented as an unannotated corpus. Recently Ptaszynski et al. (2012b) annotated it with syntactic information, such as POS, dependency structure or named entity recognition. An example of the original blog structure in XML is represented in Figure 1. Some statistics about the corpus are represented in Table 2.

4 Affective Information Annotation Tools

Emotive Expression Dictionary (Nakamura, 1993) is a collection of over two thousand expressions describing emotional states collected manually from a wide range of literature. It is not a tool *per se*, but

Figure 2: Output examples for ML-Ask and CAO.

Table 3: Distribution of separate expressions across emotion classes in Nakamura's dictionary (overall 2100 ex.).

emotion class	nunber of expressions	emotion class	nunber of expressions
dislike	532	fondness	197
excitement	269	fear	147
sadness	232	surprise	129
joy	224	relief	106
anger	199	shame	65
		sum	**2100**

was converted into an emotive expression database by Ptaszynski et al. (2009c). Since YACIS is a Japanese language corpus, for the affect annotation we needed the most appropriate lexicon for the language. The dictionary, developed for over 20 years by Akira Nakamura, is a state-of-the art example of a hand-crafted emotive expression lexicon. It also proposes a classification of emotions that reflects the Japanese culture: 喜 *ki/yorokobi*[5] (joy), 怒 *dō/ikari* (anger), 哀 *ai/aware* (sorrow, sadness, gloom), 怖 *fu/kowagari* (fear), 恥 *chi/haji* (shame, shyness), 好 *kō/suki* (fondness), 厭 *en/iya* (dislike), 昂 *kō/takaburi* (excitement), 安 *an/yasuragi* (relief), and 驚 *kyō/odoroki* (surprise). All expressions in the dictionary are annotated with one emotion class or more if applicable. The distribution of expressions across all emotion classes is represented in Table 3.

ML-Ask (Ptaszynski et al., 2009a; Ptaszynski et al., 2009c) is a keyword-based language-dependent system for affect annotation on sentences in Japanese. It uses a two-step procedure: **1)** specifying whether an utterance is emotive, and **2)** annotating the particular emotion classes in utterances described as emotive. The emotive sentences are detected on the basis of *emotemes*, emotive features like: interjections, mimetic expressions, vulgar language, emoticons

[5] Separation by "/" represents two possible readings of the character.

Table 4: Evaluation results of ML-Ask and CAO.

	emotive/ non-emotive	emotion classes	2D (valence and activation)
ML-Ask	98.8%	73.4%	88.6%
CAO	97.6%	80.2%	94.6%
ML-Ask+CAO	100.0%	89.9%	97.5%

and emotive markers. The examples in Japanese are respectively: *sugee* (great!), *wakuwaku* (heart pounding), *-yagaru* (syntactic morpheme used in verb vulgarization), (^_^) (emoticon expressing joy) and '!', '??' (markers indicating emotive engagement). Emotion class annotation is based on Nakamura's dictionary. ML-Ask is also the only present system for Japanese recognized to implement the idea of Contextual Valence Shifters (CVS) (Zaenen and Polanyi, 2005) (words and phrases like "not", or "never", which change the valence of an evaluative word). The last distinguishable feature of ML-Ask is implementation of Russell's two dimensional affect model (Russell, 1980), in which emotions are represented in two dimensions: valence (positive/negative) and activation (activated/deactivated). An example of negative-activated emotion could be "anger"; a positive-deactivated emotion is, e.g., "relief". The mapping of Nakamura's emotion classes on Russell's two dimensions was proved reliable in several research (Ptaszynski et al., 2009b; Ptaszynski et al., 2009c; Ptaszynski et al., 2010b). With these settings ML-Ask detects emotive sentences with a high accuracy (90%) and annotates affect on utterances with a sufficiently high Precision (85.7%), but low Recall (54.7%). Although low Recall is a disadvantage, we assumed that in a corpus as big as YACIS there should still be plenty of data.

CAO (Ptaszynski et al., 2010b) is a system for affect analysis of Japanese emoticons, called *kaomoji*. Emoticons are sets of symbols used to convey emotions in text-based online communication, such as blogs. CAO extracts emoticons from input and determines specific emotions expressed by them. Firstly, it matches the input to a predetermined raw emoticon database (with over ten thousand emoticons). The emoticons, which could not be estimated with this database are divided into semantic areas (representations of "mouth" or "eyes"). The areas are automatically annotated according to their co-occurrence in the database. The performance of CAO was evaluated as close to ideal (Ptaszynski et al., 2010b) (over 97%). In this research we used CAO as a supporting procedure in ML-Ask to improve the overall performance and add detailed information about emoticons.

Table 5: Statistics of emotive sentences.

# of emotive sentences	233,591,502
# of non-emotive sentence	120,408,023
ratio (emotive/non-emotive)	1.94
# of sentences containing emoteme class:	
- interjections	171,734,464
- exclamative marks	89,626,215
- emoticons	49,095,123
- endearments	12,935,510
- vulgarities	1,686,943
ratio (emoteme classes in emotive sentence)	1.39

5 Annotation Results and Evaluation

It is physically impossible to manually evaluate all annotations on the corpus[6]. Therefore we applied three different types of evaluation. First was based on a sample of 1000 sentences randomly extracted from the corpus and annotated by laypeople. In second we compared YACIS annotations to other emotion corpora. The third evaluation was application based and is be described in section 6.

Evaluation of Affective Annotations: Firstly, we needed to confirm the performance of affect analysis systems on YACIS, since the performance is often related to the type of test set used in evaluation. ML-Ask was positively evaluated on separate sentences and on an online forum (Ptaszynski et al., 2009c). However, it was not yet evaluated on blogs. Moreover, the version of ML-Ask supported by CAO has not been evaluated thoroughly as well. In the evaluation we used a test set created by Ptaszynski et al. (2010b) for the evaluation of CAO. It consists of thousand sentences randomly extracted from YACIS and manually annotated with emotion classes by 42 layperson annotators in an anonymous survey. There are 418 emotive and 582 non-emotive sentences. We compared the results on those sentences for ML-Ask, CAO (described in detail by Ptaszynski et al. (2010b)), and both systems combined. The results showing accuracy, cal-

[6]Having one sec. to evaluate one sentence, one evaluator would need 11.2 years to verify the whole corpus (354 mil.s.).

Table 6: Emotion class annotations with percentage.

emotion class	# of sentences	%	emotion class	# of sentences	%
joy	16,728,452	31%	excitement	2,833,388	5%
dislike	10,806,765	20%	surprize	2,398,535	5%
fondness	9,861,466	19%	gloom	2,144,492	4%
fear	3,308,288	6%	anger	1,140,865	2%
relief	3,104,774	6%	shame	952,188	2%

Table 7: Comparison of positive and negative sentences between KNB and YACIS.

		positive	negative	ratio
KNB*	emotional attitude	317	208	1.52
	opinion	489	289	1.69
	merit	449	264	1.70
	acceptation or rejection	125	41	3.05
	event	43	63	0.68
	sum	1,423	865	1.65
YACIS**	only	22,381,992	12,837,728	1.74
	only+mostly	23,753,762	13,605,514	1.75

* p<.05, ** p<.01

culated as a ratio of success to the overall number of samples, are summarized in Table 4. The performance of discrimination between emotive and non-emotive sentences of ML-Ask baseline was a high 98.8%, which is much higher than in original evaluation of ML-Ask (around 90%). This could indicate that sentences with which the system was not able to deal with appear much less frequently on Ameblo. As for CAO, it is capable of detecting the presence of emoticons in a sentence, which is partially equivalent to detecting emotive sentences in ML-Ask, since emoticons are one type of features determining sentence as emotive. The performance of CAO was also high, 97.6%. This was due to the fact that grand majority of emotive sentences contained emoticons. Finally, ML-Ask supported with CAO achieved remarkable 100% accuracy. This was a surprisingly good result, although it must be remembered that the test sample contained only 1000 sentences (less than 0.0003% of the whole corpus). Next we verified emotion class annotations on sentences. The baseline of ML-Ask achieved slightly better results (73.4%) than in its primary evaluation (Ptaszynski et al., 2009c) (67% of balanced F-score with P=85.7% and R=54.7%). CAO achieved 80.2%. Interestingly, this makes CAO a better affect analysis system than ML-Ask. However, the condition is that a sentence must contain an emoticon. The best result, close to 90%, was achieved by ML-Ask supported with CAO. We also checked the results when only the dimensions of valence and activation were taken into account. ML-Ask achieved 88.6%, CAO nearly 95%. Support of CAO to ML-Ask again resulted in the best score, 97.5%.

Statistics of Affective Annotations: There were nearly twice as many emotive sentences than non-emotive (ratio 1.94). This suggests that the corpus is biased in favor of emotive contents, which could be considered as a proof for the assumption that blogs make a good base for emotion related research. When it comes to statistics of each emotive feature (emoteme), the most frequent class were interjections. Second frequent was the exclamative marks class, which includes punctuation marks suggesting emotive engagement (such as "!", or "??"). Third frequent emoteme class was emoticons, followed by endearments. As an interesting remark, emoteme class that was the least frequent were vulgarities. As one possible interpretation of this result we propose the following. Blogs are social space, where people describe their experiences to be read and commented by other people (friends, colleagues). The use of vulgar language could discourage potential readers from further reading, making the blog less popular. Next, we checked the statistics of emotion classes annotated on emotive sentences. The results are represented in Table 6. The most frequent emotions were joy (31%), dislike (20%) and fondness (19%), which covered over 70% of all annotations. However, it could happen that the number of expressions included in each emotion class database influenced the number of annotations (database containing many expressions has higher probability to gather more annotations). Therefore we verified if there was a correlation between the number of annotations and the number of emotive expressions in each emotion class database. The verification was based on Spearman's rank correlation test between the two sets of numbers. The test revealed no statistically significant correlation between the two types of data, with ρ=0.38.

Comparison with Other Emotion Corpora: Firstly, we compared YACIS with KNB. The KNB corpus was annotated mostly for the need of sentiment analysis and therefore does not contain any

Table 8: Comparison of number of emotive expressions in three different corpora including ratio within this set of emotions and results of Spearman's rank correlation test.

	Minato et al.	YACIS	Nakamura
dislike	355 (26%)	14,184,697 (23%)	532 (32%)
joy	295 (21%)	22,100,500 (36%)	224 (13%)
fondness	205 (15%)	13,817,116 (22%)	197 (12%)
sorrow	205 (15%)	2,881,166 (5%)	232 (14%)
anger	160 (12%)	1,564,059 (3%)	199 (12%)
fear	145 (10%)	4,496,250 (7%)	147 (9%)
surprise	25 (2%)	3,108,017 (5%)	129 (8%)
	Minato et al. and Nakamura	**Minato et al. and YACIS**	**YACIS and Nakamura**
Spearman's ρ	0.88	0.63	0.25

information on specific emotion classes. However, it is annotated with emotion valence for different categories valence is expressed in Japanese, such as *emotional attitude* (e.g., "to feel sad about X" [NEG], "to like X" [POS]), *opinion* (e.g., "X is wonderful" [POS]), or *positive/negative event* (e.g., "X broke down" [NEG], "X was awarded" [POS]). We compared the ratios of sentences expressing positive to negative valence. The comparison was made for all KNB valence categories separately and as a sum. In our research we do not make additional subcategorization of valence types, but used in the comparison ratios of sentences in which the expressed emotions were of only positive/negative valence and including the sentences which were mostly (in majority) positive/negative. The comparison is presented in table 7. In KNB for all valence categories except one the ratio of positive to negative sentences was biased in favor of positive sentences. Moreover, for most cases, including the ratio taken from the sums of sentences, the ratio was similar to the one in YACIS (around 1.7). Although the numbers of compared sentences differ greatly, the fact that the ratio remains similar across the two different corpora suggests that the Japanese express in blogs more positive than negative emotions.

Next, we compared the corpus created by Minato et al. (2006). This corpus was prepared on the basis of an emotive expression dictionary. Therefore we compared its statistics not only to YACIS, but also to the emotive lexicon used in our research (see section 4 for details). Emotion classes used in Minato et al. differ slightly to those used in our research (YACIS and Nakamura's dictionary). For example, they use class name "hate" to describe what in YACIS is called "dislike". Moreover, they have no classes such as excitement, relief or shame. To make the comparison possible we used only the emotion classes appearing in both cases and unified all class names. The results are summarized in Table 8. There was no correlation between YACIS and Nakamura (ρ=0.25), which confirms the results calculated in previous paragraph. A medium correlation was observed between YACIS and Minato et al. (ρ=0.63). Finally, a strong correlation was observed between Minato et al. and Nakamura (ρ=0.88), which is the most interesting observation. Both Minato et al. and Nakamura are in fact dictionaries of emotive expressions. However, the dictionaries were collected in different times (difference of about 20 years), by people with different background (lexicographer vs. language teacher), based on different data (literature vs. conversation) assumptions and goals (creating a lexicon vs. Japanese language teaching). The only similarity is in the methodology. In both cases the dictionary authors collected expressions considered to be emotion-related. The fact that they correlate so strongly suggests that for the compared emotion classes there could be a tendency in language to create more expressions to describe some emotions rather than the others (dislike, joy and fondness are often some of the most frequent emotion classes). This phenomenon needs to be verified more thoroughly in the future.

6 Applications

6.1 Extraction of Evaluation Datasets

In evaluation of sentiment and affect analysis systems it is very important to provide a statistically reliable random sample of sentences or documents as a test set (to be further annotated by laypeople). The larger is the source, the more statistically reliable is the test set. Since YACIS contains 354 mil. sentences in 13 mil. documents, it can be considered sufficiently reliable for the task of test set extraction, as probability of extracting twice the same sentence is close to zero. Ptaszynski et al. (2010b) already used YACIS to randomly extract a 1000 sentence sample and used it in their evaluation of emoticon analysis system. The sample was also used in this research and is described in more detail in section 5.

6.2 Generation of Emotion Object Ontology

One of the applications of large corpora is to extract from them smaller sub-corpora for specified tasks. Ptaszynski et al. (2012a) applied YACIS for their task of generating an robust emotion object ontology. They used cross-reference of annotations of emotional information described in this paper and syntactic annotations done by Ptaszynski et al. (2012b) to extract only sentences in which expression of emotion was proceeded by its cause, like in the example below.

彼女に振られたから悲しい...
Kanojo ni furareta ***kara*** *kanashii...*
Girlfriend DAT dump PAS CAUS sad ...
I'm sad **because** my girlfriend dumped me...

The example can be analyzed in the following way. Emotive expression (*kanashii*, "sad") is related with the sentence contents (*Kanojo ni furareta*, "my girlfriend dumped me") with a causality morpheme (***kara***, "**because**"). In such situation the sentence contents represent the object of emotion. This can be generalized to the following meta-structure,

$$O_E \ CAUS \ X_E,$$

where O_E=[Emotion object], $CAUS$=[**causal form**], and X_E=[expression of emotion].

The cause phrases were cleaned of irrelevant words like stop words to leave only the object phrases. The evaluation showed they were able to extract nearly 20 mil. object phrases, from which 80% was extracted correctly with a reliable significance. Thanks to rich annotations on YACIS corpus the ontology included such features as emotion class (joy, anger, etc.), dimensions (valence/activation), POS or semantic categories (hypernyms, etc.).

6.3 Retrieval of Moral Consequence of Actions

Third application of the YACIS corpus annotated with affect- and sentiment-related information has been in a novel research on retrieval of moral consequences of actions, first proposed by Rzepka and Araki (2005) and recently developed by Komuda et al. (2010)[7]. The moral consequence retrieval agent was based on the idea of Wisdom of Crowd. In particular Komuda et al. (2010) used a Web-mining technique to gather consequences of actions applying causality relations, like in the research described in section 6.2, but with a reversed algorithm and lexicon containing not only emotional but also ethical notions. They cross-referenced emotional and ethical information about a certain phrase (such as "To kill a person.") to obtain statistical probability for emotional ("feeling sad", "being in joy", etc.) and ethical consequences ("being punished", "being praised", etc.). Initially, the moral agent was based on the whole Internet contents. However, multiple queries to search engine APIs made by the agent caused constant blocking of IP address an in effect hindered the development of the agent.

The agent was tested on over 100 ethically-significant real world problems, such as "killing a man", "stealing money", "bribing someone", "helping people" or "saving environment". In result 86% of recognitions were correct. Some examples of the results are presented in the Appendix on the end of this paper.

[7] See also a mention in *Scientific American*, by Anderson and Anderson (2010).

7 Conclusions

We performed automatic annotation of a five-billion-word corpus of Japanese blogs with information on affect and sentiment. A survey in emotion blog corpora showed there has been no large scale emotion corpus available for the Japanese language. We chose YACIS, a large-scale blog corpus and annotated it using two systems for affect analysis for word- and sentence-level affect analysis and for analysis of emoticons. The annotated information included affective features like sentence subjectivity (emotive/non-emotive) or emotion classes (joy, sadness, etc.), useful in affect analysis and information on sentence valence/polarity (positive/negative) useful in sentiment analysis obtained as generalizations of those features on a 2-dimensional model of affect. We evaluated the annotations in several ways. Firstly, on a test set of thousand sentences extracted and evaluated by over forty respondents. Secondly, we compared the statistics of annotations to other existing emotion corpora. Finally, we showed several tasks the corpus has already been applied in, such as generation of emotion object ontology or retrieval of emotional and moral consequences of actions.

Acknowledgments

This research was supported by (JSPS) KAKENHI Grant-in-Aid for JSPS Fellows (Project Number: 22-00358).

References

Ahmed Abbasi and Hsinchun Chen. "Affect Intensity Analysis of Dark Web Forums", Intelligence and Security Informatics 2007, pp. 282-288, 2007

Saima Aman and Stan Szpakowicz. 2007. "Identifying Expressions of Emotion in Text". In *Proceedings of the 10th International Conference on Text, Speech, and Dialogue (TSD-2007)*, Lecture Notes in Computer Science (LNCS), Springer-Verlag.

Michael Anderson and Susan Leigh Anderson. 2010. "Robot be Good", *Scientific American*, October, pp. 72-77.

Dipankar Das, Sivaji Bandyopadhyay, "Labeling Emotion in Bengali Blog Corpus ? A Fine Grained Tagging at Sentence Level", Proceedings of the 8th Workshop on Asian Language Resources, pages 47?55, 2010.

Marco Baroni, Silvia Bernardini, Adriano Ferraresi, Eros Zanchetta. 2008. "The WaCky Wide Web: A Collection of Very Large Linguistically Processed Web-Crawled Corpora", Kluwer Academic Publishers, Netherlands.

Marco Baroni and Motoko Ueyama. 2006. "Building General- and Special-Purpose Corpora by Web Crawling", In *Proceedings of the 13th NIJL International Symposium on Language Corpora: Their Compilation and Application*, www.tokuteicorpus.jp/result/pdf/2006_004.pdf

Jürgen Broschart. 1997. "Why Tongan does it differently: Categorial Distinctions in a Language without Nouns and Verbs." *Linguistic Typology*, Vol. 1, No. 2, pp. 123-165.

Eugene Charniak, Don Blaheta, Niyu Ge, Keith Hall, John Hale and Mark Johnson. 2000. "BLLIP 1987-89 WSJ Corpus Release 1", Linguistic Data Consortium, Philadelphia, http://www.ldc.upenn.edu/Catalog/CatalogEntry.jsp?catalogId=LDC2000T43

Paul Ekman. 1992. "An Argument for Basic Emotions". *Cognition and Emotion*, Vol. 6, pp. 169-200.

Irena Srdanovic Erjavec, Tomaz Erjavec and Adam Kilgarriff. 2008. "A web corpus and word sketches for Japanese", *Information and Media Technologies*, Vol. 3, No. 3, pp.529-551.

Katarzyna Głowińska and Adam Przepiórkowski. 2010. "The Design of Syntactic Annotation Levels in the National Corpus of Polish", In *Proceedings of LREC 2010*.

Peter Halacsy, Andras Kornai, Laszlo Nemeth, Andras Rung, Istvan Szakadat and Vikto Tron. 2004. "Creating open language resources for Hungarian". In *Proceedings of the LREC*, Lisbon, Portugal.

Chikara Hashimoto, Sadao Kurohashi, Daisuke Kawahara, Keiji Shinzato and Masaaki Nagata. 2011. "Construction of a Blog Corpus with Syntactic, Anaphoric, and Sentiment Annotations" [in Japanese], *Journal of Natural Language Processing*, Vol 18, No. 2, pp. 175-201.

Ichiro Hiejima. 1995. *A short dictionary of feelings and emotions in English and Japanese*, Tokyodo Shuppan.

Paul J. Hopper and Sandra A. Thompson. 1985. "The Iconicity of the Universal Categories 'Noun' and 'Verbs'". In *Typological Studies in Language: Iconicity and Syntax*. John Haiman (ed.), Vol. 6, pp. 151-183, Amsterdam: John Benjamins Publishing Company.

Daisuke Kawahara and Sadao Kurohashi. 2006. "A Fully-Lexicalized Probabilistic Model for Japanese Syntactic and Case Structure Analysis", *Proceedings of the Human Language Technology Conference of the North American Chapter of the ACL*, pp. 176-183.

Radoslaw Komuda, Michal Ptaszynski, Yoshio Momouchi, Rafal Rzepka, and Kenji Araki. 2010. "Machine Moral Development: Moral Reasoning Agent Based on Wisdom of Web-Crowd and Emotions", *Int. Journal of Computational Linguistics Research*, Vol. 1 , Issue 3, pp. 155-163.

Taku Kudo and Hideto Kazawa. 2009. "Japanese Web N-gram Version 1", Linguistic Data Consortium, Philadelphia, http://www.ldc.upenn.edu/Catalog/CatalogEntry.jsp?catalogId=LDC2009T08

Vinci Liu and James R. Curran. 2006. "Web Text Corpus for Natural Language Processing", In *Proceedings of the 11th Meeting of the European Chapter of the Association for Computational Linguistics (EACL)*, pp. 233-240.

Maciejewski, J., Ptaszynski, M., Dybala, P. 2010. "Developing a Large-Scale Corpus for Natural Language Processing and Emotion Processing Research in Japanese", In *Proceedings of the International Workshop on Modern Science and Technology (IWMST)*, pp. 192-195.

Kazuyuki Matsumoto, Yusuke Konishi, Hidemichi Sayama, Fuji Ren. 2011. "Analysis of Wakamono Kotoba Emotion Corpus and Its Application in Emotion Estimation", *International Journal of Advanced Intelligence*, Vol.3,No.1,pp.1-24.

Junko Minato, David B. Bracewell, Fuji Ren and Shingo Kuroiwa. 2006. "Statistical Analysis of a Japanese Emotion Corpus for Natural Language Processing", *LNCS* 4114.

Gilad Mishne. 2005. "Experiments with Mood Classification in Blog Posts". In *The 1st Workshop on Stylistic Analysis of Text for Information Access*, at *SIGIR 2005*, August 2005.

Akira Nakamura. 1993. "Kanjo hyogen jiten" [Dictionary of Emotive Expressions] (in Japanese), Tokyodo Publishing, Tokyo, 1993.

Jan Pomikálek, Pavel Rychlý and Adam Kilgarriff. 2009. "Scaling to Billion-plus Word Corpora", In *Advances in Computational Linguistics, Research in Computing Science*, Vol. 41, pp. 3-14.

Michal Ptaszynski, Pawel Dybala, Wenhan Shi, Rafal Rzepka and Kenji Araki. 2009. "A System for Affect Analysis of Utterances in Japanese Supported with Web Mining", *Journal of Japan Society for Fuzzy Theory and Intelligent Informatics*, Vol. 21, No. 2, pp. 30-49 (194-213).

Michal Ptaszynski, Pawel Dybala, Wenhan Shi, Rafal Rzepka and Kenji Araki. 2009. "Towards Context Aware Emotional Intelligence in Machines: Computing Contextual Appropriateness of Affective States". In *Proceedings of Twenty-first International Joint Conference on Artificial Intelligence (IJCAI-09)*, Pasadena, California, USA, pp. 1469-1474.

Michal Ptaszynski, Pawel Dybala, Rafal Rzepka and Kenji Araki. 2009. "Affecting Corpora: Experiments with Automatic Affect Annotation System - A Case Study of the 2channel Forum -", In *Proceedings of the Conference of the Pacific Association for Computational Linguistics (PACLING-09)*, pp. 223-228.

Michal Ptaszynski, Rafal Rzepka and Kenji Araki. 2010a. "On the Need for Context Processing in Affective Computing", In *Proceedings of Fuzzy System Symposium (FSS2010)*, Organized Session on Emotions, September 13-15.

Michal Ptaszynski, Jacek Maciejewski, Pawel Dybala, Rafal Rzepka and Kenji Araki. 2010b. "CAO: Fully Automatic Emoticon Analysis System", In *Proc. of the 24th AAAI Conference on Artificial Intelligence (AAAI-10)*, pp. 1026-1032.

Michal Ptaszynski, Rafal Rzepka, Kenji Araki and Yoshio Momouchi. 2012a. "A Robust Ontology of Emotion Objects", In *Proceedings of The Eighteenth Annual Meeting of The Association for Natural Language Processing (NLP-2012)*, pp. 719-722.

Michal Ptaszynski, Rafal Rzepka, Kenji Araki and Yoshio Momouchi. 2012b. "Annotating Syntactic Information on 5.5 Billion Word Corpus of Japanese Blogs", In *Proceedings of The 18th Annual Meeting of The Association for Natural Language Processing (NLP-2012)*, pp. 385-388.

Changqin Quan and Fuji Ren. 2010. "A blog emotion corpus for emotional expression analysis in Chinese", *Computer Speech & Language*, Vol. 24, Issue 4, pp. 726-749.

Rafal Rzepka, Kenji Araki. 2005. "What Statistics Could Do for Ethics? - The Idea of Common Sense Processing Based Safety Valve", AAAI Fall Symposium on Machine Ethics, *Technical Report FS-05-06*, pp. 85-87.

James A. Russell. 1980. "A circumplex model of affect". *J. of Personality and Social Psychology*, Vol. 39, No. 6, pp. 1161-1178.

Peter D. Turney and Michael L. Littman. 2002. "Unsupervised Learning of Semantic Orientation from a Hundred-Billion-Word Corpus", National Research Council, Institute for Information Technology, *Technical Report ERB-1094*. (NRC #44929).

Masao Utiyama and Hitoshi Isahara. 2003. "Reliable Measures for Aligning Japanese-English News Articles and Sentences". *ACL-2003*, pp. 72-79.

Janyce Wiebe, Theresa Wilson and Claire Cardie. 2005. "Annotating expressions of opinions and emotions in language". *Language Resources and Evaluation*, Vol. 39, Issue 2-3, pp. 165-210.

Theresa Wilson and Janyce Wiebe. 2005. "Annotating Attributions and Private States", In *Proceedings of the ACL Workshop on Frontiers in Corpus Annotation II*, pp. 53-60.

Annie Zaenen and Livia Polanyi. 2006. "Contextual Valence Shifters". In *Computing Attitude and Affect in Text*, J. G. Shanahan, Y. Qu, J. Wiebe (eds.), Springer Verlag, Dordrecht, The Netherlands, pp. 1-10.

Appendix. Examples of emotional and ethical consequence retrieval.

emotional conseq.	results	score	ethical conseq.	results	score
SUCCESS CASES					
"To hurt somebody."					
anger	13.01/54.1	0.24	penalty/ punishment	4.01/7.1	0.565
fear	12.01/54.1	0.22			
sadness	11.01/54.1	0.2			
"To kill one's own mother."					
sadness	9.01/35.1	0.26	penalty/ punishment	5.01/5.1	0.982
surprise	6.01/35.1	0.17			
anger	5.01/35.1	0.14			
"To steal an apple."					
surprise	2.01/6.1	0.33	reprimand/ scold	3.01/3.1	0.971
anger	2.01/6.1	0.33			
"To steal money."					
anger	3.01/9.1	0.33	penalty/punish.	3.01/6.1	0.493
sadness	2.01/9.1	0.22	reprimand/sco.	2.01/6.1	0.330
"To kill an animal."					
dislike	7.01/23.1	0.3	penalty/ punishment	36.01/45.1	0.798
sadness	5.01/23.1	0.22			
"To drive after drinking."					
fear	6.01/19.1	0.31	penalty/punish.	24.01/36.1	0.665
"To cause a war."					
dislike	7.01/15.1	0.46	illegal	2.01/3.1	0.648
fear	3.01/15.1	0.2			
"To stop a war."					
joy	6.01/13.1	0.46	forgiven	1.01/1.1	0.918
surprise	2.01/13.1	0.15			
"To prostitute oneself."					
anger	6.01/19.1	0.31	illegal	12.01/19.1	0.629
sadness	5.01/19.1	0.26			
"To have an affair."					
sadness	10,01/35.1	0.29	penalty/punish.	8.01/11.1	0.722
anger	9.01/35.1	0.26			
INCONSISTENCY BETWEEN EMOTIONS AND ETHICS					
"To kill a president."					
joy	2.01/4.1	0.49	penalty/ punishment	2.01/2.1	0.957
likeness	1.01/4.1	0.25			
"To kill a criminal."					
joy	8.01/39.1	0.2	penalty/ punishment	556/561	0.991
excite	8.01/39.1	0.2			
anger	7.01/39.1	0.18			
CONTEXT DEPENDENT					
"To act violently."					
anger	4.01/11.1	0.36	penalty/punish.	1.01/2.1	0.481
fear	2.01/11.1	0.18	agreement	1.01/2.1	0.481
NO ETHICAL CONSEQUENCES					
"Sky is blue."					
joy	51.01/110,1	0.46	none	0	0
sadness	21.01/110,1	0.19			

How to Evaluate Opinionated Keyphrase Extraction?

Gábor Berend
University of Szeged
Department of Informatics
Árpád tér 2., Szeged, Hungary
berendg@inf.u-szeged.hu

Veronika Vincze
Hungarian Academy of Sciences
Research Group on Artificial Intelligence
Tisza Lajos krt. 103., Szeged, Hungary
vinczev@inf.u-szeged.hu

Abstract

Evaluation often denotes a key issue in semantics- or subjectivity-related tasks. Here we discuss the difficulties of evaluating opinionated keyphrase extraction. We present our method to reduce the subjectivity of the task and to alleviate the evaluation process and we also compare the results of human and machine-based evaluation.

1 Introduction

Evaluation is a key issue in natural language processing (NLP) tasks. Although for more basic tasks such as tokenization or morphological parsing, the level of ambiguity and subjectivity is essentially lower than for higher-level tasks such as question answering or machine translation, it is still an open question to find a satisfactory solution for the (automatic) evaluation of certain tasks. Here we present the difficulties of finding an appropriate way of evaluating a highly semantics- and subjectivity-related task, namely opinionated keyphrase extraction.

There has been a growing interest in the NLP treatment of subjectivity and sentiment analysis – see e.g. Balahur et al. (2011) – on the one hand and on keyphrase extraction (Kim et al., 2010) on the other hand. The tasks themselves are demanding for automatic systems due to the variety of the linguistic ways people can express the same linguistic content. Here we focus on the evaluation of subjective information mining through the example of assigning opinionated keyphrases to product reviews and compare the results of human- and machine-based evaluation on finding opinionated keyphrases.

2 Related Work

As the task we aim at involves extracting keyphrases that are responsible for the author's opinion toward the product, aspects of both keyphrase extraction and opinion mining determine our methodology and evaluation procedure. There are several sentiment analysis approaches that make use of manually annotated review datasets (Zhuang et al., 2006; Li et al., 2010; Jang and Shin, 2010) and Wei and Gulla (2010) constructed a sentiment ontology tree in which attributes of the product and sentiments were paired.

For evaluating scientific keyphrase extraction, several methods have traditionally been applied. In the case of exact match, the gold standard keywords must be in perfect overlap with the extracted keywords (Witten et al., 1999; Frank et al., 1999) – also followed in the SemEval-2010 task on keyphrase extraction (Kim et al., 2010), while in other cases, approximate matches or semantically similar keyphrases are also accepted (Zesch and Gurevych, 2009; Medelyan et al., 2009). In this work we applied the former approach for the evaluation of opinion phrases and made a thorough comparison with the human judgement.

Here, we use the framework introduced in Berend (2011) and conducted further experiments based on it to point out the characteristics of the evaluation of opinionated keyphrase extraction. Here we pinpoint the severe differences in performance measures when the output is evaluated by humans compared to strict exact match principles and also examine the benefit of hand-annotated corpus as opposed to an automatically crawled one. In addition, the extent to which original author keyphrases resemble those of independent readers' is also investigated in this paper.

3 Methodology

In our experiments, we used the methodology described in Berend (2011) to extract opinionated keyphrase candidates from the reviews. The system treats it as a supervised classification task using Maximum Entropy classifier, in which certain n-grams of the product reviews are treated as classification instances and the task is to classify them as proper or improper ones. It incorporates a rich feature set, relying on the usage of SentiWordNet (Esuli et al., 2010) and further orthological, morphological and syntactic features. Next, we present the difficulties of opinionated keyphrase extraction and offer our solutions to the emerging problems.

3.1 Author keyphrases

In order to find relevant keyphrases in the texts, first the reviews have to be segmented into analyzable parts. We made use of the dataset described in Berend (2011), which contains 2000 product reviews each from two quite different domains, i.e. mobile phone and video film reviews from the review portal `epinions.com`. In the free-text parts of the reviews, the author describes his subjective feelings and views towards the product, and in the sections *Pros and cons* and *Bottomline* he summarizes the advantages and disadvantages of the product, usually by providing some keyphrases or short sentences. However, these pros and cons are noisy since some authors entered full sentences while others just wrote phrases or keywords. Furthermore, the segmentation also differs from review to review or even within the same review (comma, semicolon, ampersand etc.). There are also non-informative comments such as *none* among cons. For the above reasons, the identification of the appropriate gold standard phrases is not unequivocal.

We had to refine the pros and cons of the reviews so that we could have access to a less noisy database. Refinement included segmenting pros and cons into keyphrase-like units and also bringing complex phrases into their semantically equivalent, yet much simpler forms, e.g. instead of *'even I found the phones menus to be confusing'*, we would like to have *'confusing phones menus'*. Refinement was carried out both automatically by using hand-crafted transformation rules (based on POS patterns and parse trees) and manual inspection. The annotation guidelines for the human refinement and various statistics on the dataset can be accessed at `http://rgai.inf.u-szeged.hu/proCon`.

	$Auth.$	Ann_1	Ann_2	Ann_3
$Auth.$	–	0.415	0.324	0.396
Ann_1	0.601	–	0.679	0.708
Ann_2	0.454	0.702	–	0.713
Ann_3	0.525	0.690	0.688	–

Table 1: Inter-annotator agreement among the author's and annotators' sets of opinion phrases. Elements above and under the main diagonal refer to the agreement rates in Dice coefficient for pro and con phrases, respectively.

3.2 Annotator keyphrases

The second problem with regard to opinionated keyphrase extraction is the subjectivity of the task. Different people may have different opinions on the very same product, which is often reflected in their reviews. On the other hand, people can gather different information from the very same review due to differences in interpretation, which again complicates the way of proper evaluation.

In order to evaluate the difficulty of identifying opinion-related keyphrases, we decided to apply the following methodology. We selected 25 reviews related to the mobile phone Nokia 6610, which were also collected from the website `epinions.com`. The task for three linguists was to write positive and negative aspects of the product in the form of keyphrases, similar to the original pros and cons. In order not to be influenced by the keyphrases given by the author of the review, the annotators were only given the free-text part of the review, i.e. the original *Pros and cons* and *Bottomline* sections were removed. In this way, three different pro and con annotations were produced for each review, besides, those of the original author were also at hand. The inter-annotator agreement rate is in Table 1.

Concerning the subjectivity of the task, pro and con phrases provided by the three annotators and

Eval	Ref	Top-5	Top-10	Top-15
$3Ann_\cup$	man	32.14	44.66	53.92
$3Ann_\cup$	auto	27.68	38.17	45.78
$Merged_\cup$	man	28.52	41.09	52.18
$Merged_\cup$	auto	27.39	37.67	46.34
$3Ann_\cap$	man	34.89	43.31	44.92
$3Ann_\cap$	auto	29.96	34.34	35.54
$Merged_\cap$	man	24.75	26.12	22.22
$Merged_\cap$	auto	21.39	20.94	21.89
$Author$	man	27.14	33.5	35.24
$Author$	auto	20.61	22.34	25.03

Table 2: F-scores of the human evaluation of the automatically extracted opinion phrases. Columns Eval and Ref show the way gold standard phrases were obtained and if they were refined manually or automatically.

the original author showed a great degree of variety although they had access to the very same review. Sometimes it happened that one annotator did not give any pro or con phrases for a review whereas the others listed a bunch of them, which reflects that the very same feature can be judged as still tolerable, neutral or absolutely negative for different people. Thus, as even human annotations may differ from each other to a great extent, it is not unequivocal to decide which human annotation should be regarded as the gold standard upon evaluation.

3.3 Evaluation methodology

Since the comparison of annotations highlighted the subjectivity of the task, we voted for smoothing the divergences of annotations. We wanted to take into account all the available annotations which were manually prepared and regarded as acceptable. Thus, an annotator formed the union and the intersection of the pro and con features given by each annotator either including or excluding those defined by the original author. With this, we aimed at eliminating subjectivity since in the case of union, every keyphrase mentioned by at least one annotator was taken into consideration while in the case of intersection, it is possible to detect keyphrases that seem to be the most salient for the annotators as regards the given document. Thus, four sets of pros and cons were finally yielded for each review depending on whether the unions or intersections were determined purely on the phrases of the annotators excluding the original phrases of the author or including them. The following example illustrates the way new sets were created based on the input sets (in italics):

Pro_1: *radio, organizer, phone book*
Pro_2: *radio, organizer, loudspeaker*
Pro_3: *radio, organizer, calendar*
Union: radio, organizer, calendar, loudspeaker, phone book
Intersection: radio, organizer
Pro_{author}: *clear, fun*
Merged_Union: radio, organizer, calendar, loudspeaker, phone book, clear, fun
Merged_Intersection: $\emptyset$

The reason behind this methodology was that it made it possible to evaluate our automatic methods in two different ways. Comparing the automatic keyphrases to the union of human annotations means that a bigger number of keyphrases is to be identified, however, with a bigger number of gold standard keywords it is more probable that the automatic keywords occur among them. At the same time having a larger set of gold standard tags might affect the recall negatively since there are more keyphrases to return. On the other hand, in the case of intersection it can be measured whether the most important features (i.e. those that every annotator felt relevant) can be extracted from the text. Note that our strategy is similar to the one applied in the case of BLEU/ROUGE score (Papineni et al., 2002; Lin, 2004) with respect to the fact that multiple good solutions are taken into account whereas the application of union and intersection is determined by the nature of the task: different annotators may attach several outputs (in other words, different numbers of keyphrases) to the same document in the case of keyphrase extraction, which is not realistic in the case of machine translation or summarization (only one output is offered for each sentence / text).

3.4 Results

In our experiments, we used the opinion phrase extraction system based on the paper of Berend (2011). Results vary whether the manually or the automatically refined set of the original sets of pros and cons were regarded as positive training examples and also whether the evaluation was carried out

	Mobiles			Movies		
A/A	9.95	9.55	8.61	7.58	7.1	6.24
A/M	13.51	12.73	11.2	9.95	9.05	7.72
M/A	10.15	9.7	8.69	7.52	6.92	5.97
M/M	15.27	14.11	12.17	12.22	10.63	8.67

Table 3: F-scores achieved with different keyphrase refinement strategies. A and M as the first (second) character indicate the fact that the training (testing) was based on the automatically and manually defined sets of gold standard expressions, respectively.

against purely the original set of author-assigned keyphrases or the intersection/union of the manual annotations including and excluding the author-assigned keyphrases on the 25 mobile phone reviews. Results of the various combinations in the experiments for the top 5, 10 and 15 keyphrases are reported in Table 2 containing both cases when human and automatic refinement of the gold standard opinion phrases were carried out. Automatic keyphrases were manually compared to the above mentioned sets of keyphrases, i.e. human annotators judged them as acceptable or not. Human evaluation had the advantage over automated ones, that they could accept the extracted term '*MP3*' when there was only its mistyped version '*MP+*' in the set of gold standard phrases (as found in the dataset).

Table 3 presents the results of our experiments on keyphrase refinement on the mobiles and movies domains. In these settings strict matches were required instead of human evaluation. Results differ with respect to the fact whether the automatically or manually refined sets of the original author phrases were utilized for training and during the strict evaluation. Having conducted these experiments, we could examine the possibility of a fully automatic system that needs no manually inspected training data, but it can create it automatically as well.

4 Discussion and conclusions

Both human and automatic evaluation reveal that the results yielded when the system was trained on manually refined keyphrases are better. The usage of manually refined keyphrases as the training set leads to better results (the difference being 5.9 F-score on average), which argues for human annotation as opposed to automatic normalization of the gold standard opinion phrases. Note, however, that even though results obtained with the automatic refinement of training instances tend to stay below the results that are obtained with the manual refinement of gold standard phrases, they are still comparable, which implies that with more sophisticated rules, training data could be automatically generated.

If the inter-annotator agreement rates are compared, it can be seen that the agreement rates between the annotators are considerably higher than those between a linguist and the author of the product review. This may be due to the fact that the linguists were to conform to the annotation guidelines whereas the keyphrases given by the authors of the reviews were not limited in any way. Still, it can be observed that among the author-annotator agreement rates, the con phrases could reach higher agreement than the pro phrases. This can be due to psychological reasons: people usually expect things to be good hence they do not list all the features that are good (since they should be good by nature), in contrast, they list negative features because this is what deviates from the normal expectations.

In this paper, we discussed the difficulties of evaluating opinionated keyphrase extraction and also conducted experiments to investigate the extent of overlap between the keyphrases determined by the original author of a review and those assigned by independent readers. To reduce the subjectivity of the task and to alleviate the evaluation process, we presented our method that employs several independent annotators and we also compared the results of human and machine-based evaluation. Our results reveal that for now, human evaluation leads to better results, however, we believe that the proper treatment of polar expressions and ambiguous adjectives might improve automatic evaluation among others.

Besides describing the difficulties of the automatic evaluation of opinionated keyphrase extraction, the impact of training on automatically crawled gold standard opinionated phrases was investigated. Although not surprisingly they lag behind the ones obtained based on manually refined training data, the automatic creation of gold standard keyphrases can be a much cheaper, yet feasible option to manually refined opinion phrases. In the future, we plan to reduce the gap between manual and automatic evaluation of opinionated keyphrase extraction.

Acknowledgments

This work was supported in part by the NIH grant (project codename MASZEKER) of the Hungarian government.

References

Alexandra Balahur, Ester Boldrini, Andres Montoyo, and Patricio Martinez-Barco, editors. 2011. *Proceedings of the 2nd Workshop on Computational Approaches to Subjectivity and Sentiment Analysis (WASSA 2.011)*. ACL, Portland, Oregon, June.

Gábor Berend. 2011. Opinion expression mining by exploiting keyphrase extraction. In *Proceedings of 5th International Joint Conference on Natural Language Processing*, pages 1162–1170, Chiang Mai, Thailand, November. Asian Federation of Natural Language Processing.

Andrea Esuli, Stefano Baccianella, and Fabrizio Sebastiani. 2010. Sentiwordnet 3.0: An enhanced lexical resource for sentiment analysis and opinion mining. In *Proceedings of the Seventh conference on International Language Resources and Evaluation (LREC'10)*, Valletta, Malta, May. European Language Resources Association (ELRA).

Eibe Frank, Gordon W. Paynter, Ian H. Witten, Carl Gutwin, and Craig G. Nevill-Manning. 1999. Domain-specific keyphrase extraction. In *Proceeding of 16th International Joint Conference on Artificial Intelligence*, pages 668–673. Morgan Kaufmann Publishers.

Hayeon Jang and Hyopil Shin. 2010. Language-specific sentiment analysis in morphologically rich languages. In *Coling 2010: Posters*, pages 498–506, Beijing, China, August. Coling 2010 Organizing Committee.

Su Nam Kim, Olena Medelyan, Min-Yen Kan, and Timothy Baldwin. 2010. Semeval-2010 task 5: Automatic keyphrase extraction from scientific articles. In *Proceedings of the 5th International Workshop on Semantic Evaluation*, SemEval '10, pages 21–26, Morristown, NJ, USA. ACL.

Fangtao Li, Chao Han, Minlie Huang, Xiaoyan Zhu, Ying-Ju Xia, Shu Zhang, and Hao Yu. 2010. Structure-aware review mining and summarization. In *Proceedings of the 23rd International Conference on Computational Linguistics (Coling 2010)*, pages 653–661, Beijing, China, August. Coling 2010 Organizing Committee.

Chin-Yew Lin. 2004. Rouge: A package for automatic evaluation of summaries. In Stan Szpakowicz Marie-Francine Moens, editor, *Text Summarization Branches Out: Proceedings of the ACL-04 Workshop*, pages 74–81, Barcelona, Spain, July. ACL.

Olena Medelyan, Eibe Frank, and Ian H. Witten. 2009. Human-competitive tagging using automatic keyphrase extraction. In *Proceedings of the 2009 Conference on Empirical Methods in Natural Language Processing*, pages 1318–1327, Singapore, August. ACL.

Kishore Papineni, Salim Roukos, Todd Ward, and Wei-Jing Zhu. 2002. Bleu: a method for automatic evaluation of machine translation. In *Proceedings of 40th Annual Meeting of the ACL*, pages 311–318, Philadelphia, Pennsylvania, USA, July. ACL.

Wei Wei and Jon Atle Gulla. 2010. Sentiment learning on product reviews via sentiment ontology tree. In *Proceedings of the 48th Annual Meeting of the ACL*, pages 404–413, Uppsala, Sweden, July. ACL.

Ian H. Witten, Gordon W. Paynter, Eibe Frank, Carl Gutwin, and Craig G. Nevill-Manning. 1999. Kea: Practical automatic keyphrase extraction. In *ACM DL*, pages 254–255.

Torsten Zesch and Iryna Gurevych. 2009. Approximate Matching for Evaluating Keyphrase Extraction. In *Proceedings of the 7th International Conference on Recent Advances in Natural Language Processing*, pages 484–489, September.

Li Zhuang, Feng Jing, and Xiao-Yan Zhu. 2006. Movie review mining and summarization. In *Proceedings of the 15th ACM international conference on Information and knowledge management*, CIKM '06, pages 43–50, New York, NY, USA. ACM.

Semantic frames as an anchor representation for sentiment analysis

Josef Ruppenhofer
Department of Information Science
and Natural Language Processing
University of Hildesheim, Germany
ruppenho@uni-hildesheim.de

Ines Rehbein
SFB 632: Information Structure
German Department
Potsdam University, Germany
irehbein@uni-potsdam.de

Abstract

Current work on sentiment analysis is characterized by approaches with a pragmatic focus, which use shallow techniques in the interest of robustness but often rely on ad-hoc creation of data sets and methods. We argue that progress towards deep analysis depends on a) enriching shallow representations with linguistically motivated, rich information, and b) focussing different branches of research and combining ressources to create synergies with related work in NLP. In the paper, we propose SentiFrameNet, an extension to FrameNet, as a novel representation for sentiment analysis that is tailored to these aims.

1 Introduction

Sentiment analysis has made a lot of progress on more coarse-grained analysis levels using shallow techniques. However, recent years have seen a trend towards more fine-grained and ambitious analyses requiring more linguistic knowledge and more complex statistical models. Recent work has tried to produce relatively detailed summaries of opinions expressed in news texts (Stoyanov and Cardie, 2011); to assess the impact of quotations from business leaders on stock prices (Drury et al., 2011); to detect implicit sentiment (Balahur et al., 2011); etc. Accordingly, we can expect that greater demands will be made on the amount of linguistic knowledge, its representation, and the evaluation of systems.

Against this background, we argue that it is worthwhile to complement the existing shallow and pragmatic approaches with a deep, lexical-semantics based one in order to enable deeper analysis. We report on ongoing work in constructing SentiFrameNet, an extension of FrameNet (Baker et al., 1998) offering a novel representation for sentiment analysis based on frame semantics.

2 Shallow and pragmatic approaches

Current approaches to sentiment analysis are mainly pragmatically oriented, without giving equal weight to semantics. One aspect concerns the identification of sentiment-bearing expressions. The annotations in the MPQA corpus (Wiebe et al., 2005), for instance, were created without limiting what annotators can annotate in terms of syntax or lexicon. While this serves the spirit of discovering the variety of opinion expressions in actual contexts, it makes it difficult to match opinion expressions when using the corpus as an evaluation dataset as the same or similar structures may be treated differently. A similar challenge lies in distinguishing so-called polar facts from inherently sentiment-bearing expressions. For example, out of context, one would not associate any of the words in the sentence *Wages are high in Switzerland* with a particular evaluative meaning. In specific contexts, however, we may take the sentence as reason to either think positively or negatively of Switzerland: employees receiving wages may be drawn to Switzerland, while employers paying wages may view this state of affairs negatively. As shown by the inter-annotator agreement results reported by (Toprak et al., 2010), agreement on distinguishing polar facts from inherently evaluative language is low. Unsurprisingly, many efforts at automatically building up sentiment lexica simply harvest expressions that frequently occur as part of polar facts without resolving whether the subjectivity clues extracted are inherently evaluative or merely associated with statements of polar fact.

Pragmatic considerations also lead to certain expressions of sentiment or opinion being excluded from analysis. (Seki, 2007), for instance, annotated sentences as "not opinionated" if they contain indirect hearsay evidence or widely held opinions.

In the case of targets, the work by (Stoyanov and Cardie, 2008) exhibits a pragmatic focus as well. These authors distinguish between (a) the **topic** of a fine-grained opinion, defined as the real-world object, event or abstract entity that is the subject of the opinion as *intended* by the opinion holder; (b) the **topic span** associated with an opinion expression is the closest, minimal span of text that mentions the topic; and (c) the **target span** defined as the span of text that covers the syntactic surface form comprising the contents of the opinion. As the definitions show, (Stoyanov and Cardie, 2008) focus on text-level, pragmatic relevance by paying attention to what the author intends, rather than concentrating on the explicit syntactic dependent (their target span) as the topic. This pragmatic focus is also in evidence in (Wilson, 2008)'s work on contextual polarity classification, which uses features in the classification that are syntactically independent of the opinion expression such as the number of subjectivity clues in adjoining sentences.

Among lexicon-driven approaches, we find that despite arguments that word sense distinctions are important to sentiment analysis (Wiebe and Mihalcea, 2006), often-used resources do not take them into account and new resources are still being created which operate on the more shallow lemma-level (e.g. (Neviarouskaya et al., 2009)). Further, most lexical resources do not adequately represent cases where multiple opinions are tied to one expression and where presuppositions and temporal structure come into play. An example is the verb *despoil*: there is a positive opinion by the reporter about the despoiled entity in its former state, a negative opinion about its present state, and (inferrable) negative sentiment towards the despoiler. In most resources, the positive opinion will not be represented.

The most common approach to the task is an information extraction-like pipeline. Expressions of opinion, sources and targets are often dealt with separately, possibly using separate resources. Some work such as (Kim and Hovy, 2006) has explored the connection to role labeling. One reason not to pursue this is that "in many practical situations, the annotation beyond opinion holder labeling is too expensive" (Wiegand, 2010, p.121). (Shaikh et al., 2007) use semantic dependencies and composition rules for sentence-level sentiment scoring but do not deal with source and target extraction. The focus on robust partial solutions, however, prevents the creation of an integrated high-quality resource.

3 The extended frame-semantic approach

We now sketch a view of sentiment analysis on the basis of an appropriately extended model of frame semantic representation.[1]

Link to semantic frames and roles Since the possible sources and targets of opinion are usually identical to a predicate's semantic roles, we add *opinion frames* with slots for Source, Target, Polarity and Intensity to the FrameNet database. We map the Source and Target opinion roles to semantic roles as appropriate, which enables us to use semantic role labeling systems in the identification of opinion roles (Ruppenhofer et al., 2008).

In SentiFrameNet all lexical units (LUs) that are inherently evaluative are associated with *opinion frames*. The language of polar facts is not associated with opinion frames. However, we show in the longer version of this paper (cf. footnote 1) how we support certain types of inferred sentiment. With regard to targets, our representation selects as targets of opinion the target spans of (Stoyanov and Cardie, 2008) rather than their opinion topics (see Section 2). For us, opinion topics that do not coincide with target spans are inferential opinion targets.

Formal diversity of opinion expressions For fine-grained sentiment-analysis, handling the full variety of opinion expressions is indispensable. While adjectives in particular have often been found to be very useful cues for automatic sentiment analysis (Wiebe, 2000; Benamara et al., 2007), evaluative meaning pervades all major lexical classes. There are many subjective multi-words and idioms such as *give away the store* and evaluative meaning also attaches to grammatical constructions, even ones without obligatory lexical material. An exam-

[1]We present a fuller account of our ideas in an unpublished longer version of this paper, available from the authors' websites.

ple is the construction exemplified by *Him be a doctor?* The so-called *What, me worry?*-construction (Fillmore, 1989) consists only of an NP and an infinitive phrase. Its rhetorical effect is to express the speaker's surprise or incredulity about the proposition under consideration. The FrameNet database schema accommodates not only single and multiwords but also handles data for a constructicon (Fillmore et al., to appear) that pairs grammatical constructions with meanings.

Multiple opinions We need to accommodate multiple opinions relating to the same predicate as in the case of *despoil* mentioned above. Predicates with multiple opinions are not uncommon: in a 100-item random sample taken from the Pittsburgh subjectivity clues, 17 involved multiple opinions.

The use of opinion frames as described above enables us to readily represent multiple opinions. For instance, the verb *brag* in the modified *Bragging* frame has two opinion frames. The first one has positive polarity and represents the frame-internal point of view. The SPEAKER is the Source relative to the TOPIC as the Target. The second opinion frame has negative polarity, representing the reporter's point of view. The SPEAKER is the Target but the Source is unspecified, indicating that it needs to be resolved to an embedded source. For a similar representation of multiple opinions in a Dutch lexical resource, see (Maks and Vossen, 2011).

Event structure and presuppositions A complete representation of subjectivity needs to include event and presuppositional structure. This is necessary, for instance, for predicates like *come around (on)* in (1), which involve changes of opinion relative to the *same* target by the *same* source. Without the possibility of distinguishing between attitudes held at different times, the sentiment associated with these predicates cannot be modeled adequately.

(1) Newsom is still against extending weekday metering to evenings, but has COME AROUND on Sunday enforcement.

For *come around (on)*, we want to to distinguish its semantics from that of predicates such as *ambivalent* and *conflicted*, where a COGNIZER *simultaneously* holds opposing valuations of (aspects of) a target. Following FrameNet's practice, we model presupposed knowledge explicitly in SentiFrameNet by

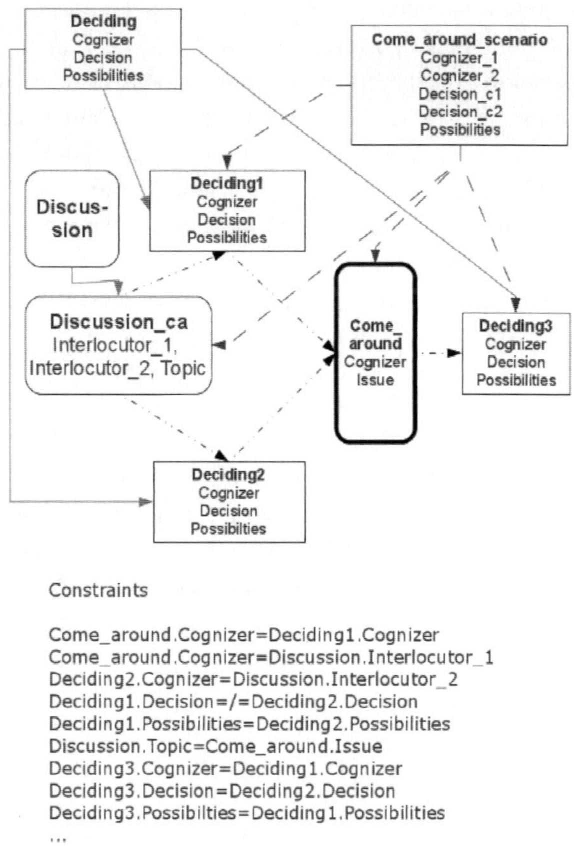

Figure 1: Frame analysis for "Come around"

using additional frames and frame relations. A partial analysis of *come around* is sketched in Figure 1.

We use the newly added *Come around scenario* frame as a background frame that ties together all the information we have about instances of coming around. Indicated by the dashed lines are the SUBFRAMES of the scenario. Among them are three instances of the *Deciding* frame (solid lines), all related temporally (dashed-dotted) and in terms of content to an ongoing *Discussion*. The initial difference of opinion is encoded by the fact that *Deciding*1 and *Deciding*2 share the same POSSIBILITIES but differ in the DECISION. The occurrence of *Come_around* leads to *Deciding*3, which has the same COGNIZER as *Deciding*1 but its DECISION is now identical to that in *Deciding*2, which has been unchanged. The sentiment information we need is encoded by simply stating that there is a sentiment of positive polarity of the COGNIZER (as source) towards the DECISION (as target) in the *Deciding* frame. (This opinion frame is not displayed in the graphic.) The *Come around* frame itself is not associated with sentiment information, which seems right given that it does not include a DECISION as a frame element but only includes the ISSUE.

For a discussion of how SentiFrameNet captures factuality presuppositions by building on (Saurí, 2008)'s work on event factuality, we refer the interested reader to the longer version of the paper.

Modulation, coercion and composition Speakers can shift the valence or polarity of sentiment-bearing expressions through some kind of negation operator, or intensify or attenuate the impact of an expression. Despite these interacting influences, it is desirable to have at least a partial ordering among predicates related to the same semantic scale; we want to be able to find out from our resource that *good* is less positive than *excellent*, while there may be no ordering between *terrific* and *excellent*. In SentiFrameNet, an ordering between the polarity strength values of different lexical units is added on the level of frames.

The frame semantic approach also offers new perspectives on sentiment composition. We can, for instance, recognize cases of presupposed sentiment, as in the case of the noun *revenge*, which are not amenable to shifting by negation: *She did not take revenge* does not imply that there is no negative evaluation of some injury inflicted by an offender.

Further, many cases of what has been called valence shifting for us are cases where the evaluation is wholly contained in a predicate.

(2) Just barely AVOIDED an accident today.

(3) I had served the bank for 22 years and had AVOIDED a promotion since I feared that I would be transferred out of Chennai city.

If we viewed *avoid* as a polarity shifter and further treated nouns like *promotion* and *accident* as sentiment-bearing (rather than treating them as denoting events that affect somebody positively or negatively) we should expect that while (2) has positive sentiment, (3) has negative sentiment. But that is not so: accomplished intentional avoiding is always positive for the avoider. Also, the reversal analysis for *avoid* cannot deal with complements that have no inherent polarity. It readily follows from the coercion analysis that *I avoid running into her* is negative but that cannot be derived in e.g. (Moilanen and Pulman, 2007)'s compositional model which takes into account inherent lexical polarity, which *run (into)* lacks. The fact that *avoid* imposes a negative evaluation by its subject on its object can easily be modeled using opinion frames.

4 Impact and Conclusions

Deep analysis Tying sentiment analysis to frame semantics enables immediate access to a deeper lexical semantics. Given particular application-interests, for instance, identifying statements of uncertainty, frames and lexical units relevant to the task can be pulled out easily from the general resource. A frame-based treatment also improves over resources such as SentiWordNet (Baccianella et al., 2008), which, while representing word meanings, lacks any representation of semantic roles.

Theoretical insights New research questions await, among them: whether predicates with multiple opinions can be distinguished automatically from ones with only one, and whether predicates carrying factivity or other sentiment-related presuppositions can be discovered automatically. Further, our approach lets us ask how contextual sentiment is, and how much of the analysis of pragmatic annotations can be derived from lexical and syntactic knowledge.

Evaluation With a frame-based representation, the units of annotation are pre-defined by a general frame semantic inventory and systems can readily know what kind of units to target as potential opinion-bearing expressions. Once inherent semantics and pragmatics are distinguished, the correctness of inferred (pragmatic) targets and the polarity towards them can be weighted differently from that of immediate (semantic) targets and their polarity.

Synergy On our approach, lexically inherent sentiment information need not be annotated, it can be imported automatically once the semantic frame's roles are annotated. Only pragmatic information needs to be labeled manually. By expanding the FrameNet inventory and creating annotations, we improve a lexical resource and create role-semantic annotationsas well as doing sentiment analysis.

We have proposed SentiFrameNet as a linguistically sound, deep representation for sentiment analysis, extending an existing resource. Our approach complements pragmatic approaches, allows us to join forces with related work in NLP (e.g. role labeling, event factuality) and enables new insights into the theoretical foundations of sentiment analysis.

References

S. Baccianella, A. Esuli, and F. Sebastiani. 2008. SENTIWORDNET 3.0: An enhanced lexical resource for sentiment analysis and opinion mining. In *Proceedings of the Seventh conference on International Language Resources and Evaluation LREC10*, pages 2200–2204. European Language Resources Association (ELRA).

Collin F. Baker, Charles J. Fillmore, and John B. Lowe. 1998. The Berkeley Framenet Project. In *Proceedings of the 36th Annual Meeting of the Association for Computational Linguistics and 17th International Conference on Computational Linguistics-Volume 1*, pages 86–90. Association for Computational Linguistics.

Alexandra Balahur, Jesús M. Hermida, and Andrés Montoyo. 2011. Detecting implicit expressions of sentiment in text based on commonsense knowledge. In *Proceedings of the 2nd Workshop on Computational Approaches to Subjectivity and Sentiment Analysis (WASSA 2.011)*, pages 53–60, Portland, Oregon, June. Association for Computational Linguistics.

Farah Benamara, Sabatier Irit, Carmine Cesarano, Napoli Federico, and Diego Reforgiato. 2007. Sentiment analysis : Adjectives and adverbs are better than adjectives alone. *In Proc of Int Conf on Weblogs and Social Media*, pages 1–4.

Brett Drury, Gaël Dias, and Luís Torgo. 2011. A contextual classification strategy for polarity analysis of direct quotations from financial news. In *Proceedings of the International Conference Recent Advances in Natural Language Processing 2011*, pages 434–440, Hissar, Bulgaria, September. RANLP 2011 Organising Committee.

Charles J. Fillmore, Russell Lee-Goldman, and Russell Rhodes, to appear. *Sign-based Construction Grammar*, chapter The FrameNet Constructicon. CSLI, Stanford, CA.

Charles J. Fillmore. 1989. Grammatical construction theory and the familiar dichotomies. In R. Dietrich and C.F. Graumann, editors, *Language processing in social context*, pages 17–38. North-Holland/Elsevier, Amsterdam.

S.M. Kim and E. Hovy. 2006. Extracting opinions, opinion holders, and topics expressed in online news media text. In *Proceedings of the Workshop on Sentiment and Subjectivity in Text*, pages 1–8. Association for Computational Linguistics.

Isa Maks and Piek Vossen. 2011. A verb lexicon model for deep sentiment analysis and opinion mining applications. In *Proceedings of the 2nd Workshop on Computational Approaches to Subjectivity and Sentiment Analysis (WASSA 2.011)*, pages 10–18, Portland, Oregon, June. Association for Computational Linguistics.

Karo Moilanen and Stephen Pulman. 2007. Sentiment composition. In *Proceedings of RANLP 2007*, Borovets, Bulgaria.

A. Neviarouskaya, H. Prendinger, and M. Ishizuka. 2009. Sentiful: Generating a reliable lexicon for sentiment analysis. In *Affective Computing and Intelligent Interaction and Workshops, 2009. ACII 2009. 3rd International Conference on*, pages 1–6. Ieee.

J. Ruppenhofer, S. Somasundaran, and J. Wiebe. 2008. Finding the sources and targets of subjective expressions. In *LREC*, Marrakech, Morocco.

Roser Saurí. 2008. *A Factuality Profiler for Eventualities in Text*. Ph.d., Brandeis University.

Yohei Seki. 2007. Crosslingual opinion extraction from author and authority viewpoints at ntcir-6. In *Proceedings of NTCIR-6 Workshop Meeting*, Tokyo, Japan.

Mostafa Shaikh, Helmut Prendinger, and Ishizuka Mitsuru. 2007. Assessing sentiment of text by semantic dependency and contextual valence analysis. *Affective Computing and Intelligent Interaction*, pages 191–202.

Veselin Stoyanov and Claire Cardie. 2008. Topic identification for fine-grained opinion analysis. In *Proceedings of the 22nd International Conference on Computational Linguistics - Volume 1*, COLING '08, pages 817–824, Stroudsburg, PA, USA. Association for Computational Linguistics.

Veselin Stoyanov and Claire Cardie. 2011. Automatically creating general-purpose opinion summaries from text. In *Proceedings of RANLP 2011*, pages 202–209, Hissar, Bulgaria, September.

Cigdem Toprak, Niklas Jakob, and Iryna Gurevych. 2010. Sentence and expression level annotation of opinions in user-generated discourse. In *Proceedings of ACL-10, the 48th Annual Meeting of the Association for Computational Linguistics*, Portland. Association for Computational Linguistics.

Janyce Wiebe and Rada Mihalcea. 2006. Word sense and subjectivity. In *Proceedings of the 21st International Conference on Computational Linguistics and the 44th annual meeting of the Association for Computational Linguistics*, ACL-44, pages 1065–1072, Stroudsburg, PA, USA. Association for Computational Linguistics.

Janyce Wiebe, Theresa Wilson, and Claire Cardie. 2005. Annotating expressions of opinions and emotions in language. *Language Resources and Evaluation*, 39(2/3):164–210.

Janyce Wiebe. 2000. Learning subjective adjectives from corpora. In *Proceedings of the Seventeenth National Conference on Artificial Intelligence (AAAI-2000)*, pages 735–740, Austin, Texas.

Michael Wiegand. 2010. *Hybrid approaches to sentiment analysis*. Ph.D. thesis, Saarland University, Saarbrücken.

Theresa Ann Wilson. 2008. *Fine-grained Subjectivity and Sentiment Analysis: Recognizing the Intensity, Polarity, and Attitudes of Private States*. Ph.D. thesis, University of Pittsburgh.

On the Impact of Sentiment and Emotion Based Features in Detecting Online Sexual Predators

Dasha Bogdanova
University of
Saint Petersburg
dasha.bogdanova
@gmail.com

Paolo Rosso
NLE Lab - ELiRF
Universitat
Politècnica de València
prosso@dsic.upv.es

Thamar Solorio
CoRAL Lab
University of
Alabama at Birmingham
solorio@cis.uab.edu

Abstract

According to previous work on pedophile psychology and cyberpedophilia, sentiments and emotions in texts could be a good clue to detect online sexual predation. In this paper, we have suggested a list of high-level features, including sentiment and emotion based ones, for detection of online sexual predation. In particular, since pedophiles are known to be emotionally unstable, we were interested in investigating if emotion-based features could help in their detection. We have used a corpus of predators' chats with pseudo-victims downloaded from www.perverted-justice.com and two negative datasets of different nature: cybersex logs available online and the NPS chat corpus. Naive Bayes classification based on the proposed features achieves accuracies of up to 94% while baseline systems of word and character n-grams can only reach up to 72%.

1 Introduction

Child sexual abuse and pedophilia are both problems of great social concern. On the one hand, law enforcement is working on prosecuting and preventing child sexual abuse. On the other hand, psychologists and mental specialists are investigating the phenomenon of pedophilia. Even though the pedophilia has been studied from different research points, it remains to be a very important problem which requires further research, especially from the automatic detection point of view.

Previous studies report that in the majority of cases of sexual assaults the victims are underaged (Snyder, 2000). On the Internet, attempts to solicit children have become common as well. Mitchell (2001) found out that 19% of children have been sexually approached online. However, manual monitoring of each conversation is impossible, due to the massive amount of data and privacy issues. A good alternative is the development of reliable tools for detecting pedophilia in online social media is of great importance.

In this paper, we address the problem of detecting pedophiles with natural language processing (NLP) techniques. This problem becomes even more challenging because of the chat data specificity. Chat conversations are very different not only from the written text but also from other types of social media interactions, such as blogs and forums, since chatting in the Internet usually involves very fast typing. The data usually contains a large amount of mistakes, misspellings, specific slang, character flooding etc. Therefore, accurate processing of this data with automated syntactic analyzers is rather challenging.

Previous research on pedophilia reports that the expression of certain emotions in text could be helpful to detect pedophiles in social media (Egan et al., 2011). Following these insights we suggest a list of features, including sentiments as well as other content-based features. We investigate the impact of these features on the problem of automatic detection of online sexual predation. Our experimental results show that classification based on such features discriminates pedophiles from non-pedophiles with high accuracy.

The remainder of the paper is structured as follows: Section 2 overviews related work on the topic,

Section 3 outlines the profile of a pedophile based on the previous research. Our approach to the problem of detecting pedophiles in social media on the basis of high-level features is presented in Section 4. Experimental data is described in Section 5. We show the results of the conducted experiments in Section 6; they are followed by discussion and plans for future research in Section 7. We finally draw some conclusions in Section 8.

2 Related Research

The problem of automatic detection of pedophiles in social media has been rarely addressed so far. In part, this is due to the difficulties involved in having access to useful data. There is an American foundation called Perverted Justice (PJ). It investigates cases of online sexual predation: adult volunteers enter chat rooms as juveniles (usually 12-15 year old) and if they are sexually solicited by adults, they work with the police to prosecute the offenders. Some chat conversations with online sexual predators are available at www.perverted-justice.com and they have been the subject of analysis of recent research on this topic.

Pendar (2007) experimented with PJ data. He separated the lines written by pedophiles from those written by pseudo-victims and used a kNN classifier based on word n-grams to distinguish between them.

Another related research has been carried out by McGhee et al. (2011). The chat lines from PJ were manually classified into the following categories:

1. Exchange of personal information
2. Grooming
3. Approach
4. None of the listed above classes

Their experiments have shown that kNN classification achieves up to 83% accuracy and outperforms a rule-based approach.

As it was already mentioned, pedophiles often create false profiles and pretend to be younger or of another gender. Moreover, they try to copy children's behavior. Automatically detecting age and gender in chat conversations could then be the first step in detecting online predators. Peersman et al. (2011) have analyzed chats from the Belgium Netlog social network. Discrimination between those who are older than 16 from those who are younger based on a Support Vector Machine classification yields 71.3% accuracy. The accuracy is even higher when the age gap is increased (e.g. the accuracy of classifying those who are less than 16 from those who are older than 25 is 88.2%). They have also investigated the issues of the minimum amount of training data needed. Their experiments have shown that with 50% of the original dataset the accuracy remains almost the same, and with only 10% it is still much better than the random baseline performance.

NLP techniques were as well applied to capture child sexual abuse data in P2P networks (Panchenko et al., 2012). The proposed text classification system is able to predict with high accuracy if a file contains child pornography by analyzing its name and textual description.

Our work neither aims at classification of chat lines into categories as it was done by McGhee et al. (2011) nor at discriminating between victim and predator as it was done by Pendar (2007), but at distinguishing between pedophile's and not pedophile's chats, in particular, by utilizing clues provided by psychology and sentiment analysis.

3 Profiling the Pedophile

Pedophilia is a "disorder of adult personality and behavior" which is characterized by sexual interest in prepubescent children (International statistical classification of diseases and related health problems, 1988). Even though solicitation of children is not a medical diagnosis, Abel and Harlow (2001) reported that 88% of child sexual abuse cases are committed by pedophiles. Therefore, we believe that understanding behavior of pedophiles could help to detect and prevent online sexual predation. Even though an online sexual offender is not always a pedophile, in this paper we use these terms as synonyms.

Previous research reports that about 94% of sexual offenders are males. With respect to female sexual molesters, it is reported, that they tend to be young and, in these cases, men are often involved as well (Vandiver and Kercher, 2004). Sexual assault offenders are more often adults (77%), though in 23% of cases children are solicited by other juveniles.

Analysis of pedophiles' personality characterizes them with feelings of inferiority, isolation, loneliness, low self-esteem and emotional immaturity. Moreover, 60%-80% of them suffer from other psychiatric illnesses (Hall and Hall, 2007). In general, pedophiles are less emotionally stable than mentally healthy people.

3.1 Profile of the Online Sexual Predator

Hall and Hall (2007) noticed that five main types of computer-based sexual offenders can be distinguished: (1) the stalkers, who approach children in chat rooms in order to get physical access to them; (2) the cruisers, who are interested in online sexual molestation and not willing to meet children offline; (3) the masturbators, who watch child pornography; (4) the networkers or swappers, who trade information, pornography, and children; and (5) a combination of the four types. In this study we are interested in detecting stalkers (type (1)) and cruisers (type (2)).

The language sexual offenders use was analyzed by Egan et al. (2011). The authors considered the chats available from PJ. The analysis of the chats revealed several characteristics of predators' language:

- Implicit/explicit content. On the one hand, predators shift gradually to the sexual conversation, starting with more ordinary compliments:

  Predator: hey you are really cute
  Predator: u are pretty
  Predator: hi sexy

  On the other hand, the conversation then becomes overtly related to sex. They do not hide their intentions:

  Predator: can we have sex?

  Predator: you ok with sex with me and drinking?

- Fixated discourse. Predators are not willing to step aside from the sexual conversation. For example, in this conversation the predator almost ignores the question of pseudo-victim and comes back to the sex-related conversation:

  Predator: licking dont hurt
  Predator: its like u lick ice cream
  Pseudo-victim: do u care that im 13 in march and not yet? i lied a little bit b4
  Predator: its all cool
  Predator: i can lick hard

- Offenders often understand that what they are doing is not moral:

  Predator: i would help but its not moral

- They transfer responsibility to the victim:

  Pseudo-victim: what ya wanta do when u come over
  Predator: whatever–movies, games, drink, play around–it's up to you–what would you like to do?
  Pseudo-victim: that all sounds good
  Pseudo-victim: lol
  Predator: maybe get some sexy pics of you :-P
  Predator: would you let me take pictures of you? of you naked? of me and you playing? :-D

- Predators often behave as children, copying their linguistic style. Colloquialisms appear often in their messages:

  Predator: howwwww dy
  ...
  Predator: i know PITY MEEEE

- They try to minimize the risk of being prosecuted: they ask to delete chat logs and warn victims not to tell anyone about the talk:

Predator: don't tell anyone we have been talking
Pseudo-victim: k
Pseudo-victim: lol who would i tell? no one's here.
Predator: well I want it to be our secret

- Though they finally stop being cautious and insist on meeting offline:

Predator: well let me come see you
Pseudo-victim: why u want 2 come over so bad?
Predator: i wanna see you

In general Egan et al. (Egan et al., 2011) have found online solicitation to be more direct, while in real life children seduction is more deceitful.

4 Our Approach

We address the problem of automatic detection of online sexual predation. While previous studies were focused on classifying chat lines into different categories (McGheeet al., 2011) or distinguishing between offender and victim (Pendar, 2007), in this work we address the problem of detecting sexual predators.

We formulate the problem of detecting pedophiles in social media as the task of binary text categorization: given a text (a set of chat lines), the aim is to predict whether it is a case of cyberpedophilia or not.

4.1 Features

On the basis of previous analysis of pedophiles' personality (described in previous section), we consider as features those emotional markers that could unveil a certain degree of emotional instability, such as feelings of inferiority, isolation, loneliness, low self-esteem and emotional immaturity.

On the one hand, pedophiles try to be nice with a victim and make compliments, at least in the beginning of a conversation. Therefore, the use of positive words is expected. On the other hand, as it was described earlier, pedophiles tend to be emotionally unstable and prone to lose temper, hence they might start using words expressing anger and negative lexicon. Other emotions can be as well a clue to detect pedophiles. For example, offenders often demonstrate fear, especially with respect to being prosecuted, and they often lose temper and express anger:

Pseudo-victim: u sad didnt car if im 13. now u car.
Predator: well, *I am just scared* about being in trouble or going to jail
Pseudo-victim: u sad run away now u say no. i gues i dont no what u doin
Predator: *I got scared*
Predator: we would get caugth sometime

In this example pseudo-victim is not answering:

Predator: hello
Predator: r u there
Predator:
Predator: thnx a lot
Predator: thanx a lot
Predator:
Predator: *u just wast my time*
Predator: drive down there
Predator: can u not im any more

Here the offender is angry because the pseudo-victim did not call him:

Predator: u didnt call
Predator: *i m angry with u*

Therefore, we have decided to use markers of basic emotions as features. At the SemEval 2007 task on "Affective Text" (Strapparava and Mihalcea, 2007) the problem of fine-grained emotion annotation was defined: given a set of news titles, the system is to label each title with the appropriate emotion out of the following list: ANGER, DISGUST, FEAR, JOY, SADNESS, SURPRISE. In this research work we only use the percentages of the markers of each emotion.

We have also borrowed several features from McGhee et al. (2011):

- Percentage of *approach words*. Approach words include verbs such as *come* and *meet* and such nouns as *car* and *hotel*.
- Percentage of *relationship words*. These words refer to dating (e.g. *boyfriend*, *date*).

- Percentage of *family words*. These words are the names of family members (e.g. *mum, dad, brother*).

- Percentage of *communicative desensitization words*. These are explicit sexual terms offenders use in order to desensitize the victim (e.g. *penis, sex*).

- Percentage of *words expressing sharing information*. This implies sharing basic information, such as age, gender and location, and sending photos. The words include *asl, pic*.

Since pedophiles are known to be emotionally unstable and suffer from psychological problems, we consider features reported to be helpful to detect neuroticism level by Argamon et al. (2009). In particular, the features include *percentages of personal* and *reflexive pronouns* and *modal obligation verbs* (have to, has to, had to, must, should, mustn't, and shouldn't).

We consider the use of imperative sentences and emoticons to capture the predators tendencies to be dominant and copy childrens' behaviour respectively.

The study of Egan et al. (Egan et al., 2011) has revealed several recurrent themes that appear in PJ chats. Among them, *fixated discourse:* the unwillingness of the predator to change the topic. In (Bogdanova et al., 2012) we present experiments on modeling the fixated discourse. We have constructed lexical chains (Morris and Hirst, 1991) starting with the anchor word "sex" in the first WordNet meaning: "sexual activity, sexual practice, sex, sex activity (activities associated with sexual intercourse)". We have finally used as a feature the l*ength of the lexical chain* constructed with the Resnik similarity measure (Resnik, 1995) with the threshold = 0.7.

The full list of features is presented in Table 1.

5 Datasets

Pendar (2007) has summarized the possible types of chat interactions with sexually explicit content:

1. Predator/Other
   (a) Predator/Victim (victim is underaged)
   (b) Predator/Volunteer posing as a children
   (c) Predator/Law enforcement officer posing as a child
2. Adult/Adult (consensual relationship)

The most interesting from our research point of view is data of the type 1a, but obtaining such data is not easy. However, the data of the type 1b is freely available at the web site www.perverted-justice.com. For our study, we have extracted chat logs from the perverted-justice website. Since the victim is not real, we considered only the chat lines written by predators.

Since our goal is to distinguish sex related chat conversations where one of the parties involved is a pedophile, the ideal negative dataset would be chat conversations of type 2 (consensual relations among adults) and the PJ data will not meet this condition for the negative instances. We need additional chat logs to build the negative dataset. We used two negative datasets in our experiments: cybersex chat logs and the NPS chat corpus.

We downloaded the cybersex chat logs available at www.oocities.org/urgrl21f/. The archive contains 34 one-on-one cybersex logs. We have separated lines of different authors, thereby obtaining 68 files.

We have also used the subset the of NPS chat corpus (Forsythand and Martell, 2007), though it is not of type 2. We have extracted chat lines only for those adult authors who had more than 30 lines written. Finally the dataset consisted of 65 authors. From each dataset we have left 20 files for testing.

6 Experiments

To distinguish between predators and not predators we used a Naive Bayes classifier, already successfully utilized for analyzing chats by previous research (Lin, 2007). To extract positive and negative words, we used SentiWordNet (Baccianella et al., 2010). The features borrowed from McGhee et al. (2011), were detected with the list of words authors made available for us. Imperative sentences were detected as affirmative sentences starting with verbs. Emoticons were captured with simple regular expressions.

Our dataset is imbalanced, the majority of the chat logs are from PJ. To make the experimental data more balanced, we have created 5 subsets of PJ cor-

Feature Class	Feature	Example	Resource
Emotional Markers	Positive Words	*cute, pretty*	SentiWordNet (Baccianella et al., 2010)
	Negative Words	*dangerous, annoying*	
	JOY words	*happy, cheer*	WordNet-Affect (Strapparava and Valitutti, 2004)
	SADNESS words	*bored, sad*	
	ANGER words	*annoying, furious*	
	SURPRISE words	*astonished, wonder*	
	DISGUST words	*yucky, nausea*	
	FEAR words	*scared, panic*	
Features borrowed from McGhee et al. (2011)	Approach words	*meet, car*	McGhee et al. (2011)
	Relationship nouns	*boyfriend, date*	
	Family words	*mum, dad*	
	Communicative desensitization words	*sex. penis*	
	Information words	*asl, home*	
Features helpful to detect neuroticism level	Personal pronouns	*I, you*	Argamon et al. (2009)
	Reflexive pronouns	*myself, yourself*	
	Obligation verbs	*must, have to*	
Features derived from pedophile's psychological profile	Fixated Discourse	see in Section 3.1	Bogdanova et al. (2012)
Other	Emoticons	*8), :(*	
	Imperative sentences	*Do it!*	

Table 1: Features used in the experiments.

pus, each of which contained chat lines from 60 randomly selected predators.

For the cybersex logs, half of the chat sessions belong to the same author. We used this author for training, and the rest for testing, in order to prevent the classification algorithm from learning to distinguish this author from pedophiles.

For comparison purposes, we experimented with several baseline systems using low-level features based on n-grams at the word and character level, which were reported as useful features by related research (Peersman et al., 2011). We trained naive Bayes classifiers using word level unigrams, bigrams and trigrams. We also trained naive Bayes classifiers using character level bigrams and trigrams.

The classification results are presented in Tables 2 and 3. The high-level features outperform all the low-level ones in both the cybersex logs and the NPS chat datasets and achieve 94% and 90% accuracy on these datasets respectively.

Cybersex chat logs are data of type 2 (see previous section), they contain sexual content and, therefore, share same of the same vocabulary with the perverted-justice data, whilst the NPS data generally is not sex-related. Therefore, we expected low-level features to provide better results on the NPS data. The experiments have shown that, except for the character bigrams, all low-level features considered indeed work worse in case of cybersex logs (see the average rows in both tables). The average accuracy in this case varies between 48% and 58%. Surprisingly, low-level features do not work as good as we expected in case of the NPS chat dataset: bag of words provides only 61% accuracy. Among other low-level features, character trigrams provide the highest accuracy of 72%, which is still much lower than the one of the high-level features (90%). The high-level features yield a lower accuracy (90% accuracy) on the PJ-NPS dataset than in the case of PJ-cybersex logs (94% accuracy). This is probably due to the data diversity: cybersex chat is a very particular type of a conversation, though NPS chat corpora can contain any type of conversations up to sexual predation.

	Accuracy					
	High-level features	**Bag of words**	**Term bigrams**	**Term trigrams**	**Character bigrams**	**Character trigrams**
Run 1	0.93	0.38	0.55	0.60	0.73	0.78
Run 2	0.95	0.40	0.50	0.53	0.75	0.45
Run 3	0.95	0.70	0.45	0.53	0.48	0.50
Run 4	0.98	0.43	0.53	0.53	0.50	0.38
Run 5	0.90	0.50	0.48	0.53	0.45	0.50
Average	**0.94**	**0.48**	**0.50**	**0.54**	**0.58**	**0.52**

Table 2: Results of Naive Bayes classification applied to perverted-justice data and cybersex chat logs.

	Accuracy					
	High-level features	**Bag of words**	**Term bigrams**	**Term trigrams**	**Character bigrams**	**Character trigrams**
Run 1	0.93	0.73	0.60	0.60	0.68	0.75
Run 2	0.95	0.68	0.53	0.53	0.48	0.45
Run 3	0.95	0.58	0.53	0.53	0.48	0.85
Run 4	0.98	0.53	0.53	0.53	0.23	0.80
Run 5	0.90	0.53	0.53	0.53	0.25	0.75
Average	**0.92**	**0.61**	**0.54**	**0.54**	**0.42**	**0.72**

Table 3: Results of Naive Bayes classification applied to perverted-justice data and NPS chats.

7 Discussion and Future Work

We have conducted experiments on detecting pedophiles in social media with a binary classification algorithm. In the experiments we used two negative datasets of different nature: the first one is more appropriate, it contains one-on-one cybersex conversations, while the second dataset is extracted from the NPS chat corpus and contains logs from chat rooms, and, therefore, is less appropriate since the conversations are not even one on one.

It is reasonable to expect that in the case of the negative data consisting of cybersex logs, distinguishing cyberpedophiles is a harder task, than in the case of the NPS data. The results obtained with the baseline systems support this assumption: we obtain higher accuracy for the NPS chats in all but character bi-grams. The interesting insight from these results is that our proposed higher-level features are able to boost accuracy to 94% on the seemingly more challenging task.

Our error analysis showed that the NPS logs misclassified with the high-level features are also misclassified by the baseline systems. These instances either share the same lexicon or are about the same topics. Therefore they are more similar to cyberpedophiles training data than the training data of the NPS corpus, which is very diverse. These examples are taken from misclassified NPS chat logs:

User: love me like a bomb baby come on get it on

...

User: ryaon so sexy
User: you are so anal
User: obviously i didn't get it
User: just loosen up babe

...

User: i want to make love to him

User: right field wrong park lol j/k
User: not me i put them in the jail lol
User: or at least tell the cops where to go to get the bad guys lol

In the future we plan to further investigate the misclassified data. The feature extraction we have implemented does not use any word sense disambiguation. This can as well cause mistakes since the markers are not just lemmas but words in particular senses, since for example the lemma "fit" can be either a positive marker ("a fit candidate") or negative ("a fit of epilepsy"), depending on the context. Therefore we plan to employ word sense disambiguation techniques during the feature extraction phase.

So far we have only seen that the list of features we have suggested provides good results. They outperform all thelow-level features considered. Among those low-level features, character trigrams provide the best results on the NPS data (72% accuracy), though on the cybersex logs they achieve only 54%. We plan to merge low-level and high-level features in order to see if this could improve the results.

In the future we plan also to explore the impact of each high-level feature. To better understand which ones carry more discriminative power and if we can reduce the number of features. All these experiments will be done employing naive Bayes as well as Support Vector Machines as classifiers.

8 Conclusions

This paper presents some results of an ongoing research project on the detection of online sexual predation, a problem the research community is interested in, as the PAN task on Sexual Predator Identification[1] suggests.

Following the clues given by psychological research, we have suggested a list of high-level features that should take into account the level of emotional instability of pedophiles, as well as their feelings of inferiority, isolation, loneliness, low self-esteem etc. We have considered as well such low-level features as character bigrams and trigrams and word unigrams, bigrams and trigrams. The Naive Bayes classification based on high-level features achieves 90% and 94% accuracy when using NPS chat corpus and the cybersex chat logs as a negative dataset respectively, whereas low-level features achieve only 42%-72% and 48%-58% accuracy on the same data.

Acknowledgements

The research of Dasha Bogdanova was carried out during the 3-month internship at the Universitat Politècnica de València (scholarship of the University of St.Petersburg). Her research was partially supported by Google Research Award. The collaboration with Thamar Solorio was possible thanks to her one-month research visit at the Universitat Politècnica de València (program PAID-PAID-02-11 award n. 1932). The research work of Paolo Rosso was done in the framework of the European Commission WIQ-EI IRSES project (grant no. 269180) within the FP 7 Marie Curie People, the MICINN research project TEXT-ENTERPRISE 2.0 TIN2009-13391-C04-03(Plan I+D+i), and the VLC/CAMPUS Microcluster on Multimodal Interaction in Intelligent Systems.

[1]http://pan.webis.de/

References

Gene G. Abel and Nora Harlow. The Abel and Harlow child molestation prevention study. Philadelphia, Xlibris, 2001.

Shlomo Argamon, Moshe Koppel, James Pennebaker, and Jonathan Schler. Automatically profiling the author of an anonymous text. *Communications of the ACM*, 52 (2):119–123, 2009.

Stefano Baccianella, Andrea Esuli, and Fabrizio Sebastiani. Sentiwordnet 3.0: An enhanced lexical resource for sentiment analysis and opinion mining. *the Seventh International conference on Language Resources and Evaluation*, 2010.

Regina Barzilay and Michael Elhadad. Using lexical chains for text summarization. *In Proceedings of the Intelligent Scalable Text Summarization Workshop*, 1997.

Dasha Bogdanova, Paolo Rosso, Thamar Solorio. Modelling Fixated Discourse in Chats with Cyberpedophiles. *Proceedings of the Workshop on Computational Approaches to Deception Detection, EACL*, 2012.

Vincent Egan, James Hoskinson, and David Shewan. Perverted justice: A content analysis of the language used by offenders detected attempting to solicit children for sex. *Antisocial Behavior: Causes, Correlations and Treatments*, 2011.

Eric N Forsythand and Craig H Martell. Lexical and discourse analysis of online chat dialog. *International Conference on Semantic Computing ICSC 2007*, pages 19–26, 2007.

Michel Galley and Kathleen McKeown. Improving word sense disambiguation in lexical chaining. *In Proceedings of IJCAI-2003*, 2003.

Ryan C. W. Hall and Richard C. W. Hall. A profile of pedophilia: Definition, characteristics of offenders, recidivism, treatment outcomes, and forensic issues. *Mayo Clinic Proceedings*, 2007.

David Hope. Java wordnet similarity library. http://www.cogs.susx.ac.uk/users/drh21.

Claudia Leacock and Martin Chodorow. C-rater: Automated scoring of short-answer questions. *Computers and the Humanities*, 37(4):389–405, 2003.

Timothy Leary. *Interpersonal diagnosis of personality; a functional theory and methodology for personality evaluation*. Oxford, England: Ronald Press, 1957.

Jane Lin. *Automatic author profiling of online chat logs*. PhD thesis, 2007.

India McGhee, Jennifer Bayzick, April Kontostathis, Lynne Edwards, Alexandra McBride and Emma Jakubowski. Learning to identify Internet sexual predation. *International Journal on Electronic Commerce* 2011.

Kimberly J. Mitchell, David Finkelhor, and Janis Wolak. Risk factors for and impact of online sexual solicitation of youth. *Journal of the American Medical Association*, 285:3011–3014, 2001.

Jane Morris and Graeme Hirst. Lexical cohesion computed by thesaural relations as an indicator of the structure of text. *Computational Linguistics*, 17(1):21–43, 1991.

Ted Pedersen, Siddharth Patwardhan, Jason Michelizzi, and Satanjeev Banerjee. Wordnet:similarity. http://wn-similarity.sourceforge.net/.

Claudia Peersman, Walter Daelemans, and Leona Van Vaerenbergh. Predicting age and gender in online social networks. *In Proceedings of the 3rd Workshop on Search and Mining User-Generated Contents*, 2011.

Nick Pendar. Toward spotting the pedophile: Telling victim from predator in text chats. *In Proceedings of the International Conference on Semantic Computing*, pages 235–241, Irvine, California, 2007.

Alexander Panchenko, Richard Beaufort, Cedrick Fairon. Detection of Child Sexual Abuse Media on P2P Networks: Normalization and Classification of Associated Filenames. *In Proceedings of the LREC Workshop on Language Resources for Public Security Applications*, 2012.

Philip Resnik. Using information content to evaluate semantic similarity in a taxonomy. In *IJCAI*, pages 448–453, 1995.

Howard N. Snyder. Sexual assault of young children as reported to law enforcement: Victim, incident, and offender characteristics. a nibrs statistical report. *Bureau of Justice Statistics Clearinghouse*, 2000.

Carlo Strapparava and Rada Mihalcea. Semeval-2007 task 14: affective text. *In Proceedings of the 4th International Workshop on Semantic Evaluations, SemEval'07*, pages 70–74, 2007.

Carlo Strapparava and Alessandro Valitutti. Wordnet-affect: an affective extension of wordnet. *In Proceedings of the 4th International Conference on Language Re-sources and Evaluation*, 2004.

Frederik Vaassen and Walter Daelemans. Automatic emotion classification for interpersonal communication. In *Proceedings of the 2nd Workshop on Computational Approaches to Subjectivity and Sentiment Analysis (WASSA 2.011)*, pages 104–110. Association for Computational Linguistics, 2011.

Donna M. Vandiver and Glen Kercher. Offender and victim characteristics of registered female sexual offenders in Texas: A proposed typology of female sexual offenders. *Sex Abuse*, 16:121–137, 2004

World health organization, international statistical classification of diseases and related health problems: Icd-10 section f65.4: Paedophilia. 1988.

Author Index